FLANAGAN'S
VERSION

FLANAGAN'S VERSION

A Spectator's Guide to Science
on the Eve of the 21st Century

DENNIS FLANAGAN

VINTAGE BOOKS

A Division of Random House, Inc.
New York

Grateful acknowledgment is made to the following for permission to
reprint previously published material:

ALFRED A. KNOPF, INC.: "III. The Dance of the Solids" from
"Midpoint," in *Midpoint and Other Poems* by John Updike. Copyright
© 1969 by John Updike. Reprinted by permission of Alfred A. Knopf,
Inc.

RANDOM HOUSE, INC.: "A New Year Greeting" from *W. H. Auden:
Collected Poems*, edited by Edward Mendelson. Copyright © 1969 by
W. H. Auden. Reprinted by permission of Random House, Inc.

VIKING PENGUIN, INC.: Excerpt from *Lives of a Cell* by Lewis
Thomas. Copyright © 1971 by Lewis Thomas. Originally it appeared
in *The New England Journal of Medicine*. All rights reserved. Reprinted by permission of Viking Penguin, Inc.

Library of Congress Cataloging-in-Publication Data
Flanagan, Dennis, 1919–
Flanagan's version.
1. Science. 2. Science—History. I. Title
[Q158.5.F53 1989]   500   88-82385
ISBN 0-679-72156-8 (pbk.)

Manufactured in the United States of America
10 9 8 7 6 5 4 3 2 1

This book is dedicated
to Barbara

CONTENTS

Contents

ACKNOWLEDGMENTS

I once heard a horror story about acknowledgments, one that is particularly pertinent to this book: Scientist X wrote a book and sent the manuscript to Scientist Y for criticism. Scientist Y pointed out a conceptual error that spoiled the book's entire argument. Scientist X then published the book without change. In it he effusively thanked Scientist Y, thus implicating him in the crime.

The seven pieces in my own book were read in whole or in part by a substantial number of knowledgeable people. If the book commits any crimes, however, the fault is not theirs but mine. Nevertheless they, and others who did not actually see the manuscript, gave me an enormous amount of help and deserve my grateful thanks. They are, in alphabetical order: Francisco J. Ayala, John Tyler Bonner, Donald Christiansen, I. Bernard Cohen, Nathan H. Cook, James F. Crow, Arnold L. Demain, Michael Feirtag, George B. Field, Cara Flanagan, John G. Flanagan, Susan Roberts Flanagan, J. Charles Forman, William A. Fowler, Lee Friedman, Martin Gardner, Owen Gingerich, Jack R. Harlan, Norman G. Heatley, Edward Hutchings, Jr., Fritz Kalhammer, Robert Kunzig, Bruce V. Lewenstein, Robert G. Lewis, Stanley Meltzoff, Philippe Monod, Philip Morrison, David Ogilvy,

Heinz R. Pagels, Melba Phillips, Keith R. Porter, John Purcell, Jean Ritchie, Steven N. Shore, Raymond Siever, Cyril Stanley Smith, Laurence A. Soderblom, A. P. Speiser, Kosta Tsipis, W. E. van Heyningen, Hugh Williams, Barbara Williams, Robert R. Wilson, C. R. Woese and Chia-Shun Yih.

To Vicky Wilson, my editor at Alfred A. Knopf, to Brian Hayes and to Harriet Wasserman I owe special thanks. Without their encouragement and their counsel on the manuscript the book would never have seen the light of day.

FLANAGAN'S
VERSION

A MASTER KEY
TO MODERN SCIENCE

Some years ago I attended a luncheon talk by Pauline Kael, the film critic of *The New Yorker*. Miss Kael arrived early, and so did I; indeed, for a few minutes we were the only people present. After pausing at the bar, I introduced myself. Miss Kael asked me what I did. I said: "I am the editor of *Scientific American* magazine." She said: "That's nice." There was a moment's silence. Then she added: "You know, I know absolutely nothing about science." I had heard this remark many times before, and so I emitted my stock answer: "Miss Kael, what ever became of the idea that an educated person is supposed to know a little something about everything?" Visibly annoyed, she replied: "Oh, you're a *Renaissance* hack."

It was a genial insult, and I had a good laugh. Actually I like the idea of being a Renaissance hack. If tombstones were still in style, I would want to have the two words chiseled right under my name. In an age of specialization people are proud to be able to do one thing well, but if that is all they know about, they are missing out on much else life has to offer. To be sure, to be able to do more than one thing well is hard, so that outside of one's main line of work one may have to be satisfied with being a kind of hack.

Modern science, it is said, is hard to understand. In a limited sense this is true; new concepts are by definition strange, and even the nouns they call for can be unfamiliar. In my view, however, the work of modern science can be described in terms anyone can follow. And following the work of modern science as a spectator can be one of life's deepest pleasures, fully comparable with the pleasures of literature, painting and music. Of equal importance is that following the work of modern science, which penetrates all the rest of life, enables one to better comprehend and cope with the modern world.

The reason I hold the view that the work of modern science can be described in terms anyone can follow is that if I can follow it, anyone can. Before I wrote this book I had been editor of *Scientific American* for thirty-seven years. (*Scientific American* had been founded in 1845, but in 1948 a new version of it was brought out by Gerard Piel, Donald H. Miller, Jr., and me, under the leadership of Piel.) Before that I had been science editor of *Life*. Any nonscientist reading these pages may be comforted to know that my qualifications for those jobs were nil. I was an English-major type and destitute of formal knowledge in hard subjects such as physics and chemistry.

Lacking any background, how was I to gauge the importance of scientific topics—to choose the ones that had to be covered in the magazine? Over the years I arrived at the conclusion that the best touchstone was whether or not the subject came as a surprise. After all, if it came as a surprise to me, it would come as a surprise to any equally innocent person.

An example comes to mind. In the late 1950s I heard of some work being done by the historian of science Derek de Solla Price. In 1900 sponge divers had found in an ancient shipwreck off the Greek island of Antikythera the corroded remains of a bronze mechanism. Dated to the first century B.C., the mechanism consisted of shafts and gearing resembling the works of a grandfather's clock. Nothing else like it is known from the ancient world.

What was it? Over the years scholars peered at it, X-rayed it, teased debris out of it and analyzed how its parts meshed. Then came the surprise: It was an analogue computer for predicting the motions of the stars, the sun, the moon and the planets! I invited Price to tell the readers of *Scientific American* about it, and we published his article in 1959. In those days Gerard Piel, as publisher of the magazine, wrote for our advertising sales staff a monthly memorandum describing the articles in the forthcoming issue. He commented about the Greek computer-builders of the Price article: "What did they think of next?"

Surprise is the most precious of all journalistic commodities; for the journalist the moment of truth is when the reader stiffens in the chair and says something like: "Wow! That's the damndest thing I ever heard." In science some of the surprises, such as the double helix of DNA, are big ones. Some, such as what makes thunder roll, are small but nonetheless delightful for that.

A spectacular example of how one article came as a surprise to a reader of *Scientific American* is the following. In 1969 the magazine published an article by Mary J. Marples titled "Life on the Human Skin." It was an account of all the small creatures that, largely unbeknownst to us, make their home *on* us. W. H. Auden was so taken with it that he chose it as the theme of a year-end greeting to his friends:

> On this day tradition allots
>   to taking stock of our lives,
> my greetings to all of you, Yeasts,
>   Bacteria, Viruses,
> Aerobics and Anaerobics:

A Very Happy New Year
to all for whom my ectoderm
   is as Middle-Earth to me.

For creatures your size I offer
   a free choice of habitat,
so settle yourselves in the zone
   that suits you best, in the pools
of my pores or the tropical
   forests of arm-pit and crotch,
in the deserts of my fore-arms,
   or the cool woods of my scalp.

Build colonies: I will supply
   adequate warmth and moisture,
the sebum and lipids you need,
   on condition you never
do me annoy with your presence,
   but behave as good guests should,
not rioting into acne
   or athlete's-foot or a boil.

Does my inner weather affect
   the surfaces where you live?
Do unpredictable changes
   record my rocketing plunge
from fairs when the mind is in tift
   and relevant thoughts occur
to fouls when nothing will happen
   and no one calls and it rains?

I should like to think that I make
   a not impossible world,
but an Eden it cannot be:
   my games, my purposive acts,

may turn to catastrophes there.
  If you were religious folk,
how would your dramas justify
  unmerited suffering?

By what myths would your priests account
  for the hurricanes that come
twice every twenty-four hours,
  each time I dress or undress,
when, clinging to keratin rafts,
  whole cities are swept away
to perish in space, or the Flood
  that scalds to death when I bathe?

Then, sooner or later, will dawn
  A Day of Apocalypse,
when my mantle suddenly turns
  too cold, too rancid, for you,
appetising to predators
  of a fiercer sort, and I
am stripped of excuse and nimbus,
  a Past, subject to Judgement.

Not all surprises in science are easy to recognize. In order to have been surprised by the discovery that DNA is a double helix you had to know that biologists were confronted with a profound mystery: How do all the characteristics of a living organism emerge from a microscopic package of material bequeathed by the preceding generation? In other words, you needed some kind of context. It is as though the entire subject were some familiar epic tale and you were able to recognize that something totally new had been added to it.

All scientific subjects are epic tales. It is my aim in this book to discuss four subjects that in my lifetime have been revolutionized: physics, astronomy, geology and biology. For good measure I shall do the same for technology and for a realm largely (but not entirely) beyond the borders of modern science, the realm of the irrational.

The tales of modern science, like Chaucer's tales, are tales of travelers on a common road. The physicist's tale, the astronomer's tale, the geologist's tale and the biologist's tale are tales of evolution—past, present and future. In telling those tales in a single book it is possible to show how all of modern science hangs together, how all modern scientists are traveling toward the same Canterbury: a unified understanding of the universe, including ourselves.

To many people the word "evolution" immediately suggests biological evolution, but of course the word has a much broader meaning. In recent years our entire tale of the universe has become an evolutionary one. Starting with the big bang between 10 and 20 billion years ago, the fundamental forces of nature evolved, the fundamental particles of matter evolved, galaxies and stars evolved. Then 4.6 billion years ago the sun and its planets came into being, and 3.5 billion years ago life arose on the earth.

Those dates were won only in the past fifty years, and they are a monumental achievement in establishing the context of everything in the universe. Even more important than evolution as history, however, is evolution as process. Until recently the short span of human life predisposed human beings to regard the universe as unchanging, with the planets, the stars and the galaxies wheeling endlessly in some kind of cosmic clockwork. Even geologists, whose subject has always been strongly historical, were slow to recognize that the very earth is an evolutionary process that began with the origin of the universe. That life on the earth is an evolutionary process was discovered in the nineteenth century, but the shock of that discovery is by no means fully absorbed.

What may cut closest to the bone is that human societies and individual human beings too are process. Recently I ran across a penetrating comment by the philosopher Georg Lukács: "The humanization of man is the content of history which—very variously—is realized in the course of every human life. Thus every individual—no matter how consciously—is an active ingredient in this total historical process, of which he is at the same time the product." *In short, all is evolutionary process, and evolutionary process is the master key to modern science and all other human knowledge.*

Wetenschap Is Wat Wetenschappers Doen

What is science anyway? It is a remarkable fact that almost everyone has a clear picture of what it is, and yet scarcely any two of the pictures are alike. It is the fable of the blind men and the elephant raised to a higher power.

I have always thought that the spectacle of journalists interviewing journalists was somewhat comical, and yet once I assented to being interviewed by a Dutch journalist. After the interview he sent me a copy of his story in a Dutch newspaper. I cannot, of course, read Dutch, but one sentence sprang out at me: *Wetenschap is wat Wetenschappers doen.* What I had said was that one definition of science is that science is what scientists do. Somehow it looked so much better in Dutch that I had the sentence enlarged and pinned it to the bulletin board in my office.

The definition has much to recommend it, but most people have other ideas. A worldly scientist once said to me: "Science is what *I* do." Many nonscientists have firm convictions about what scientists *should* do.

Congressmen, when the time comes to appropriate money for science, often express themselves as regarding science as something that should contribute directly to the public welfare, as in health and agriculture. In this regard they doubtless reflect the opinion of most of their constituents. The trouble with this view is that it leaves no room for the fact that most scientific discoveries that have contributed to the public welfare could not have been predicted. If a scientist of the 1920s had applied for a grant to study the biology of molds, would anyone have known that the work might lead to antibiotics?

The journalism of science has an odd feature: It abounds in contests and awards. Philanthropic organizations are rightly concerned with the public understanding of science, and accordingly they have established numerous prizes to encourage those who write about science for the public. A friend of mine once got a large anatomical drawing of the human body and entered on it the amounts of the prizes one could get for writing about various parts of the body and their disorders: $1,000 from the American Heart Association, $1,000 from the American Diabetes Association, $1,000 from the American Dental Association and similar awards from half a dozen others.

If one has been around science journalism long enough to grow long white whiskers, one inevitably gets asked to judge such contests. Over the years I have judged at least fifty of them, and they have afforded a survey of what writers, or at least the editors of the newspapers and magazines they write for, think science is. The overwhelming majority of stories submitted are about medical subjects. Depending on the year, second place goes to such subjects as the environment, computers, overpopulation, drug addiction, toxic wastes, the activities of NASA and the safety of nuclear reactors. They are all reasonable subjects, but there is not much in them about what scientists do.

Science too abounds in prizes, notably the Nobel. Do the Nobel prizes help define science? Curiously they do not recognize many important scientific subjects: mathematics, astronomy (except when it occasionally sneaks in as physics), most of biology and all the social sciences except economics. On the whole the Nobel prizes are a distorted mirror of science. That does not subtract from their vast prestige. One indication among many is a story from 1957, when the Nobel prize in physics was awarded to C. N. Yang and T. D. Lee. Lee often ate lunch in a Chinese restaurant near Columbia University. The day after he and Yang won the prize there appeared in the window of the restaurant a hand-lettered sign: "Eat here, win Nobel prize."

Over the years I have been particularly interested in the view of science presented by flamboyant magazines such as *Omni*. They seem to be wistfully asking: "What is human life going to be like in the future," and making the assumption that that is what scientists do. It is remarkable how many of the cover illustrations on such magazines depict a shapely, bald female robot made of what appears to be stainless steel.

Are scientists perhaps those people who apply the scientific method? If they are, what *is* the scientific method? The physicist Percy Bridgman doubted that such a thing existed. "The scientific method," he said, "is doing one's damndest with one's mind."

Is a useful definition of science supplied by the dictionary? Not really, but the origins of the word are haunting. Older dictionaries derive it from the Latin verb *scire*, to know. My main dictionary, the American Heritage, has an excellent Indo-European appendix that goes deeper. *Scire* comes from the Indo-European root *skei-*, to cut, split. To know is to separate one thing from another.

One thing most modern scientists do is teach. This fact structures the entire institution of science. I have heard scientists grumble that they are so busy teaching they do not have enough time for research. It is hard to see how the two activities can be separated. If a university is to offer a course on a science, who can teach it but one of the science's practitioners? In the secondary schools science is taught by professional teachers, but who is to teach *them?*

Of equal importance is the fact that the interaction between scientists and their students is part of science itself. Getting a Ph.D. in science typically takes four years, and many new Ph.D.s work as postdoctoral fellows for some years after that. In this period they are not only students but also colleagues. Graduate students and postdoctoral fellows do much of the work in modern science. Some even make the great discoveries. In 1973 Brian Josephson received a Nobel prize in physics for discovering what is now known as the Josephson effect; at the time of the discovery he was a graduate student.

In the United States the symbiosis between scientists and their students generates social tensions that have to do with money. Since most scientists work in universities, and since most of the support for science comes from the public, public funds for science flow through the universities. And since the public and its representatives tend to view science as something that should contribute directly to the public welfare, the share of the money that goes to those in the universities who do that kind of work is disproportionate.

In the modern world the public welfare has come to include national defense. Public funds for science in the universities are disbursed by such federal agencies as the National Science Foundation, the National Institutes of Health and the National Aeronautics and Space Administration. Large amounts are also disbursed by the Department of Energy (incorporating the former Atomic Energy Commission) and the Department of Defense. Among other things the latter departments support military work in the universities and hire universities to operate military laboratories. As an example, the great nuclear-weapons laboratories at Los Alamos and Livermore are run under contract by the University of California. Such activities distort American universities, which are supposed to be communities of students and scholars.

What Is the Question?

But is a scientist a scholar? Absolutely. Sometimes I wish there were a court where I could appeal the academic dichotomy between "the sciences" and "the humanities." It suggests that scientists are technicians and other members of the faculty deal with the finer things of life, the things of real interest to human beings. But the nature of human beings and the world they live in is the most humane of subjects, and it is the province of the sciences. The sciences *are* humanities.

A modern scholar is a person who undertakes to master a body of knowledge and extend its limits. *Whatever else scientists do, the most significant thing they do is to try to find out things that are not known.* When you stop to think about it, it is quite a trick. Most of us, when we need to find out something we don't know, look it up in a book or ask someone about it. But what if no one knows the answer?

Gertrude Stein is said to have asked on her deathbed: "What is the answer?" Getting no answer, she said: "In that case, what is the question?" Scientists not only seek answers but formulate questions. People who have the habit of asking good questions of nature have a distinct place in human society. If they did not exist, nothing new would ever be learned.

Since all is evolutionary process, science itself can be regarded as such a process. It is a great pity that many intelligent people have the impression that science is a collection of facts. Science is the process of all processes: a perpetual reshaping of what human beings know about the universe and themselves.

The facts and principles of yesteryear give way to new facts and principles, and they always will.

The interplay of facts and principles in the human mind is as old as the ability to learn from experience. Science as we know it today dates back only four centuries to Galileo Galilei, a great artist at observing nature, raising questions and figuring out ways to get the answers. It is only over the past two centuries, however, that science has become a full-fledged social institution.

Populations of living organisms tend to evolve characteristics that make them more successful in a particular environment. Biologists speak of such a characteristic as an adaptation. The long neck of the giraffe is an adaptation that enables the animal to forage in trees. Human social institutions such as kinship systems and law and medicine are also adaptations; they make the society more successful than it would be without them. Science too is a social adaptation.

Like other social institutions science has its guiding principles. To quote the famous line from Francis Bacon: " 'What is truth?' said jesting Pilate; and would not stay for an answer." Scientists worth their salt must stay not for an answer but for many answers. When a scientist gets an answer to a question, the answer immediately gives rise to another question: "Is it true?"

How, in fact, do we know what is true? The great invention of modern science is that when scientists get an answer they *think* is true, they submit it to their peers for their judgment. Other scientists in effect repeat the question and try to get the same answer. The process has given rise to an almost incredible number of scientific journals. The Library of Congress receives upwards of 55,000 scientific periodicals, and it estimates that there are at least 15,000 more.

The best example of how the system works is in sciences that rely heavily on experiment, such as physics and chemistry. When the result of an experiment is published in a scientific journal, it is assumed that other people will repeat the experiment to determine whether or not the result is true. If other people cannot get the same result, the assumption is made that the result is *not* true. For someone who has done an experiment and published the result the most devastating of all words are "not reproducible."

This system too can be regarded as an evolutionary adaptation. There is no shortage of hot ideas in science. If that was all there was to it, the textbooks would be quickly filled with captivating garbage. Scientists who have survived the Darwinian selection of their education and apprenticeship are keenly aware that they must be merciless with their brainchildren; if it is not possible to demonstrate their validity, they must be strangled in the crib. That also is quite an intellectual and emotional trick.

A handsome picture of the life of a scientist is given in Wordsworth's *The Prelude*: ". . . Newton with his prism and his silent face, / The marble index of a mind forever / Voyaging through strange seas of thought alone." The picture is wrong. It is true that in the deepest sense scientists, like all other human beings, are alone with the processes going on in their head, but for the rest science is intensely social.

In an active scientific discipline everyone knows everyone else, if not in person, then by their writings and reputation. Scientists attend at least as many meetings and conventions as salesmen. I have always been amazed at how quickly news of an important discovery in science travels through the community of workers in that science. I do believe the time of propagation can be measured in hours, even less time than it takes a good joke to travel through the advertising community. The scientific papers come later.

An interesting consequence of science's being social is that it is international. An experiment in Chicago can be repeated in Paris as well as it can be repeated in Los Angeles. The scientific community has been international since its beginnings. Indeed, the community of scientists is the closest thing human beings have to a world culture. This is no romantic ideal. Scientists have done much, both behind the scenes and in front of them, to improve relations between nations.

Science is culture not only in the anthropological sense but also in the everyday one. Many young people take up science because it is a cultural activity, like writing plays or composing music. Here again there is tension between what scientists do and what other people think they should do.

Some years ago the Congressional Joint Committee on Atomic Energy was holding a public hearing. An official of the Atomic Energy Commission was testifying about the giant particle accelerator that was then being built at the Fermi National Accelerator Laboratory in Illinois. Senator John O. Pastore of Connecticut, known for his irascibility, was giving the official a hard time. In the audience was the director of the laboratory, Robert R. Wilson. The AEC man was not defending the accelerator well, and according to the transcript Wilson, quite out of order, erupted.

"Senator Pastore, I and my colleagues will be spending a good part of our lives building and using this machine. We have a deep and very personal commitment to it." He launched into an impassioned argument for the accelerator, and Senator Pastore was being impassioned right back. Among other things the senator said: "Is there anything connected [with] this accelerator that in any way involves the security of the country?" Wilson responded: "No, sir; I do not believe so." Senator Pastore persisted: "Nothing at all?" Finally Wilson said: "[The accelerator] has to do with: Are we good painters, good sculptors, great poets? . . . It has nothing to do with defending our country, *except to make it worth defending*." (The emphasis is mine.)

The Tribes of Science

Yet another definition of science is that it is the collection of scientific subjects taught in universities. Over the years, however, several scientists have remarked to me that I should not take scientific disciplines—physics, chemistry, geology and the like —too seriously. They are arbitrary provinces of knowledge; in the real world there is no sharp boundary between one discipline and another. The fact remains that the people working in each scientific discipline are a kind of tribe, in some instances a group almost as different from the groups in other disciplines as the Trobriand Islanders of the South Pacific are from the Chukchi of Siberia. Most chemists live in laboratories, paleontologists spend much of their time trudging across the landscape looking for fossils, epigraphers brood in the office over ancient inscriptions. The epic tale of each tribe has a different sound, as Mozart sounds different from Vivaldi.

In relating tales of four tribes I shall be doing an injustice to the others. Even though in my lifetime physicists, astronomers, geologists and biologists have been having most of the adventures, in the long run the adventures of other tribes may be fully as exciting. Let me, therefore, pay my respects to those tribes.

Take mathematicians. My earliest memory of their subject goes back to the age of eight, when one of my contemporaries who went to another school said to me: "Have you got to gazinta?" "Gazinta?" I asked. It turned out he was saying "goes into" and referring to division. My last formal acquaintance with mathematics was with plane geometry in the second year of high school.

One cannot say a great deal about mathematics without using it. Still, there are analogies that yield fascinating intimations. One is the Möbius strip. As you may have seen, if you take a strip of paper and paste its ends together, the resulting loop has two sides and two edges. Then if you take the same kind of strip, give one end a half twist and paste the two ends together, the loop has only one side and one edge! You can verify it by running your finger along the side or the edge.

What is going on here? Are you changing a three-dimensional object into a two-dimensional one? (One dimension is the thickness of the paper.) Well, not exactly, but if a two-sided, two-edged object can be converted into a one-sided, one-edged one, it gives you a glimpse of one of the great achievements of mathematics. To mathematics our everyday world of three dimensions is no limitation. Mathematicians have built logical systems having four, five or even an infinite number of dimensions.

Another mathematical analogy I like concerns Fourier analysis, which plays a most important role in science and technology. I owe the thought to the physicist Banesh Hoffmann.

You are listening to a recording of Beethoven's Fifth Symphony. Let us say it is not a tape recording or a compact disk but an old-style phonograph record. The sound waves being generated by all the instruments in the orchestra—violins, French horns, bassoons and so on—come in an enormous number of different frequencies, to say nothing of the fact that the frequencies and their amplitudes are constantly changing. Nevertheless, all those frequencies can be dissected into a collection of sine waves—that is, pure tones—by Fourier analysis.

Think for a minute about the tip of the phonograph needle. As it travels along the groove of the record it describes a single line, a single curve. In other words, all the curves of all the frequencies of all the instruments playing Beethoven's Fifth have been combined into a single curve! That we can call Fourier synthesis.

When you play the record, of course, you hear not the

single curve but all the original curves that went into it. In other words, when you play the record, the curve described by the phonograph needle is being analyzed in the ear and the brain by a process similar to Fourier analysis. It is much more difficult to do it mathematically, but that is what Fourier analysis is capable of doing.

Mathematics is the language of physics. This does not mean that the two subjects are the same. Philip Morrison, physicist and peerless explainer of science to the layman, once told me that when he was an undergraduate at the Carnegie Institute of Technology he formed the impression that modern advances in mathematics were well exploited by physics. Then, as a graduate student of J. Robert Oppenheimer's at Berkeley, he encountered a new mathematics textbook: *A Survey of Modern Algebra*, by Garrett Birkhoff and Saunders MacLane. He found that all the modern algebra utilized by physicists occupied only two chapters out of ten. And algebra is only one branch of mathematics.

The essence of mathematics, it seems to this layman, is that it is not confined by the universe of space and time; it is any internally consistent logical system that can be created in the human head. Hence mathematics is an enterprise with even more of an individual human constituent than sciences such as physics and biology, which are not lacking in individual human constituents.

Certain mathematical innovators have a Mozartean quality: It is hard to imagine how they are able to do what they do. An example is the life and work of Srinivasa Ramanujan, an uneducated Indian mathematical prodigy. Brought to the University of Cambridge in 1914 by the mathematician G. H. Hardy, he did important research in the theory of numbers until after five years he died at age thirty-two. Once when he was gravely ill he was visited by Hardy, who later said: "I had ridden in taxicab No. 1729, and remarked that the number seemed to me rather a dull one, and that I hoped it was not an unfavorable omen.

'No,' [Ramanujan] replied, 'it is a very interesting number; it is the smallest number expressible as the sum of two cubes in two different ways.' "

Oracles and Social Scientists

One of the icons of science is a picture of a great innovator such as Darwin or Einstein. Curiously the picture is usually one of the man long after he did the work that made him famous. In Darwin's case the man appears with long whiskers, usually white; in Einstein's he appears with the wild hair of an Indian cult leader. One of the small pleasures of working at *Scientific American* was seeking out pictures of such men at the time they did their work, long before they had become oracles. A watercolor of Darwin at the time of the voyage of the *Beagle*, when he was thirty-one, shows him as a clean-shaven, slender redhead. A photograph of Einstein in his *annus mirabilis* of 1905, when he was twenty-six, shows him with well-combed jet-black hair and a sharp plaid suit. It was these young fellows, not the gurus they later became, who shook the world.

Whether or not Einstein wanted to be an oracle, society demanded it of him. Wherever he went, newspapermen and others sought his opinion about everything under the sun. As a result there is a large corpus of Einstein remarks, some of which he may never have made. Even they, however, have become folklore. They say in Italy: *Se non è vero, è ben' trovato*, which may be rendered: Even if it isn't true, it is well founded.

Once Einstein is said to have been asked: "Why is it, Dr. Einstein, that so much progress has been made in physics and so little has been made in the social sciences?" He is said to have responded: "Physics is much simpler than social science."

Denigration of the social sciences is unjust. Many people

seem to think that they consist largely of sociology. Actually sociology, measured in the number of its practitioners, is a rather small social science. Among the many other sciences classified as being social are psychology, demography, geography, economics, anthropology and archaeology. All have made deep contributions to human knowledge and human ways of thinking.

Take archaeology. Sometimes it seems that the heroic age of the discipline was the excavation of palaces and the opening of royal tombs, as when Arthur Evans excavated the Minoan palace at Knossos and Howard Carter opened the tomb of Tutankhamen. In a way this was a mere extension of the traditional picture of human history: a succession of civilizations and dynasties. It also gave rise to a public image of archaeology characterized by such films as *Indiana Jones and the Temple of Doom*.

The true heroic period of archaeology is now, when archaeologists take a few burnt kernels of grain or a discoloration in the soil where once a post had been implanted and from such clues derive a picture of how ordinary people lived before history was preserved by writing. The greatest achievement of modern archaeology has been the working out of how nomadic hunters and gatherers across the world took up agriculture and settled life and then civilization. What we now take for granted about it was scarcely known fifty years ago.

Even the allegedly softer social sciences offer surprises. One is the following simple experiment devised by the psychologist Solomon Asch. Calling in a small group of students, he asked them to join in the experiment as his confederates. Another student would later be joining them who would not know what Asch was about to tell them.

In the experiment, Asch said, he would be displaying a series of pairs of display cards. On one card of each pair would be a single vertical line. On the second card would be three vertical lines, one of them quite distinctly the same length as the line on the first card. The three lines would be labeled by number. Each student would be asked to identify which of the three lines on the second card of each pair was equal in length to the line on the first card. The student who was not a confederate would be told it was an experiment in visual perception.

Asch then instructed his confederates to respond to certain of his questions with an answer that would be unanimously *wrong*. For example, if in one pair of cards the line on the second card that was equal in length to the line on the first card was Line 3, the confederates would all say that the line that was equal was Line 2. For each pair of cards the student who was not a confederate would be asked to respond after several others had responded. He or she would therefore be confronted with a dilemma: Should I respond according to what I can see with my own eyes or should I go along with the group? *Over a series of experiments close to 75 percent chose to go along with the group.* The result is food for thought for anyone who assumes that people tend to put more faith in the evidence of their senses than in majority opinion.

A not unfamiliar expression in the description of human relations is "the Hawthorne effect." Many people assume that the Hawthorne somehow refers to a story by Nathaniel Hawthorne, but actually it is the Hawthorne Works of the Western Electric Company in Chicago. There in 1924 C. E. Snow of the National Research Council undertook to study the influence of lighting on the productivity of industrial workers, in this case women working on assembly lines making telephone components such as electrical relays.

At first Snow and his colleagues measured the productivity at the normal level of illumination. Then they raised the level of illumination. The productivity of the workers increased. Then they raised the level again; the productivity increased again. They raised it still more; the productivity continued to increase.

Being good scientists, Snow and his colleagues now *lowered* the level of illumination below what it had been at first. To their surprise, the productivity continued to increase. They lowered the level of illumination still more, with the same result. Finally when the level was so low that the workers could hardly see what they were doing, the productivity fell off. It suddenly dawned on everyone. The workers were not responding to the changes in illumination. *They were responding to someone's paying attention to them.* That is the Hawthorne effect.

The most familiar of all the social sciences is economics. Even so, it too is unjustly denigrated. If economists know so much, many people feel, why can't they do more to solve the world's economic problems? I was once striking a similar note with the eminent economist Wassily Leontief. He said to me with mild asperity: "You must understand, economists do not run economies!"

To economists we owe, among other things, deep perceptions of the nature of society. As an example, when I was growing up in the 1920s and 1930s, the word "worker" summoned up mental images of people working in manufacturing, construction, mining or farming. Even then, however, a substantial fraction of the workers had jobs not in factories, at construction sites, in mines or on farms but in such places as stores and offices. They were producing not goods but services.

It was economists, notably Eli Ginzberg, who pointed out that a modern economy is *overwhelmingly* a service economy. As of 1985, 72.5 percent of the people in the U.S. labor force worked in the service sector. Only 19.9 percent worked in manufacturing, 4.8 percent in construction, 1 percent in mining and an incredibly small 1.8 percent in farming. This seems to make some people—including government officials here and abroad —nervous, as though workers are no longer doing real work but are serving hamburgers or goofing off around the water cooler.

The service economy is a development only to be expected in countries where much physical work is mechanized and the main business of society is the processing of information.

The Impractical and the Practical

In much of the foregoing I have been emphasizing the point that science is a cultural activity. This does not mean it is all fun and games. Even if science does not normally contribute directly to the public welfare, it is the wellspring of technology. If science is the social institution for finding out things that are not known, technology is the social institution for applying things that *are* known. Technology without science would evolve very slowly indeed.

There was a time, a century and more ago, when there was no real distinction between science and technology. In many instances practical people made basic scientific discoveries and impractical people (for want of a better term) applied them. Benjamin Franklin, a printer, discovered that there are two aspects of electricity: positive and negative. Samuel F. B. Morse, a painter, invented the first workable electric telegraph.

Even today the street between science and technology runs both ways. Scientists are heavily dependent on instrumental technology, from the astronomer's great telescopes to the biologist's exquisite gear for separating molecules that are very much alike. Sometimes great generalizations, for example modern information theory, are opened up not by scientists but by engineers.

A two-way street of equal importance is the one between science and medicine. I am not devoting a separate piece to it largely because it seems to me that the big excitement has yet to come. Over the centuries physicians have made basic discoveries about the physiology of human beings and other animals, and scientists have made basic discoveries that revolutionized medicine. William Harvey, a physician, discovered the circulation of the blood. Louis Pasteur, a chemist, demonstrated that disease can be caused by microorganisms.

The big excitement that has yet to come is the full impact of molecular biology on medicine. Susceptibility to one illness or another, including mental illness, is largely a matter of genes. It has been only in the past thirty years that the connection between the genes of the cells that make up the human body and the functioning of those cells has come into focus. Already the faulty genes that are responsible for certain grave hereditary disorders, for example a common form of muscular dystrophy, have been identified. It seems likely that in time, although no one could say how much time, there will be gene therapies.

The same thirty years have seen other kinds of technical advance, such as coronary-bypass surgery and a host of new medications. Such advances can be a blessing to the individual, and no one would want to be without them, but they do not have a great deal to do with the overall health of the population. To me this was brought home a few years ago in a somewhat oblique way.

In his book *The Lives of a Cell* the eminent medical scientist Lewis Thomas proposes a survey of physicians. In the survey the physicians would be asked: "How many times in the last five years have the members of your family, including yourself, had any kind of laboratory test? How many complete physical examinations? X rays? Electrocardiograms? How often, in a year's turning, have you prescribed antibiotics of any kind for yourself and your family? How many hospitalizations? How much surgery? How many consultations with a psychiatrist? How many formal visits to a doctor, any doctor, including yourself?"

Thomas continues: "I will bet that if you got this kind of information, and added everything up, you would find quite a

different set of figures from the ones now being projected in
official circles for the population at large. I have tried it already,
in an unscientific way, by asking around among my friends. My
data, still soft but fairly consistent, reveal that none of my internist
friends have had a routine physical examination since military
service; very few have been X-rayed except by dentists; almost all
have resisted surgery; laboratory tests for anyone in the family are
extremely rare. They use a lot of aspirin, but they seem to write
very few prescriptions and almost never treat family fever with
antibiotics. This is not to say that they do not become ill; these
families have the same incidence of chiefly respiratory and gastro-
intestinal illness as everyone else, the same number of anxieties
and bizarre notions, and the same number—on balance, a small
number—of frightening or devastating diseases. . . .

"The great secret, known to internists and learned early in
marriage by internists' wives, but still hidden from the general
public, is that most things get better by themselves. Most things,
in fact, are better by morning."

The greatest contribution medicine has made to human
health is in the prevention of infectious disease. Inoculation against
smallpox was practiced even before Edward Jenner's time at the
end of the eighteenth century. It was done by rubbing into a
scratch in the skin material scraped from a pustule of someone
suffering from smallpox. Usually the result was a mild infection
that immunized the inoculated individual against future infection, but sometimes it was a dangerous full-fledged infection.
Jenner's contribution was to use material from a milkmaid in-
fected by a cow suffering from a milder form of the disease—
cowpox. The term "vaccination" is from the Latin *vacca*, cow.
Much later it was discovered that the two diseases are caused by
closely related viruses.

Jenner's approach is still one of the beacons of preventive
medicine. It ultimately led to the campaign of the World Health

Organization that by 1976 had eradicated smallpox from the face of the earth. I have often wondered why more is not made of this stunning human triumph. Think of it! A disease that had brought intense pain, terrible disfigurement, blindness and death to millions of human beings since prehistory is totally gone. As late as the 1940s I can remember the shudder that went through New York when it was discovered that a few cases of smallpox had arrived from abroad. Throughout the city tens of thousands of people stood in line for booster vaccinations.

The idea of using one virus to immunize people against another is still at the frontier of efforts to prevent infectious disease. When a virus enters the body, it is "recognized" by a receptor on the surface of a specialized cell that mobilizes the immune system of the body to attack the invader. The receptor does not, however, recognize the entire virus particle. It recognizes only a certain array of atoms, characteristic of that virus, on the virus particle's surface. Therefore if two viruses have the same array of atoms on their surface, one virus can mobilize the immune system to attack not only it but also the other virus.

What is even more interesting is that a fragment of a virus particle that incorporates the same array of atoms can accomplish the same thing. Such fragments can now be created by the techniques of genetic engineering. The advantage of using them in vaccines instead of using whole virus particles is that there is always some danger that a whole virus particle will cause an infection. The Food and Drug Administration has already approved such a vaccine, produced by genetically engineered yeast cells, against the serious disease hepatitis B.

In the past century the health of those who are lucky enough to live in one of the economically developed countries has improved even more dramatically than most people realize. In the United States between 1900 and 1986 the life expectancy at birth increased from 47 years to 75 years. The death of an infant, among other things the heaviest of all psychic blows to anyone who is a parent, has become a far rarer event; in the United States between 1915 and 1984 the death rate for children under one year of age decreased from 100 per 1,000 births to 11.

The remarkable thing is that most of this historic advance has come without medicine, preventive or otherwise. Even infectious diseases against which no widespread preventive or therapeutic measures have been taken—for example, tuberculosis—have become comparatively rare. *The advance in health has clearly come as the result of the advance in living conditions: better nutrition, better sanitation, higher income, less residential crowding, shorter working hours, better conditions in the workplace, fewer hazardous jobs, less child labor, better education, more recreation—all the ordinary things human beings seek for themselves.*

The fact remains that these advances are not yet shared by three-fourths of the people in the world. As of 1983 half of the people lived in countries with a gross national product per capita of less than $400. (The equivalent figure for the United States was $15,500.) A tenth of the people lived in countries where the life expectancy at birth was under 50 years. A sixth of the people lived in countries where the infant mortality rate was above 100 per 1,000 births. The situation has remained unchanged.

It is well known that the prime requirement for the economic development of the poor countries is capital investment. The rich countries have not been entirely remiss in providing such capital, through direct grants and loans, agencies of the United Nations, the World Bank, commercial banks and private philanthropy. In recent years, however, providing capital for economic development has become less popular, particularly in the United States.

There are some in this country who argue that the fate of the less developed countries is none of our business. Those countries, it is said, would not be in the fix they are in if they had had our gifts of self-interest. This point of view ignores historical accidents, such as the edge in technology that enabled Europeans to take over a virgin North America from its earlier immigrants.

What is more to the point, the people in the less developed countries don't go away. Indeed, their high rates of population growth ensure that every year there will be more of them. Their economies are embedded in the world economy, and their economic troubles are trouble for everyone. Their poverty energizes their high rates of population growth, since poor people need offspring in order to survive. It generates tensions that in an unstable world could lead even to a catastrophic world war. The economic development of the less developed countries is therefore of critical importance to the world community.

For me this is the larger context of modern science. Pursuing their own curiosity, scientists increase our knowledge of the universe. Although one cannot predict what they will discover, what they do discover, translated into technology, can make the difference between human misery and human well-being.

The subject of economic development brings to mind an example. Capital investment in plant breeding created new strains of wheat and rice that starting in the 1960s greatly increased the food supply of the less developed countries. One century earlier Gregor Mendel, an unknown Moravian monk studying the patterns of heredity in pea plants, was discovering the principles of plant breeding that led directly to that "green revolution."

Who could have known what kind of principles should be discovered? Who could have known that Mendel was the man to discover them? Who could have known what consequences the discovery would bring?

PHYSICS SEEKS ITS HOLY GRAIL

One of the characters in *The Third Policeman*, by the Irish novelist Flann O'Brien, is a universal scholar named de Selby. In the novel de Selby points out that when you look at yourself in a mirror, what you see is a person slightly younger than you are. The reason is that it takes a finite time for light to travel from your face to the mirror and back again to your eye.

De Selby set up two large mirrors opposite each other, like the mirrors in a barbershop. He could therefore see smaller and smaller images of his head in infinite regress. He then set up a powerful telescope and trained it on the images. He maintained he could follow them backward in time until he saw himself as a boy of twelve. At that point, he said, he could not see any farther "owing to the curvature of the earth."

To be serious, we *do* look backward in time. It takes light, traveling at 186,000 miles per second, eight minutes to get from the sun to the earth. Therefore we see the sun not as it is now but as it was eight minutes ago. When we photograph a distant galaxy, we see it not as it is today but as it was when the light we record left billions of years ago. Retrospection of this kind enables us to look back toward the origin of the universe, where the epic tale of physics begins.

Physics is not traditionally a historical and evolutionary

subject, as geology and biology are. It normally deals with things that are happening at the moment. Today it has become the most historical and evolutionary of all subjects. The universe we observe in telescopes, between 10 and 20 billion years old, began with an unimaginably hot flash: the big bang. Physics is now seeking its Holy Grail early in the flash's first second. That's historical!

The Holy Grail (some physicists actually use the term) is the unification of everything about matter and energy in a single all-embracing mathematical theory. There are separate theories for the three known forces of nature: gravity, the strong force and the electroweak force. (The last used to be two forces: the electromagnetic force and the weak force. They are now linked in a single theory.) A single all-embracing theory must also include the fundamental particles of nature.

There are two kinds of particles: fermions and bosons. Fermions may be regarded as particles of matter. When there is a force between fermions, they are exchanging bosons. The process has been likened to two moving ice skaters tossing a basketball back and forth. Each of the three forces has its own characteristic bosons. The bosons of the electroweak force are the photon (for the electromagnetic component) and the W and Z particles (for the weak-force component). The bosons of the strong force are gluons. The boson of gravity is the graviton.

There are two kinds of fermions: leptons and quarks. Only leptons and quarks? What ever became of the other particles of matter: the electron, the proton and the neutron, to say nothing of the many more exotic particles discovered over the past fifty years? Well, the electron is still there. It is simply listed according to its properties under a more meaningful heading—lepton. The proton and the neutron are seen to be composite: made up of particles more fundamental than they are.

The leptons are six in number: they are the electron, the

muon, the tauon and three kinds of neutrino. They "feel" only the electroweak force and gravity, not the strong force. The quarks are also six; combinations of them make up the proton, the neutron and diverse unstable particles that decay in a tiny fraction of a second. The proton and the neutron each consist of three quarks; the unstable particles consist of either three quarks or two.

It was the three quarks of the proton and the neutron that led Murray Gell-Mann to take the name quark from a line in James Joyce's *Finnegans Wake*: "Three quarks for Muster Mark!" Later many people pointed out that in German *Quark* means cottage cheese, which seemed to spoil the fun. A learned friend of mine, Brian Hayes, points out that on the contrary it adds to the fun.

Joyce was fluent in German. The line is actually uttered by gulls "shrillgleescreaming" above Howth Castle, and Hayes is convinced that the three quarks they bestow on Muster Mark are bird droppings. Hayes writes: "Whether quark is curd or turd, it is a good choice for the fundamental stuff of matter."

Quarks have never been observed in isolation, but there is a wealth of evidence indicating that they exist. They, and the particles made up of them, feel not only the electroweak force and gravity but also the strong force. It is because of the strong force that protons and neutrons, which are made up of quarks, cleave together in the nucleus of the atom.

Each of the leptons, the quarks and the particles made up of quarks has an antiparticle. When a particle and its antiparticle encounter each other, the two fermions are annihilated and transformed into bosons such as photons. By the same token, a boson with the appropriate amount of energy can be transformed into a pair consisting of a particle and its antiparticle.

Three forces and two kinds of particle; that does not seem

like so many to build an entire universe. It is certainly a lot better than the mélange of conceptions of the world human beings had before physics got on the job. To be sure, other forces and other particles may yet be discovered. Quarks, for example, may be made up of particles still more fundamental. Be that as it may, physicists are lured by the unification of the known forces and particles as the Arthurian knights were lured by that chalice of red gold.

The Fading Whimper

The universe is a dark and cold place, but it is not quite as dark and cold as you might think. Quite apart from the light of stars and other celestial objects, the sky shines with a faint glow that appears to extend across all wavelengths. If one assumes that the glow is emitted by something, the temperature of that something would be 3 degrees Kelvin (3 degrees C. above absolute zero).

What is the glow's origin? One of the most startling discoveries of this century, made after the First World War by Edwin P. Hubble, is that the universe is expanding, that on the average the galaxies are rushing away from one another. This being the case, if you could run the cosmic movie backward, the galaxies would be rushing toward one another. Between 10 and 20 billion years ago they would coalesce; indeed, all the matter in the universe would coalesce.

Not only all the matter would coalesce but also all the energy. The primordial universe would therefore be fantastically hot. To run the film forward again, the expansion of the primordial universe is the big bang. As the universe expanded, the density of the energy in it was diluted, another way of saying that the temperature dropped. The 3-degree glow is the remnant of the primordial energy. It is the big bang's fading whimper.

Let us run the film backward again. If the dilute energy of the 3-degree glow were reconcentrated, the universe would be so hot that the leptons and quarks would in effect melt. What is more, gravity, the electroweak force and the strong force would blend into one another. That is why physicists seek their Holy Grail early in the first second of the universe. At that time everything may have been in a unified state, and if one could mathematically describe that state, one might have succeeded in describing all matter and energy in a unified theory.

Let us run the film forward again. As the primordial universe expands, first the three forces part company. Then the quarks and leptons freeze out, like so many snowflakes freezing out of water vapor. The time required for these processes is impressively short; gravity separates from the other forces at 10^{-44} second. (That's .0000000000000000000000000000000000000000001 second. Don't bother to count the zeros; there are 43 of them.) The electroweak force and the strong force separate at 10^{-36} second. The quarks freeze out at about the same time. Then the quarks combine into heavier particles at 10^{-11} second. The leptons freeze out at 10^{-4} second.

The term "freeze" is almost fanciful. At the time the quarks freeze out the temperature is 10^{14} degrees Kelvin, and at the time the leptons freeze out it is 10^{12} degrees. The universe is still far too hot for the formation of atoms; that doesn't happen until it cools to 3,000 degrees after 300,000 years. Then the universe is filled with a gas, and it becomes possible for stars and galaxies to materialize. For what happens afterward the reader will have to wait for the next piece in this book, "Astronomy Explores an Evolutionary Universe."

The Long Arm of the Law

How do we know all this is true? Even though observing distant galaxies with telescopes enables us to see backward in time, we could not see back to the big bang however powerful our telescopes were. The reason is that until 300,000 years after the big bang the density of energy in the universe would have been so great that the universe would have been opaque.

The question "How do we know all this is true?" brings up the nature of scientific theories. It is a funny thing about the word "theory"; in everyday language it means a speculation, as in "I have a theory about why baseball players are hitting more home runs than they used to." In science it means something different; a theory is a substantial, internally consistent body of reasoning. We have, for example, a general theory of relativity and a quantum theory of electrodynamics. They are not speculations or hypotheses, although, like all other theories, they are subject to being refined or superseded.

Embedded in many theories are principles that have come to be called laws. For example, we have the law of the conservation of energy, which states that energy can be neither created nor destroyed; it can only be transformed. Nowadays it is understood that one form of energy is matter. Accordingly matter can be created out of other forms of energy, and vice versa. The overall energy content, however, is always conserved. (The relation is expressed in Einstein's $E = mc^2$: energy equals mass times the speed of light squared.)

There is something immensely comforting about scientific laws. When we observe a double star 10,000 light-years away, the two stars are going around each other in precise accord with the same law that governs the earth's going around the sun. The same can be said about many other laws: they work not only here on earth but also out to the most distant galaxy we can observe. We live in a lawful and logical universe, not one full of occult and capricious powers.

Einstein made a famous remark about it: *"Raffiniert ist der Herr Gott, aber boshaft ist er nicht."* ("God is subtle, but He is not malicious.") Speaking on another occasion of the logical system of ancient Greek geometry, he wrote: "This marvelous accomplishment of reason gave the human spirit the confidence it needed for its future achievements." So it is with the universality of scientific laws: it breeds confidence for future achievements.

The Theorist and the Experimentalist

In the preceding piece I likened scientists in different disciplines to members of different tribes. The tribe of physicists has a highly developed cultural characteristic. It has two major clans: theorists and experimentalists. Other scientific tribes show tendencies toward the same division of labor, but none have carried it nearly as far as physicists.

I had an uncle who was a theoretical physicist: Otto Laporte of the University of Michigan. Once he took me on a tour of his department and introduced me to two of its leading members. David Dennison was a theorist, Richard Crane an experimentalist.

Both men were clearly the salt of the earth. Professor Dennison was forthcoming, even loquacious. He explained what he was doing with clarity and elegance. His hands moved in response to the ideas and words. Professor Crane was shyer and perhaps more modest. He explained what he was doing in few words and with gestures at objects on the laboratory bench. (He was presiding at the building of a particle accelerator.) After we had left the building, my uncle said to me: "And so you see, Dennis, what the difference is between a theoretical physicist and an experimental physicist."

It is also alleged that some people with a bent for physics become theorists rather than experimentalists because they are just plain clumsy. The story is told that Wolfgang Pauli, one of the founders of quantum physics, was so exceedingly maladroit that delicate apparatus shattered on his merely walking into the laboratory. Once when a particularly large and expensive piece of equipment at another institution mysteriously broke while the experimenter was out, he suspected Pauli had been visiting. He could not, however, find any evidence for it. Then he had an inspiration. Checking with Pauli's office on Pauli's travel schedule, he found that during the time when the accident happened Pauli had been on a train passing through town.

Theorists, of course, do theory; experimentalists do experiments. The relationship between the two is intensely symbiotic. Theory is meaningless without experiment, and experiment is meaningless without theory.

The modern theorist is in effect an observer of everything. The word "theory" is from the Greek *theoros*, observer. What the theorist observes may suggest a train of thought indicating that something that has not yet been observed might be observed if the observation is made in the right way. In other words, that train of thought makes a prediction. The basic task of the modern experimentalist is to determine whether or not the prediction is true. At the same time the experimentalist engaged in the task is always on the lookout for something that has not been predicted. In modern physics the task may be a heroic one, calling for scores of experimentalists and a particle accelerator costing hundreds of millions of dollars.

"Help Me, or Else I'll Go Crazy"

The language of both theory and experiment is largely mathematical. It is important to repeat, however, that modern physicists are not mathematicians. (It was not always so. Newton had to invent the calculus in order to develop his universal theory of gravitation.) The people who are in charge of the mathematical imagination are mathematicians, and they create far more mathematics than physicists would ever have any use for. I have heard many apposite stories about this, including the following.

Einstein presented his special theory of relativity in 1905. Thereafter he began to work on his general theory of relativity, which he finally presented in 1916. At the beginning he was having profound difficulty. The mathematics he was using didn't get him anywhere. In genuine despair he turned to his college friend Marcel Grossman, who had become a mathematician. He said: "Grossman, you must help me or else I'll go crazy." Grossman pointed out, among other things, that the geometry Einstein was using was Euclidean: a geometry of flat space. He recommended that Einstein use Riemannian geometry: a geometry of curved space. It worked.

So theoretical physicists are a bit like students browsing in the library of mathematics, looking for a mathematical train of thought that fits a physical problem. This is not to say that in the library of mathematics the physicist finds solutions to physical problems ready-made. In constructing mathematical relations between physical things he needs to be an artist. The theorist P. A. M. Dirac told of how in seeking a theory of quantum mechanics Erwin Schrödinger devised "a very beautiful equation." Unhappily the equation did not fit the experimentally observed facts. Later, however, a new fact was uncovered that made the equation fit. Wrote Dirac: "I think there is a moral to this story, namely that it is more important to have beauty in one's equations than to have them fit the experiment."

Why mathematics should fit the physical world so well is regarded as being something of a mystery. The theorist Eugene Wigner even wrote an essay titled "The Unreasonable Effectiveness of Mathematics in the Natural Sciences." Speaking as a layman, I like to think that mathematics is effective simply because a mathematical system is a logical one and the systems of the real world are logical.

This brings us back to why physicists have confidence in what they have achieved so far in their effort to unify everything about matter and energy. Starting with simple laws such as Newton's universal law of gravitation and repeatedly testing those laws by observation and experiment, they have erected several enormous structures of physical logic. I myself visualize these structures as a lacework resembling some supernal Crystal Palace. The struts and trusses of the lacework are mostly mathematical.

Since the unification of everything about matter and energy has not yet been achieved, some of the theoretical structures are still separate. Consider the special theory of relativity, the first of Einstein's two major theories. It is a theory of electromagnetism that is based on two postulates. The first is that there is no such thing as absolute motion—motion with respect to some fixed frame of reference. All motion is relative: motion is defined by the motion of the observer with respect to the motion of the thing observed. The second postulate is that the speed of light is the same for all observers, regardless of their relative motion. In the special theory Einstein also introduced the concept that time is a fourth dimension.

The special theory makes predictions about the real world, for example that as a particle of matter moves faster it becomes more massive. Those predictions have been verified many times over by observation and experiment. The special theory is a constituent of modern quantum theory, to which I shall be returning.

Next consider the general theory of relativity. It is a theory of gravity that introduces the concept that the four dimensions of space-time are curved. Moreover, in the vicinity of a massive body the curvature of space-time increases; the more massive the body, the greater the curvature. In other words, gravity is an expression of the curvature of space.

Like the special theory, the general theory makes predictions. An example is that a ray of light passing close to a massive body such as a star will curve in the direction of that body. Those predictions too have been verified many times over by observation and experiment. The general theory, however, has resolutely resisted being joined with quantum theory. Since general relativity is a theory of gravity, the fact that it stands separate from other theories is a reflection of the fact that the theories of the three fundamental forces—gravity, the electroweak force and the strong force—are not yet unified.

In building their structures theorists do a lot of intellectual experimentation. It is akin to the approach of the builders of the great Gothic cathedrals. Lacking a theory of large structures, the cathedral builders sometimes took a chance with, say, a lovely thin arch, and sometimes the arch fell down. Presumably the next time they made the arch stronger or tried a different kind of structure.

Theorists today refer to such an intellectual experiment as a model. In fact, much of the description of the universe at the beginning of this piece is properly called not a theory but a model. The idea that particles such as the proton and the neutron are made up of quarks is a model. It is called the quark model. The entire picture of the big bang, with its schedule of times and temperatures and what happens early in the history of the universe, is called the standard model.

It is right that such intellectual experiments should be called models. Since physicists are working so close to the edge of reality, some of their logical conclusions may turn out to be wrong. So far, however, the standard model is a sturdy structure of theory that has withstood the tests of observation and experiment.

Avoiding Quantum Brain Damage

To the layman seeking to know something of modern physics one of the most formidable words is "quantum." The term "quantum leap" has found its way into the common language, but beyond that the quantum conjures up paradoxes and new ways of thinking that threaten to injure the brain. The paradoxes undeniably exist, but much of modern quantum physics can be grasped without referring to them at all.

It goes like this. In 1897 J. J. Thomson discovered the electron: a particle of negative electric charge. He assumed that electrons must be part of atoms. In 1900 Max Planck derived a law implying that energy comes not in a continuous stream but in tiny chunks: quanta. The idea did not set the world on fire until 1905. In that year Einstein, in addition to presenting the special theory of relativity, showed that light must come in quanta: photons. In 1911 Ernest Rutherford found that atoms have a tiny massive core of positive electric charge: the nucleus. The atom was now seen as a nucleus with electrons in orbit around it like planets around the sun.

Niels Bohr wondered if there was a connection between the quanta of light and the structure of the atom. The simplest of all atoms is the atom of ordinary hydrogen. It consists of one proton and one electron. In gaseous hydrogen the atoms are paired in molecules, but the atoms can be dissociated by a high-voltage electric current. Under such conditions the single hydrogen atoms emit light. If you pass the light through a slit and then through a prism, you get a spectrum of the various colors of light the single atoms are emitting. The spectrum is a series of bright lines resembling a ladder in which the rungs get progressively closer together as you move from the violet end of the spectrum to the red.

Physicists before Bohr had found mathematical rules that fit the spacing of the lines in the spectrum of hydrogen. Bohr put forward the idea that these rules were a reflection of different orbits of the electron in the hydrogen atom. When the atom absorbed a quantum of energy, the electron shifted to a higher orbit. Conversely, when the atom emitted a quantum of energy, the electron shifted to a lower orbit. Like the lines in the hydrogen spectrum, the orbits were quite distinct from one another. There was not a smooth continuum of possible orbits but only a set of allowed ones. In other words, the orbits of the electron in the hydrogen atom were quantized.

Bohr's atom captured the imagination of physicists, but it soon became clear that his theory was not very successful. For the hydrogen atom it worked reasonably well, but for atoms with a larger number of electrons it did not. (The physicist H. A. Rowland had said that if the hydrogen atom could be regarded as a single vibrating string of a guitar, the mercury atom must be at least as complicated as a grand piano.) Still, Bohr's basic idea survived. In the 1920s other physicists, notably Werner Heisenberg and Schrödinger, devised a mathematical theory that fit the larger situation.

In this theory the electron came to be visualized not as a tiny planet circling the nucleus's central sun but as a shimmering cloud. The cloud could have different energy states. When it shifted from a higher energy state to a lower one, it emitted a quantum of light or other radiation. Furthermore, the quantum it emitted was characteristic of a particular shift in a particular atom. The red glow of a neon tube is quanta emitted when the electron cloud in the neon atom shifts from a particular state to a lower one.

This general picture is what is called quantum mechanics. There is, of course, a great deal more to the subject. *But if the general reader knows no more about quantum mechanics than this, he or she has gone a long way toward grasping modern physics.*

Quantum mechanics applies to all mechanical systems: atoms more complex than the atom of hydrogen, molecules, solids, liquids, gases, automobile engines, flying footballs, Gorgonzola cheese. Whenever the energy content of one of these systems changes, it does so in distinct quantized states. To be sure, in systems consisting of large numbers of atoms or molecules the quantized shifts are drowned out in the cacophony of large numbers of simultaneous different shifts.

An instructive exception is the laser, a quantum-mechanical device par excellence. In one kind of laser a glass tube is filled with the gases neon and helium. When an electric current is passed through the tube, the gas atoms are set in vigorous motion. When a helium atom collides with a neon atom, it excites the neon atom to a higher energy state. When the neon atom drops back to a lower energy state, it emits a quantum—a photon—of red light, as does a neon atom in an ordinary neon tube.

In the glass tube of the helium-neon laser, however, the emitted photon does more than simply go off as red light. When the photon encounters *another* excited neon atom, it stimulates the atom to drop to the same lower energy state and emit a photon of the same color. As a result there are two photons of red light where there was one, and an avalanche of photons is set in motion. What is more, the excited neon atoms are emitting photons all in step. The process is enhanced by having mirrors at the ends of the laser tube, so that the stimulating photons are reflected back and forth.

Photons make up light waves, and the two mirrors of the laser tube are carefully positioned so that the light waves in the tube are reflected back and forth also in step. In this way the laser tube acts as a small resonator. It resonates at only one frequency: the frequency of the red light emitted by the neon atom. An ordinary neon tube emits light of the same frequency, but its atoms are not emitting photons in step. Its light can therefore be likened to a harsh buzz. The light emitted by the laser tube is the purest of tones.

Quantized energy states are by no means limited to electron clouds. Consider a simple molecule such as carbon monoxide. It is a tiny dumbbell: an atom of carbon and an atom of oxygen sharing their electron clouds. The atoms can vibrate back and forth, and the entire dumbbell can rotate end over end. Both the vibrations and the rotations are quantized. Only certain rates of vibration and speeds of rotation are allowed.

The Happiest Thought

One of the two best-known anecdotes in the history of physics tells of Galileo and the Leaning Tower of Pisa. The story goes that Galileo ascended the tower and simultaneously dropped two balls, a heavy one and a light one. Whereas most people then and now would assume that the heavy ball would hit the ground ahead of the light one, the story has it that the two balls hit at the same time.

An erudite but prankish cousin of mine, Stanley Meltzoff, once repeated the experiment. During the Allied campaign in Italy in the Second World War, Stanley was a correspondent for the U.S. Army newspaper *Stars and Stripes*. When American forces entered Pisa, he quickly went to the Leaning Tower. In the souvenir shop he found two objects of the same shape but of different size and weight; they were marble models of the tower. Acquiring a large model and a small one, he went up the Leaning Tower and dropped the two objects simultaneously. He gravely reported in *Stars and Stripes* that Galileo was entirely mistaken. Instead of the two objects hitting the ground at the same time the larger and heavier object hit ahead of the smaller and lighter one.

Actually there is no convincing evidence that Galileo dropped balls from the Leaning Tower. He did, however, drop two objects of the same size and shape but different weight from an unspecified tower. He reported that the heavier object hit the ground *not* simultaneously with the lighter but "half a hand's span" ahead of it. He was quite aware of why it did so. It was because of air resistance. The surface area of a light object is greater with respect to its mass than the surface area of a heavy object; therefore the lighter object encounters more air resistance with respect to its mass. What Galileo perceived was that in the absence of air all bodies falling toward the earth, whatever their mass, would accelerate at the same rate. He described that rate in a simple mathematical law.

The other of the two best-known anecdotes in the history of physics tells of Newton and the apple. The story goes that when young Newton saw an apple fall from a tree in his garden, it came to him that what made the apple fall and what held the moon in its orbit around the earth is the same force. Newton himself told the story, but he did so long after the fact and may even have been trying to establish that he had arrived at his force concept earlier than he actually had. Whenever he arrived at it, it enabled him to describe the gravitational attraction of one body for another in a simple mathematical law.

With Michael Faraday's electrical researches in the 1830s

and 1840s came another concept: the concept of field. You have doubtless seen what happens when iron filings are sprinkled on a sheet of paper and a toy horseshoe magnet is positioned under the sheet: the particles form a pattern of fuzzy loops around the two poles of the magnet. The pattern defines a magnetic field. The strength of the field can be measured at various distances from the magnet, and it falls off with distance according to another simple mathematical law.

When an object is electrically charged, it is surrounded by an electric field. If the object is in motion, the electric field is associated with a magnetic field. James Clerk Maxwell showed that the two fields are one: the electromagnetic field.

Einstein regarded gravity as being a field, although a field of quite a different kind. An extraordinary connection between Galileo and Newton and Einstein is that Einstein perceived that the acceleration of a falling object is not the result of gravity but *the same thing as gravity*. Einstein named it the equivalence principle and called it "the happiest thought of my life." The greater the acceleration, the greater the gravity. When an object is falling toward a massive body such as the earth, its acceleration is greater than it would be if it were falling toward a less massive body such as the moon.

Einstein also perceived that acceleration and the gravitational field are relative: they are not things that can be attributed to one body in isolation. They can only be ascribed to the motion of one body with respect to another. He had a simple but powerful example. A man falling from the roof of a building feels weightless because he feels no acceleration. From his point of view the earth's gravitational field does not exist.

Hence the gravitational field is not like an electromagnetic field but is the result of a fundamental geometry of space and time. Martin Gardner, who in my estimation has written the clearest popularizations of relativity, puts it elegantly: "Gravity [is not] a 'force' in the Newtonian sense. The earth goes around the sun not because the sun tugs at it but because the sun warps space-time in such a way that the earth finds an elliptical orbit the simplest, 'straightest' path in space as it hurtles ahead in time."

Still, in modern physics all fields, including the gravitational field, are quantized. The quantum of the gravitational field is the graviton, although it is so feeble it has not yet been detected. The quantum of the electromagnetic field is the photon. In fact, even a particle of matter such as an electron is a quantum of a field—the electron field. What we regard as an electron is simply a place where the field is strongest. The same is true of all other fundamental particles. The various fields interpenetrate each other like infinitesimally thin gases. *At bottom there is nothing in the universe but fields.*

Down the Drain into a Blind Alley

In popularizations of modern physics much is made of the paradoxes presented by quantum mechanics. The question may be asked: Why worry about the paradoxes at all? Why not be satisfied with the general picture of quantum mechanics given above? In *The Cosmic Code*, the best popularization of modern physics I have ever read, Heinz Pagels cites a poignant metaphor about quantum-mechanical paradoxes mixed by Richard Feynman: "Do not keep saying to yourself, if you can possibly avoid it, 'How can it possibly be like that?' because you will go down the drain into a blind alley from which no one has yet escaped. Nobody knows how it can be like that."

All the same, the curious nonscientist deserves to know what kind of blind alley he is supposed to be avoiding going down the drain into. To the layman one of the most familiar expressions of modern physics is "the uncertainty principle." Ever since

Heisenberg first enunciated the principle it has given comfort to people who regard modern physics with suspicion. If at the level of fundamental particles things are uncertain, then the whole business could be uncertain—that is, worthless.

The uncertainty principle simply means that at the level of fundamental particles you cannot observe a particle's position and velocity *simultaneously*. At the level of larger objects the effects of the principle are undetectable. If you undertake to measure the position and velocity of a flying football with television cameras, you can measure both the position and the velocity simultaneously because you are gathering from the football vast numbers of reflected photons. If you undertake to measure the position and velocity of an electron, the electron is so small that you can only illuminate it with one photon. Therefore when you use the photon to measure the electron's position, you change the electron's velocity, and if you use the photon to measure the electron's velocity, you change the electron's position.

This, you say, is scarcely a paradox. It is simply common sense at the level of fundamental particles. So, at least, it has always seemed to me. In other words, the uncertainty principle is not paradoxical.

Still, paradoxes at the level of fundamental particles do exist. One is that an electron goes through two holes at the same time. The paradox goes as follows. Before Planck and Einstein light was regarded as a wave. Einstein showed that light consisted of quanta—not waves but particles. In fact, one can demonstrate that light is both a wave and a particle, depending on how you look at it. Bohr named this kind of situation complementarity. Two quite different descriptions of the same thing, both of them equally true and mutually exclusive, may be said to be complementary.

Before quantum mechanics the electron was regarded simply as a particle. The behavior of the electron in the quantum-mechanical atom, however, suggested that it was also a wave. Then in 1927 C. J. Davisson and Lester Germer showed by experiment that wave behavior is characteristic not only of electrons in an atom but also of free electrons moving in a beam.

If an electron is a wave, it should behave like a wave on the surface of water. Visualize a long, straight ocean wave parallel to a long, straight sea wall. The wave is moving toward the wall, at the end of which is the entrance to a harbor. When the wave encounters the sea wall, it bends around the sea wall's end. It is like a long, straight line of soldiers marching toward the wall and pivoting around the end at an angle to their original direction of march. The wave is said to diffract.

The waves in a beam of electrons diffract around an obstacle in the same way. Now visualize the equivalent of a sea wall with two openings in it. When a beam of electrons is directed toward the two openings, the electron waves diffract around four edges: the inner and outer edges of both openings. Therefore the electron waves bending around the two inner edges encounter one another at an angle. When they do so, they interfere with one another. Where the waves are in step, they interfere constructively and become larger. Where they are out of step, they interfere destructively and become smaller. The constructively and destructively interfering waves form a characteristic pattern of alternating electron-rich and electron-poor areas.

When I was young and knew even less than I know now, I was having a chat with Robert Serber, a theorist at Columbia University who was always kind and helpful to ignorant journalists. I said to him: "You know, Professor Serber, this business about the electrons in a beam interfering when they go through two holes doesn't give me any trouble. What's the problem? The waves of some of the electrons simply interfere with the waves of other electrons, no?"

Serber was too gentle a person to give me a pitying smile.

He said: "*Each* electron goes through the two holes at the same time." A light went on in my head and a sheepish grin spread across my face.

But how do physicists *know* that one electron can go through two holes at the same time? In the simplest possible way. You direct a beam of electrons at the two holes and get the diffraction pattern on the other side. Then you keep throttling the beam down until the electrons are arriving at the holes one at a time. The diffraction pattern persists!

As we have seen, an electron is not only a particle and a wave but also a field. Another way to look at its going through two holes at the same time is to visualize the field as being larger in extent than the distance between the holes. Then part of the field of a single electron goes through one hole and part goes through the other. But if that is the case, why isn't the field divided in half, with each half constituting some kind of mini-electron?

The answer is that the field of a single electron is indivisible. That is what is meant by a quantum field: there is a smallest quantity—a quantum—into which the field can be divided. The laws of nature simply require, paradoxical though it may seem, that the two parts of the field divided by the two holes somehow snap back together again.

One other quantum-mechanical paradox before we go on to less troublesome things. Assume that a quantum of light has fallen on an atom and been absorbed by it. The atom shifts to a higher energy state. Eventually the higher state decays to a lower one, in the process emitting a quantum. Exactly when does the transition from the higher state to the lower one occur? Nothing in physics can tell you. It appears to be completely random.

The same kind of thing is true of the atomic nucleus. Some nuclei decay: they are radioactive. As they decay they emit a particle. Exactly when the particle will be emitted from the nucleus, like exactly when the quantum of light will be emitted from an entire atom, cannot be predicted. The radioactive decays are random. The nucleus too behaves according to quantum laws; it is an assemblage of protons and neutrons that has quantized energy states akin to those of the electron cloud.

This is not the way it was with physics before quantum mechanics. It was always assumed that when there was a cause, it was followed by an effect. When a bat hit a baseball, the ball always went somewhere. With quantum mechanics it is as though you cannot predict whether the baseball will go somewhere or not.

As an innocent bystander I used to think that such stories —an electron going through two holes at the same time and the randomness of subatomic events—were simply an indication that reality had levels deeper than those with which we are familiar. One day, perhaps, we will uncover those levels. I like to think it may be so.

My opinion, however, is based only on superficial knowledge. Physicists used to think that there might be "hidden variables" that would supply the missing subatomic events that would make quantum randomness nonrandom and restore the comfortable world of cause and effect. Apparently it has been conclusively demonstrated that such subatomic variables cannot exist. Perhaps one should keep in mind that one should not ask "How can it be like that?" lest one go down the drain into a blind alley.

Knights Who Do Not Seek the Holy Grail

By no means all of physics is concerned with seeking the Holy Grail. There is a virtual infinity of other problems worthy of the physicist's steel. An indication of this fact is that physicists are divided not only into the clans of theoretical physics and experimental physics but also into many others: solid-state physics, astrophysics, geophysics, atmospheric physics, acoustical physics and biophysics, to name only a few. The modern chemist has become largely a physicist. He lives not only by chemical experiment but also by quantum mechanics.

Solid-state physicists have a special interest in crystals. Matter comes in three phases: gas, liquid and solid. Most solids are crystalline—that is, the atoms in them are stacked one on another like the cannonballs in a Civil War monument. If you look at a flat and polished piece of metal under the microscope, you can see that it is made up of small grains. Each grain is a single crystal: the atoms in it are stacked in a regular array.

A diamond is a single crystal of carbon atoms. Quartz is a single crystal of silicon and oxygen atoms, the sizes of which are different. There are crystals consisting of many different kinds of atoms. There are crystals consisting of molecules that themselves consist of more than 10,000 atoms. Are all of these crystals like cannonballs in a stack? The answer is no, if only because the balls in the crystal pile can come in different sizes.

The "balls" can also come in different shapes, since some crystals are made up of molecules. The interesting thing is that, however many sizes and shapes there may be, there is only a finite number of ways they can be stacked. The number of ways is exactly 230. This result is subject to a mathematical proof not different in principle from the proof of the Pythagorean theorem of high-school plane geometry. It has made some physicists wonder if such a closed system of thought might not apply to larger physical systems.

One of my favorite clans is the small clan of rheologists. Rheology is from the Greek *rhein*, to flow. It is the study of how things flow. Not only liquids and gases flow. Everything flows, given enough time. Rocks flow, diamonds flow. The flow of solid metals is a subject of practical concern; the "creep" of metals must be taken into account in the design of bridges and other structures.

There aren't many children in the world who when asked "What does your daddy do?" can answer "He's a rheologist." All the same, there are many physicists with a keen interest in rheology. Notable among them are applied physicists, who must worry about practical problems involved in the flow of fresh paint, say, or bread dough, or lubricating oil.

I once met a rheologist: Marcus Reiner of the Israel Institute of Technology. In fact, it was Reiner who originally introduced the term "rheology." He told me a charming tale of a practical problem he had been asked to solve. The makers of Swiss cheese were in despair. Swiss cheese comes in a big disk, out of which pieces are cut for retail purposes. What was happening was that when the pieces were cut out of the disk, they crumbled into fragments. Customers were querulous.

Reiner analyzed the problem as follows. First of all, the cheese that crumbled was obviously drier than usual; a moister cheese would not crumble. One could not count, however, on all the cheeses in future production being just moist enough to resist crumbling. The trouble was that as the cheese in the disk dried, it shrank. Cracks developed, leading to crumbling. What was needed was a disk that, whether the cheese was dry or not, would shrink evenly throughout.

The disks at that time were too flat to meet this requirement. What Reiner did was to calculate a new shape for the disk. It was somewhat ovoid instead of flat, and if it shrank, it did so evenly and didn't crack. Crisis was averted.

While I was visiting Reiner in his office I had a delightful layman's scientific experience. It was not quite a rheological experience, but then it was not unrheological either. I noticed on one of his shelves a strange object. It was a toy balloon fastened by a rubber band to the lower end of a fat glass tube. The tube was half filled with a colored fluid. (It turned out to be colored water.)

"What's that?" I said. Reiner responded by picking up the water-filled tube with the balloon at the bottom and giving the balloon a squeeze. When he squeezed it, the level of the water in the tube went not up, as one would expect, but down! "What is happening?" he said. "We are maybe exerting negative pressure?"

The explanation is as follows. The balloon contained sand. Sand grains tend to jostle down to a state where the spaces between them are at a minimum. Then when the grains are squeezed, the spaces open up. If the sand happens to be under water, the enlarged spaces make more room for the water. Hence when Reiner squeezed the sand in his balloon, some of the water in the tube went into the enlarged spaces instead of simply being pushed farther up the tube.

You see the same thing when you are walking on the beach at the edge of the water. When you step on sand that has just been wetted by an incoming wave, the sand around your footprint absorbs the water and looks relatively dry. (If you want to repeat Reiner's experiment, please be advised that it does not work with just any kind of sand. It has to be a well-worn sand the grains of which are on the average spherical. Otherwise the spaces between the grains do not open up all that much.)

Two Pleasures of Atmospheric Physics

For human beings one of the principal manifestations of the physical world is the planetary atmosphere in which they live. We breathe it, its currents blow on us as the wind, it forms the clouds in the sky, it sheds rain, it admits the kindly sunlight and starlight while barring the harsher radiations such as ultraviolet and X rays. It is very much a domain of physics and physicists.

One of the most familiar shapes in our mind's eye is the shape of a teardrop. It is smoothly rounded at one end and gracefully tapered at the other. It is the essence of streamlining. Actually, of course, tears do not usually form drops; they fill eyes and run down cheeks. What we are really talking about is the shape of a falling raindrop.

Does a raindrop have the shape of a teardrop? It turns out it doesn't. If the raindrop is small, it is a sphere. If it is large, it has the shape of a hamburger bun. It is flattened on the bottom and somewhat rounded on the top. The raindrop is falling through another fluid: air. If it is a small drop, the forces between the water molecules are sufficient to hold it in a sphere. If it is large, those forces are overbalanced by others, mainly the slight pressure at the bottom of the drop and the slight vacuum at the top.

The hamburger-bun shape is incontrovertibly demonstrated by high-speed photographs, made by among others MIT's incomparable Harold Edgerton. The first illustrator who visualized the teardrop shape must have assumed that a raindrop has the same shape as the drop that drips out of a faucet. The correction of the myth is not all good. It is depressing to think of a summer rain consisting of drops shaped like hamburger buns.

Why does thunder roll? Why is it not simply a loud bang of the same duration as the lightning flash? First of all, how long would you guess a bolt of lightning is? Five hundred feet? A thousand feet? A mile? Well, a typical bolt has a length of three miles, and many bolts have a length of ten miles. Furthermore, in a single bolt of lightning the mighty electric discharge goes back and forth in the channel of the bolt several times. As it does so the air along the channel is intensely heated. A typical temperature is 30,000 degrees C. The surface of the sun is only 6,000 degrees C.

Being so hot, the air expands and rushes violently outward. It generates a colossal bang. Sound, of course, doesn't travel nearly as fast as light. You can measure how far away a lightning bolt is by counting aloud "One hippopotamus, two hippopotamus, three hippopotamus . . ." until you hear the thunder. "One hippopotamus" is one second, and if you multiply the number of "hippopotamuses" by 1,100 you get the distance in feet to the lightning bolt.

Now then, the reason the thunder rolls is simply that some parts of the long lightning bolt that generates the sound are farther away from you than others. You hear the sound from the nearer parts first and the sound from the farther parts later. In addition, the path of the lightning bolt is irregular and in many instances branched. That is why the overall roll of the thunder is punctuated by rumbles and booms.

Twentieth-Century Gothic

Living with modern physics also means living with nuclear weapons. If it weren't for physicists, one might say, we wouldn't be living under the threat of nuclear destruction. One cannot forget, however, that the physicists who undertook to make the first atomic bombs had an excellent motive. They were afraid the physicists of Hitler's Germany might make one first. Even Einstein, the most humane of men, played a key role in the effort when he wrote his letter to President Roosevelt calling the President's attention to the possibilities of uranium as a source of energy.

Before the Second World War most physicists were nobodies. After the war most people regarded a physicist as a somebody who made atom bombs. One day a neighbor's wife informed me that her husband was a *nuclear* physicist. He wasn't; he was another kind of physicist, but she wanted to be sure I knew he was a man of substance.

Physics has been demeaned and distorted by its association with weapons of mass destruction. In the United States much of the support for pure physics, even theory, comes from the Department of Energy (which is in charge of the making of nuclear weapons) and the armed services. The main reason is that the public and its elected representatives have the understandable impression that physicists, having once created a revolutionary weapon, may do so again. A country has to be nice to physicists or maybe somebody else's physicists will get the drop on you.

Actually very little of current physics has to do with weapons. Even if the public support of physics is based on a misconception, the money spent on real physics has been money well spent. Scientific work is characterized by the sudden opening up of a great opportunity. One field of knowledge seems to sprint ahead of the others, with bright people, many of them remarkably young, rushing in to exploit the new discovery or new way of thinking.

Physics is such a field. Consider the particle accelerator. The reason for building bigger accelerators is simple indeed. An accelerator is a device for creating a beam of high-energy particles, and the higher the energy of the particles, the more they reveal. Larger accelerators are not built simply to provide more laboratories for more experimentalists. They make it possible to test the newest predictions of theorists, and they make discoveries that call for new theories.

For example, up to the 1960s most physicists believed that the proton—the particle that together with the neutron makes up the atomic nucleus—was fundamental: that it did not consist of smaller particles. Then a few theorists began to wonder if the proton and the neutron as well were not made up of such particles. The accelerators of the day were not powerful enough to answer the question, but then the next generation of accelerators showed that inside the proton and the neutron there were indeed three smaller particles. The particles in the beam of the accelerators bounced off the smaller particles as if they were three marbles inside a tennis ball. It is these smaller particles that were named quarks.

In other words, the accelerators were acting as giant microscopes. Particles are also waves, and the more energetic the particle, the shorter its wavelength. And the shorter the wavelength, the smaller the objects the particle waves can define.

Accelerators are not only microscopes; they are also particle factories. When fermions—matter particles such as electrons or protons—are accelerated to high energy and hit other fermions, the collisions can give rise to showers or beams of different fermions. High-energy bosons can do the same. One way to create such bosons is to allow matter particles and their antiparticles to annihilate each other. In some accelerators electrons and positrons (antielectrons) annihilate each other, in others protons and antiprotons do so. The energy of annihilation goes off in a mighty blast of photons, which can then congeal into fermions. It reverses Einstein's famous relation: $m = E/c^2$.

The energy of annihilation can also congeal into bosons. It was the energy released by the annihilation of protons and antiprotons that created the first experimentally observed W and Z particles. These bosons of the electroweak force are about 100 times more massive than the proton.

The first accelerators were built in the 1930s. In the money of the day they cost less than $10,000. The cost of accelerators now under construction or seriously proposed ranges from hundreds of millions of dollars up to six billion dollars. Scientists in other fields might well say (and some do): "Boy, we could do a lot with that kind of money." They are undoubtedly right, but there are no other fields with as clear an opportunity to gain fundamental—perhaps revolutionary—new knowledge with the building of a single piece of laboratory apparatus. One possible exception is astronomy, which currently seeks to emplace powerful new telescopes in space and on the ground. Since astronomers are basically physicists, however, they too benefit from the building of accelerators.

Robert Wilson, the man who said accelerators were the kind of cultural activity that makes the country worth defending, made his point in a *Scientific American* article about them: "From time to time in the course of history men have been swept up by intense currents of creative activity. In the pyramids of Egypt, in Greek sculpture and in Florentine painting we find monuments to such bursts of expression. My favorite example is the Gothic cathedrals that so magically sprang up in 12th- and 13th-century France. . . .

"Like physics today, religion at that time was an intense intellectual activity. It seems to me that the designer of an accelerator is moved by much the same spirit that motivated the designer of a cathedral. . . . In the Gothic cathedral the appeal is primarily in the functionality of the ogival construction—the thrust and counterthrust that is so vividly evident. So too in the accelerator we feel a technological esthetic—the spirality of the orbits of the particles, the balance of electrical and mechanical motion, the upward surge of forces and events until an ultimate of height is reached, this time in the energy of the particles."

Sleptons, Squarks and Strings

The remarkable thing about the accelerators now under construction or seriously proposed is that they will create conditions like those in the universe's first quadrillionth of a second and earlier, when fermions were still congealing out of the hot primordial soup. In other words, accelerators are not only microscopes and particle factories but also telescopes that enable us to peer back to the beginnings of the universe. By the same token they are time machines. *They are the experimental embodiment of a physics that has become evolutionary and historical.*

What are they likely to find? First of all, the new accelerator microscopes will be able to resolve an object a tenth the size of the smallest object resolved so far. Perhaps they will show that inside quarks there are particles more fundamental than quarks.

Standard quantum-mechanical theory predicts the existence of a particle that has not been observed: the Higgs boson. (It is named after the British theorist Peter Higgs.) Creating a Higgs boson calls for more energy than has been available so far. If the new particle factories can make one, it will add strong support to the standard theory.

In an effort to find their Holy Grail some theorists have turned to theories in which a particle is not a particle as we normally visualize one but a string. Some such theories call for "superstrings" with ten dimensions. When the superstring particles froze out in the big bang, the theories have it, the ten dimensions curled up into the four of familiar space-time.

Superstrings include not only fermions but also bosons. Moreover, the bosons include the graviton, the quantum of gravity. Superstrings have given rise to supersymmetry: theories that for the first time unify the electroweak force, the strong force and gravity.

Supersymmetry predicts that every particle should have a "superpartner," just as every lepton and quark has an antiparticle. The putative superpartners of leptons, quarks, photons, W particles, Z particles, gluons and gravitons have been named sleptons, squarks, photinos, winos, zinos, gluinos and gravitinos. If the particle factories can make any of them, it will be a big boost for supersymmetry.

Many physicists find supersymmetry much too speculative for their taste. "Theatrical physics," one called it. Others, however, invoke what they call the totalitarian principle, adopted from the ant colony of T. H. White's *The Sword in the Stone*: "Anything not forbidden is compulsory."

Any theory that succeeds in unifying gravity with the other two forces will be a philosophical milestone. The most successful theory of gravity—Einstein's general theory of relativity—does not even include quanta and quantization. Einstein himself never believed in the quantum-mechanical picture of nature. He could not accept that submicroscopic events occur at random. He thought every effect must have a clear-cut cause.

The fact remains that the quantum-mechanical theory is also enormously successful. It predicts what happens in electrical, magnetic, chemical and nuclear systems with extraordinary accuracy. Bohr and Einstein argued about the quantum-mechanical picture, in their sad and kindly way, for decades. It was partly a reflection of an aesthetic difference between general relativity and quantum mechanics. General relativity has the absolute quality of Greek geometry; it is complete unto itself. The astrophysicist Subrahmanyan Chandrasekhar called it "the most beautiful theory there ever was." Quantum mechanics is incomplete.

Bohr believed theories should be like that: somewhat provisional and open-ended. He even said: "It is wrong to think that the task of physics is to find out what nature is. Physics concerns what we can say about nature." It might be, however, that a successful theory of all matter and energy will have the Einsteinian absolute quality or the quality of the finite number of crystal forms.

As for what will actually emerge from the accelerator workers and the theorists, one theorist remarks that it will be surprising if it is not surprising.

ASTRONOMY EXPLORES
AN EVOLUTIONARY UNIVERSE

Many people have spoken of getting a prickling sensation at the back of the neck when they see a certain painting or hear a certain passage of music. I didn't believe it until I found myself getting the same sensation whenever I heard a certain passage in *The Magic Flute*. (For the record it is in Tamino's aria *Dies Bildniss ist bezaubernd schön*.) I also get the sensation when I see a certain photograph of the Great Nebula in Andromeda.

The Andromeda nebula is a singularly beautiful pinwheel of stars and luminous clouds of gas. It is the large galaxy closest to our own. I am not alone in my reaction to it. A friend of mine once showed a photograph of the Andromeda galaxy to the art director of a magazine on which he was working. The art director said: "That's gorgeous! But tell me. Can we get a shot of it from another angle?"

What the art director didn't know is that the distance between our own galaxy and the Andromeda galaxy is 2 million light-years: the distance light travels in 2 million years. Even if the photographic mission were undertaken with a spacecraft traveling at the speed of light, the spacecraft would not be able to deliver pictures from any substantially different angle until, to make a bit of an understatement, well after the magazine's deadline. Although the art director was an educated person, he lacked a mental image of the known universe. It is a mental image no educated person should lack; it can lead to prickling sensations at the back of the neck.

Modern astronomy, like modern physics, is an epic tale of evolution. Everything in the universe evolves: planets, stars, clusters of stars, galaxies, clusters of galaxies, clusters of clusters of galaxies, the universe itself. Everything is process. To be sure, some things are evolving faster than others, and some are evolving very slowly indeed. A small-scale example is our own planet's moon, which has changed little in 4 billion years. Yet even such inactive bodies have a markedly evolutionary past.

Cosmic evolution is not quite the same thing as biological evolution. Biological evolution is based on natural selection: the perpetual experiment in which changes in living organisms are tested for their effectiveness in enabling the organisms to reproduce in a given environment. In cosmic evolution there is no natural selection. All the same there are profound connections between cosmic evolution and biological evolution. Eighteenth-century writers spoke of a Great Chain of Being, in which everything in nature is linked to everything else. The links between cosmic and biological evolution will emerge in this piece and in the following ones: "Geology Feels for the Pulses of the Earth" and "Biology, Having Found its Holy Grail, Drinks from It."

Like physics, astronomy was not always historical. Cosmology, the study of the origin and large-scale structure of the universe, is an ancient and honorable word, but there was not much to the subject until the 1920s. In that decade observational astronomy firmly established three things. First, the sun and its planets occupy a position in a distinct system of stars: the galaxy. Second, certain of the fuzzy spots in the sky—nebulae—are galaxies outside our own. Third, the galaxies are on the average rushing away from one another; in other words, the universe is expanding.

This last fact immediately suggested that the galaxies might have a common origin. As we saw in the preceding piece, if one could reverse the outward motion of the galaxies, they would all eventually come back to one point. In short, the universe that is being observed in telescopes has an origin, a past and a future.

There was also a suggestive theory: the general theory of relativity. It was in the general theory that Einstein introduced the concept that space-time is curved. Soon after Einstein presented the general theory in 1916 he undertook to apply it to cosmology. At the time it was not known that the universe is expanding. When Einstein sought to apply certain of his equations to the cosmos, he was disappointed to discover that they didn't fit the static cosmos he knew. In order to make them fit he had to introduce a "cosmological term."

Then between 1922 and 1927 two men independently showed that if the assumption is made that the universe is expanding, Einstein's equations fit the real cosmos without the cosmological term. One of the men was Alexander Friedmann, a Russian mathematician and meteorologist. The other was Georges Lemaître, a Belgian priest. Lemaître is credited with having introduced the idea that the universe began with a single huge explosion, later named the big bang. It was not until 1929, however, that Edwin Hubble presented evidence that the universe is indeed expanding. The cosmos was now seen, and is still seen, as being an expanding Einsteinian one with curved space.

What exactly is meant by curved space? One way to look at it is as follows. Visualize two prodigiously powerful laser beams aimed into space parallel to each other. In "flat" space the two beams would, no matter how long the light in the beams continued traveling, remain parallel. In curved space the beams would either converge or diverge. The general theory of relativity does not specify which of the two curvatures it is.

Whether space is flat, positively curved or negatively curved is a matter of central importance to cosmology. If the beams converged, the universe would be "closed." It would curve back on itself. If the beams remained parallel or diverged, the universe would be "open." In a closed universe expansion would eventually end and would be followed by contraction. In an open universe the expansion would continue forever. Whichever it is, the universe is not static but evolving.

How Far Is Far?

Astronomers have worked like Trojans to estimate how old the universe is. In order to know how old it is you have to know how far away things are. It goes like this. What Hubble was working with in the 1920s were the spectra of galaxies outside our own. It was already a commonplace that when a light-emitting object such as a star or a galaxy is moving toward us, its spectrum is shifted toward the blue end, and that when the object is moving away from us, the spectrum is shifted toward the red. The greater the blue shift or red shift, the greater the object's velocity toward us or away from us.

Hubble noted that nearly all the galaxies had red shifts. Moreover, the smaller and fainter the galaxy was, the greater its red shift was. He made the assumption that on the average the galaxies actually have the same size and brightness. The smaller and fainter ones are simply farther away. On this assumption he arrived at a law: the greater the distance of the galaxy, the greater its velocity away from us.

But in order to know when the galaxies started their journey from a common point of origin it is not enough to know their velocity. You also have to know their distance in absolute terms. Say you wanted to determine when a certain automobile had left on a trip. You know that the automobile has been traveling down a straight highway at 60 miles per hour. You could not work out when it had started its journey unless you knew how many miles it had traveled.

The principal measure of distance in modern astronomy is the parsec, equal to 3.26 light-years. Here I shall be using the older measure, the light-year. Since it explicitly refers to the distance light travels in a year, it is a salutary reminder that in the universe distance is a reflection of time.

The star closest to the sun and its planets is 4.3 light-years away. Out to 100 light-years astronomers were able to measure the distance to a star by simple triangulation, based on the fact that as the earth goes around the sun the star's position in the sky shows a measurable back-and-forth shift. Out to 3,000 light-years—a distance still well within our galaxy—they were able to estimate the distance by the actual motion of stars across the sky; the smaller the star's *apparent* motion, the larger its distance. But the full-sized galaxy closest to our own—the Andromeda galaxy—is clearly much farther away than 3,000 light-years. How to measure *its* distance?

The best way is by turning to the kind of star called a Cepheid variable. Cepheid variables are named after Delta Cephei, the fourth-brightest star (alpha, beta, gamma, delta . . .) in the constellation Cepheus. In Greek mythology, by coincidence, Cepheus was the father of Andromeda. Cepheid variables are giant stars that pulse regularly in brightness. Their period of pulsation ranges from hours to days. Studying Cepheid variables within a distance of 3,000 light-years from the solar system, astronomers found that their period is related to their absolute brightness: their brightness corrected for their known distance. The slower the pulsation, the brighter the star.

What this means is that if you measure the regular pulsation of a Cepheid variable farther away than 3,000 light-years, you know its absolute brightness. And if you know its absolute brightness, you know its distance; the greater the difference between the apparent brightness and the absolute brightness, the more distant the star. With the advent of the 200-inch telescope on Palomar Mountain in 1948 the method could be applied to the Andromeda galaxy. It showed that the distance of the galaxy was 2 million light-years. With that figure, and the assumption that the more distant galaxies have the same average size and brightness, astronomers could determine the age of the universe: not less than 10 billion years and not more than 20 billion.

Creeping Murmurs

The universe has been evolving, then, for between 10 and 20 billion years. The very sentence raises large questions. What was happening *before* it started evolving? How long will it continue evolving? I shall be dealing with such questions, but for the moment I should like to get on with the tale of what happened in the course of the universe's evolution.

I should emphasize that in my telling of that tale I shall be doing something no scientist would dare to do: omitting many necessary qualifications. My account, however, does not depart from what most scientists believe is *probably* true. Still, what is probably true today may not be quite the same as what will be probably true tomorrow. The tale too evolves.

After the hot flash of the big bang the universe was rather like Shakespeare's picture (in *Henry the Fifth*) of how the world began: "Now entertain conjecture of a time, when creeping murmur and the poring dark fills the wide vessel of the universe." The "poring dark" was filled with a thin gas. The gas consisted of 73 percent hydrogen and 27 percent helium, the two lightest elements. There may also have been a tincture of the third-lightest element: lithium.

The "creeping murmur" of the thin gas somehow made it denser in some places than in others. In the vast blobs of denser gas the feeble gravitational attraction between the atoms of the gas began to pull them toward one another. The density of the gas in a blob therefore increased further. It was such a blob that in time became a galaxy.

As the overall density of the blob increased, knots of even denser gas formed. In such knots the process of contraction accelerated as the atoms of the gas drew closer and the gravitational attraction between them became stronger. In time the density of the knot increased to the point where the knot began to heat up. The gas began to glow, at first with long-wave radiation such as radio waves and infrared, then with light. A star had been born.

In the beginning the source of the energy radiated by the star was simply gravity: one of the three known forces of nature. As the gas of the star was contracting, its atoms were on the average falling toward some mutual center. And as the density of the gas rose, the atoms began to encounter one another. When a moving atom encounters another moving atom, the atoms often lose energy. In this case the energy they were losing was the energy they had gained by falling.

Since energy can be neither created nor destroyed, the atoms' energy of motion is converted into another form. In this case the energy of motion was converted into electromagnetic radiation: a manifestation of one of the other two forces of nature.

The radiation can be absorbed by other atoms, some of which dissipate it by moving faster. The net effect is for the average speed of the atoms to increase and the temperature to rise.

The star continued to contract. As its density increased, so did the frequency of encounters between its atoms. And as the encounters between atoms became more energetic, a new energy source came into play. It was nuclear energy. The nuclei of atoms have a positive electric charge, and bodies with the same electric charge repel each other. When two nuclei of hydrogen collide with sufficient energy, however, they break through the barrier of electric repulsion and cleave together. The force that now binds them is the third force of nature: the strong force.

The strong force is a lot stronger than the other forces. When two hydrogen nuclei fuse, their net energy content is less than that of the two nuclei when they were separate. Therefore energy must be dissipated, either in radiation or in an increase in the speed of the fused nucleus. The amount of energy is commensurate with the strength of the strong force, so that it is a lot of energy. The star can now remain hot after it has exhausted its gravitational energy.

The Evolution of Galaxies

Clearly the star we are talking about is evolving. As it and other stars are evolving, so is the great blob of gas that gave rise to them. If the blob was asymmetrical, it would have begun to rotate. Most things in the universe rotate. Rotational momentum, like energy, is conserved. What that means is that when a large rotating body shrinks, it rotates faster. The universal metaphor for this behavior is a spinning figure skater. As the spin starts, the skater's arms are outstretched, and as the arms are pulled in, the skater spins faster. So it is with a spinning sphere of gas: as it contracts it spins faster.

The rotating sphere differs from the skater in consisting of a fluid. The atoms in it are being simultaneously pulled downward toward the center of the sphere by gravity and outward by "centrifugal force," the tendency of bodies to continue moving in a straight line because of their inertia. As a result the sphere becomes oblate: its poles get flatter and its equator fatter. At the same time it continues to shrink. Eventually it can shrink and spin down to a small, thin disk. The word "small" is only relative: the disk might be 100,000 light-years in diameter. Such a disk, illuminated by the stars born in it, is what we call a spiral galaxy.

Not all galaxies are spiral. Many are "elliptical," ranging in form from a disk to a sphere. Such galaxies consist of old red stars and contain little or no gas. For the purposes of further discussion I shall refer only to spiral galaxies.

When the magazine art director asked for a different view of the Andromeda galaxy, he was referring to the fact that from our vantage in the solar system we see the thin disk of the galaxy at an oblique angle. Understandably he wanted to see it in all its splendor head-on. If we could view the Andromeda galaxy that way, we would see more clearly that it has luminous arms spiraling out from an even more luminous region in the center of the disk. Seeing the galaxy from an oblique angle, however, is not all bad. It reveals the bright central region as a spherical bulge. Moreover, we can see that away from the disk and arrayed spherically around the center of the galaxy are scores of globular clusters.

A globular cluster is itself a singularly beautiful object: a cluster of perhaps 100,000 stars in orbit around a common center of gravity. The concentration of stars is greatest at the center and thins out with distance from it. The cluster as a whole moves in orbit around the center of the galaxy. Globular clusters played a key role in our understanding of our own galaxy. In the years 1918–21 Harlow Shapley, working with the 60- and 100-inch telescopes on Mount Wilson, found that a third of all the known globular clusters are concentrated in less than 2 percent of the sky.

That 2 percent lay in the constellation Sagittarius. Making the assumption that the globular clusters are arrayed around the center of the galaxy, Shapley drew the conclusion that the center of the galaxy lay in the same direction. It is fitting that it should lie in Sagittarius. In myth Sagittarius is the archer, and it might be said that his arrow points toward the center of the galaxy.

On the same basis Shapley deduced that the sun is not situated anywhere near the center of the galaxy. It lies in the thin galactic disk two-thirds of the way from the center to the edge. The disk is visible to us as the Milky Way, the ghostly band of distant stars that on a clear night can be seen arching across the sky. When we look at the Milky Way, we are looking along the central plane of the galactic disk from the inside. The density of stars is therefore greater in that direction than it is in others.

The center of the galaxy, however, is not visible at all, at least not at the wavelengths of light. The center is obscured by dense clouds of dust. Since the time of Shapley's work on the globular clusters it has become clear that our galaxy, like the Andromeda galaxy, is a spiral. It has spiral arms and a central bulge. Interspersed among the stars in the arms are large quantities of gas and dust. Some of this material is visible where energetic processes make the gas luminous or where stars illuminate the dust. Much of the material is dark; it can be detected only where the dust blocks, dims or reddens the light from the stars behind it.

The Evolution of Stars

Where do the gas and dust come from? Most of the gas must be the hydrogen and helium that were originally there as the galactic blob spun down to a small disk. The dust, however, was manufactured by stars. This brings us to the next link in the great chain of being.

Stars are not only born but also die. In between they lead diverse lives, some uneventful and some dramatic. Stars range in mass roughly from a tenth the mass of the sun to 100 times the mass of the sun. Smaller stars such as the sun cook along quietly for billions of years. Larger stars burn with a hard gemlike flame. Massive stars can be born, live and die in as little as 10 million years.

When the first stars lit up, they consisted of hydrogen and helium. Their nuclear energy came from the fusion of hydrogen nuclei into helium nuclei. What happens when a star's supply of hydrogen runs out? It swells up into the large cool star called a red giant. At the same time the core of the star, the place where it is hot enough and dense enough for nuclear reactions to proceed, shrinks and gets still hotter and denser. Under those conditions the energy of the helium nuclei is sufficient for *them* to fuse.

In the process helium nuclei are built up into the nuclei of carbon and oxygen. What happens when the red giant's supply of helium runs out? It first begins to burn the carbon and then begins to burn the oxygen. In the process the carbon and oxygen nuclei are built up into still heavier elements. The switchover from one nuclear fuel to another as each runs out continues up the periodic table of the elements through silicon. When it gets to elements in the vicinity of iron, it stops. The fusion reactions that could make elements heavier than iron do not release energy, they absorb it.

How then are elements heavier than iron made, elements such as silver, gold, lead and so on up to uranium, the heaviest long-lived element? Nuclei consist of protons and neutrons. The protons have a positive electric charge, and since bodies with the same electric charge repel each other, protons are repelled by nuclei unless they have enough energy to get through the electric-charge barrier. The same is not true of neutrons. They have no electric charge, and so they can be readily absorbed by nuclei. In short, the elements up to uranium are built up through neutron absorption.

It is carbon and the other heavy elements, in chemical combination with hydrogen, that make up the dust in the space between the stars. But how do the heavy elements get out of stars into interstellar space? A large part of the answer is dramatic: the heavy elements are showered into space when a star explodes.

And why does a star explode? It seems to have to do with the star's original mass. When a star with a mass less than six to eight times the mass of the sun exhausts its nuclear fuel, it typically shrinks down into the small hot star called a white dwarf. It shrinks so much it is only about the size of the earth and the atoms in its core are packed into a solid.

If the star has a mass *more* than six to eight times the mass of the sun, other things can happen. Such a star running out of nuclear fuel may be teetering on the razor's edge between stability and instability. In a stable star the heat and pressure of the core are sufficient to hold up the outer layers, and the weight of the outer layers is sufficient to hold in the hot gas of the core. In an unstable star the balance between the two may be tipped. The more massive the star, the more likely it is to be unstable.

When a star is highly unstable, it collapses. The material

in the outer part of the core, no longer held up by the inner part, plunges headlong toward the center. It gets there in as little as a second. Indeed, its velocity is so great that it bounces back outward and floods into interstellar space.

It is such a star that is called a supernova. The event is so violent that for weeks or months the exploding star can outshine all the other stars in the galaxy of which it is a part. When it fades, it can leave behind it a luminous cloud of gas that continues expanding for tens of thousands of years. It can also leave a most extraordinary cinder: a tiny dense ball, perhaps fifteen miles in diameter, consisting of neutrons.

In any one galaxy a supernova explodes about once every 100 years. If that sounds like supernovas are rare, consider that over 10 billion years one galaxy would have had 100 million of them. The last supernova to be observed in our galaxy was one in the 1670s. (The supernova of 1987 was in a small neighboring galaxy, the Large Cloud of Magellan.) In 1604 the pioneering astronomer Johannes Kepler described a supernova in our galaxy that was visible in broad daylight. Only thirty-two years earlier, in 1572, Kepler's predecessor Tycho Brahe described another such star. A supernova observed in 1006 must have been quite a spectacle: it was as bright as the moon.

(I cannot think of Tycho Brahe without remembering an odd fact about him. Tycho was a Dane, and in the days before telescopes had been turned on the sky he built on the Danish island of Hven a "celestial palace" of nontelescopic astronomical instruments. With them he plotted the positions of the stars and the planets with unprecedented accuracy. It was those measurements that enabled Kepler to arrive at the laws of how the planets travel around the sun.

As a young man Tycho fought a duel, in the course of which his nose was cut off. Being a proud nobleman, he chose to have the missing member replaced with a prosthesis made of gold and silver. Then toward the end of his life Tycho fell out with his royal Danish patron and moved to Prague, where in 1601 he died.

In 1901, for the 300th anniversary of Tycho's death, the Prague town council ordered the restoration of his tombstone, and in the course of the work the grave was opened. Scholars who had heard about the prosthesis eagerly looked for it. The legend was confirmed, though not in quite the way they expected. There was no gold and silver, but the skull around the nose was stained with the green of copper oxide. The silver had probably been alloyed with copper and then lost to corrosion. As for the gold, the legend may have been a bit more ornate than the prosthesis.)

Since a galaxy gets a supernova about once every 100 years, is our galaxy overdue for another? Probably not. The reason is that much of the galaxy is not visible to us because of the dust in the galactic disk. If there have been other supernovas in the galaxy since the 1670s, we simply may not have been in a position to see them. Most of the same dust, of course, originates with the supernovas themselves.

A small amount of the dust originates with other stars. All stars shed some of their material into space. The sun is no exception. Since the sun is a hot, luminous mass of gas, its outer layers are constantly boiling off. In effect the atmosphere of the sun is continuously expanding.

On its outward journey the expanding gas rushes past the planets. It is apparent as a "solar wind." One manifestation of the solar wind is that it creates part of the tail of a comet. The head of a comet consists largely of frozen water; it has been described as a dirty snowball. (Spacecraft observations of Comet Halley when it swung around the sun in 1985–86 showed that *its* head is coal black, so that a better description might now be a filthy snowball.) As the head approaches the sun it is heated and starts evaporating. The evaporated stuff is driven outward from the sun by two influences: the solar wind and the palpable pressure of sunlight. The light pressure drives small dust particles outward, forming a smooth, dim part of the tail. The solar wind, consisting of electrically charged particles, excites gas atoms and molecules, forming a less regular, brighter part of the tail.

(The return of Comet Halley was a curious setback for the popular appreciation of astronomy. Most people have seen photographs of the comet made when it plunged toward the sun in 1910. At that time its orbital positions with respect to those of the earth were such that at one point its tail extended halfway from the horizon to the zenith—one of the greatest astronomical spectacles in human history. When the comet returned, its orbital positions were such that it could be seen only as a dim, fuzzy object near the horizon. Although astronomers had repeatedly pointed out that this would be the case, others could be forgiven for saying: "If that's a big moment in astronomy, don't bother me with the next one.")

Another manifestation of the solar wind is the shimmering display of the aurora. The solar wind is hot, and so it consists largely of electrons that have been removed from atoms and of atoms that have lost electrons. Both are electrically charged. The path of an electrically charged particle is bent by a magnetic field, and when the particles in the solar wind encounter the magnetic field of the earth, they are bent and trapped by it in complex ways. When enough of them spill into the earth's upper atmosphere, they energize its atoms to emit the reds, yellows, greens, purples and pinks of the aurora.

The sun, then, is constantly shedding a tiny fraction of its mass into interstellar space. Some stars shed a much larger fraction of their mass. This is particularly true of stars that have just formed. Indeed, soon after the sun formed it too may have shed much more mass than it does today.

The sun consists almost entirely of hydrogen and helium. Its spectrum, however, shows that it is salted with heavier elements. A different story is told by the spectra of the stars in globular clusters. Such stars are much poorer in the heavier elements. As we have seen, globular clusters are arrayed in a sphere around the center of our galaxy and the Andromeda galaxy. The sphere is a large one: its diameter is roughly the same as the diameter of the thin galactic disk. In other words, most of the globular clusters are not in the disk at all.

It seems likely that the stars in the globular clusters formed at a stage when the galaxy was still spinning down from a sphere to a thin disk. Therefore they are old stars. In fact, they may be almost as old as the universe.

The conclusion is clear: *the sun is not a first-generation star.* Since it contains elements heavier than hydrogen and helium, it could not have coalesced simply out of the primordial gas. It must have coalesced out of stuff sprinkled with heavier elements cooked in supernovas and other stars. It formed 5 billion years ago, and it will simmer along for another 5 billion years before it runs out of hydrogen and swells up into a red giant.

This train of thought has the deepest import for matter and energy contemplating themselves. I am referring, of course, to human beings. The cloud of gas and dust that gave birth to the sun also gave birth to the earth and the other planets. If the cloud had consisted only of hydrogen and helium, it could not have given birth to much of anything. There would have been no rocks, no water, no oxygen—no life. It has often been observed that human beings and all other forms of life consist quite literally of star dust. For human beings, at least, the last link in the great chain is themselves.

Solid Stars

We cannot take leave of supernovas without missing some of the most interesting things going on in modern astronomy. I mentioned that the cinder of a supernova can be a tiny star consisting of neutrons. A neutron star can come into being as follows: When a supernova collapses, it collapses so quickly that the sheer velocity of the material falling inward from its outer core can compress the inner core to a fantastic density. The density can be so great, in fact, that the electrons in the atoms of the core are in effect crushed into the nuclei.

Since electrons have a negative electric charge and the protons of atomic nuclei have a positive charge, the opposite charges cancel each other. The process is not as simple as that, but the net result is that the protons are converted into nuclear particles without electric charge: neutrons. In the tiny sphere of a neutron star the remnant nuclei form a rigid crust. Below that are the neutrons. In the core of the sphere all kinds of bizarre things are going on. Exactly what is not clear, but some physicists have gone so far as to suggest that the core of a neutron star is a sea of quarks, the constituents of neutrons and protons.

As the neutron star forms it is given a mighty twist by the rotational momentum of the star that gave birth to it. You will remember my remarking that most things in the universe rotate and that rotational momentum is conserved. As the knot of gas that becomes a star shrinks, it rotates faster and faster. For a star such as our sun the speed of rotation is not particularly high: the sun rotates at the equator only once every twenty-five days. For a star that has shrunk to a diameter of fifteen miles the speed can be very high indeed. Some neutron stars rotate hundreds of times per *second*.

Among the properties of a star is magnetism. The sun has a modest magnetic field; its strength is about the same as that of the earth's field. More massive stars can have a magnetic field as much as 30,000 times stronger. When such a star shrinks, its magnetic field gets commensurately more intense. The magnetic field of a neutron star can be a billion times more intense than the sun's.

Through complex physical processes in its intense magnetic field the neutron star generates radio waves. The radio waves are not broadcast from the star in all directions, as light is broadcast from a normal star. They are focused in a beam that sweeps the sky like a searchlight. Therefore when they are detected by radio telescopes on the earth they pulse regularly in time with the rotation of the star. It is such stars that have been named pulsars.

The connection between pulsars and neutron stars, and between neutron stars and supernovas, is handsomely exemplified by one object. It is the Crab Nebula, a splash of luminous gas in the constellation Taurus. The speed with which the nebula is expanding indicates that it originated with a supernova explosion about 1,000 years ago. As it happens, at the position of the nebula today astronomers in the Orient observed a brilliant "guest star" in the year 1054. At the center of the gas cloud is a pulsar rotating thirty times per second.

Some neutron stars flare up with less regularity than pulsars do. This appears to be the result of an interesting general fact about stars. Perhaps half of all stars are not single stars like our sun but are double or multiple stars in orbit around a common center of gravity. Therefore a neutron star is quite likely to be a member of a pair of stars. If the other member of the pair is at an earlier stage of stellar evolution, and if the two stars are quite close together, matter from the other star may spill onto the neutron star, setting off a stellar conflagration. The flare-up is so intense that it can emit X rays and gamma rays, radiations far more energetic than light.

Many ordinary double stars blink like pulsars, although far less rapidly. They do so, however, only when the plane in which the two stars of the pair revolve around a common center happens to coincide with the line of sight between them and us. When that is the case, one star regularly passes in front of the other, and vice versa. The timing of those periodic eclipses makes it possible to calculate the masses and the orbits of the two stars. A significant thing about such calculations is that they precisely confirm the theory of gravity that holds in the solar system.

The Evolution of Dust

In the foregoing a link in the great chain is missing. The heavier elements were cooked in the interior of stars, but how did the heavier elements become the dust that lies between the stars in the disk of our galaxy? As the galaxy spun down from a sphere to a disk, it concentrated the primordial hydrogen and helium. The gas is still, however, extremely thin. A tiny fraction of the hydrogen atoms combines into molecules: H_2. The same does not happen to the helium atoms because helium does not combine with anything. It is to the mixture of atomic and molecular hydrogen and atomic helium that the spritz of heavier elements cooked in supernovas and other stars is added.

The heavier elements combine with the hydrogen atoms and molecules to form other molecules. The main elements that do so are carbon, nitrogen and oxygen; after them in abundance come magnesium, silicon and iron. Most of the molecules are two-atom ones such as carbon monoxide (CO). Some are more complex, such as water and even ethanol (C_2H_5OH). Ethanol is drinkable alcohol, and an inevitable joke told at the time of its discovery in interstellar space had to do with the fact that the molecule was not as common as calculations had suggested it would be. The explanation was clearly that much of it had been drunk up.

Some sixty kinds of molecules have been discovered in interstellar space. The molecules too combine, forming small icy particles and the larger particles called interstellar grains. The interstellar grains themselves are not large: the largest are the size of particles in cigarette smoke. They nonetheless have a complex structure and history.

Even after molecules form in interstellar space they can be disrupted by the harsh radiation of hot stars. It is only the tougher molecules that survive. Among the toughest are silicates: compounds of silicon, oxygen and other elements. It is believed that they provide a core on which other molecules can collect. Among those molecules are water, methane and ammonia. These molecules, in turn, appear to be reworked by interstellar radiation into a complex chemical mixture. A grain with a silicate core and a layer of reworked stuff can then collect a mantle of still more unreworked stuff.

It is the interstellar grains that obscure our view of the center of the galaxy. The grains are nonetheless exceedingly sparse. It is estimated that in the disk of the galaxy there is typically one grain in a cube 100 yards on an edge. That their cumulative effect can be so great is a measure of the fact that, although the stars in the sky and in astronomical photographs seem close together, they are actually a long way apart. Over a distance of a few light-years a grain every 100 yards adds up to a lot of grains.

The Invisible Universe

Thin though it is, the interstellar gas and dust is thicker in some places than it is in others. It tends to build up in great billows that trace out the spiral pattern of the galaxy's arms. Since new stars form out of interstellar material, most of them form in that same pattern. That is why the spiral arms of our galaxy and other spiral galaxies are luminous.

The luminosity of the spiral arms comes not only from stars but also from glowing clouds of gas thousands of times larger than a star. These clouds are made luminous by brilliant young stars around them and embedded in them. They are clearly the kind of place where new stars are born. The luminous material itself, however, is not a good place. Its luminosity is an indication that it is hot, and a hot gas expands. The gestation of a star calls for material that is not expanding but contracting. Such material needs to be dark and cool.

Dark and cool material cannot be seen against a dark background, and most of the sky is dark. Against the bright background of the luminous clouds of the spiral arms, however, drifts and knots of dark material stand out. A knot of dark material is where a new star or stars would be born. Its cool interior would favor the slow drizzle of atoms, molecules and dust grains toward a common center or centers. As the density of the material increased, its temperature would rise, and in due course a new star would begin to shine.

How do the knots form in the first place? It is one of the main questions of modern astronomy. One thing that helps them form is turbulence in the interstellar gas and dust, which creates eddies where the gas and dust are denser than they are elsewhere. Perhaps the eddies are molded into protostars, as a ball of clay is molded in your hands, by the pressure of the light and stellar winds of surrounding stars; such pressure is strong in the vicinity of hot young stars. Since those stars formed out of the same large cloud of material that stars in their vicinity are forming out of, new stars may breed newer stars.

The larger knots are sometimes called nodules, the smaller

ones Bok globules. Bok was Bart J. Bok, the astronomer who introduced the term "globules." He was Dutch, and his not unpleasant accent was such that a generation of astronomers listening to his talks came to know globules as "globbles."

Our galaxy is a spiral much like the Andromeda galaxy. The demonstration for this came later than one might think: not until the 1950s. Thereafter many extraordinary new things were discovered about the galaxy.

For example, it became apparent that the thin central disk of the galaxy is embedded in a distinct sphere of gas and stars with about the same diameter as the disk. The stars are old ones, and among them are the stars of perhaps half of the 200-odd globular clusters. The sphere was named the galactic halo.

Furthermore, the halo was seen to be embedded in a still larger sphere. Nothing in that sphere is visible or otherwise directly detectable, but there is no doubting its existence. The disk of the galaxy rotates like a great flat pinwheel, and the speed with which its various detectable constituents—stars, gas and dust—revolve around the galactic center can be measured. What one would expect is that the inner constituents would be revolving faster than the outer ones, in accordance with the law Johannes Kepler formulated for the revolution of the planets around the sun. (For example, the innermost planet, Mercury, moves around the sun at a speed ten times higher than the speed of the outermost, Pluto.)

The measurements show something else. Instead of the speed of revolution falling off with distance from the center of the galaxy in accordance with the distribution of the detectable matter, the speed falls off practically not at all. There is only one conclusion: much of the galaxy's matter is not detectable.

The same seems to be true of other spiral galaxies. The edge of their visible disk is moving faster than it should be. Moreover, the galaxies in clusters of galaxies are in motion with respect to one another, and the motions are such that if the only matter present were the visible galaxies, the clusters would have long since dispersed. They are held together by matter that is invisible. Indeed, 90 percent of the matter in the universe—and perhaps as much as 99 percent—is invisible.

What is the invisible matter? It cannot simply be dust, like the dark matter in our galaxy; that much dust would be visible where it obscured galaxies outside our own. Is it perhaps bodies that coalesced out of the primordial gas but never got big enough to shine like a star? Is it stars that have burned out? The fraction of the invisible matter that would be accounted for by such bodies, according to theorists, could not be much more than 10 percent.

What is the rest? Is it perhaps unknown fundamental particles, or unknown properties of known particles? For example, if the neutrinos have a tiny mass, there are so many neutrinos in the universe that the remainder of the invisible matter might be accounted for by them alone.

Through the Dust Darkly

The galactic halo and the invisible matter turn the mind's eye outward from the galaxy. Let us now turn it inward. What is there at the center of the galaxy? As we have seen, the galactic center is screened from us by the dust that lies in the central plane of the galactic disk. Through the screen, however, we can dimly perceive the outlines of happenings dramatic and mysterious.

What enables us to see through the screen is the fact that radio waves and infrared radiation penetrate clouds of dust better than light waves do. The radio waves from the direction of the galactic center show the distribution of gas. At a distance of some 15,000 light-years from the center—roughly a third of the distance from the edge of the galactic disk—is a circle of what are called giant molecular-cloud complexes. These complexes are distinguished from the surrounding atomic gas by a high concentration of molecules. They are where dust grains—and therefore stars—form. Having a diameter of some 150 light-years and a mass of several hundred thousand suns, they are the largest and most massive bodies yet identified in the galaxy.

Closer to the galactic center, at a distance of some 10,000 light-years, is some kind of galactic smoke ring: a circle of atomic hydrogen. There is evidence that it is expanding outward, and if this is true, the ring originated with an explosion 30 million years ago. Still closer to the center, at a distance of some 5,000 light-years, is an expanding and rotating disk of both atomic and molecular hydrogen.

Still closer, at a distance of some 1,000 light-years, is another smoke ring, consisting not only of atomic hydrogen but also of molecular hydrogen and giant molecular-cloud complexes. Some of the hydrogen is hot. Still closer, at a distance of only 30 light-years, is yet another smoke ring. Curiously it appears to be cooler than the one at 1,000 light-years.

Within 10 light-years of the center are particularly enigmatic objects. They are small clouds of hot hydrogen whizzing around the center at a speed 10,000 times higher than the speed of the sun around the center. They appear to be satellites of some supermassive body at the exact center.

All this is divined from the radio waves. More comes from the infrared radiation. Infrared detectors show that within the central 10 light-years is the highest concentration of stars in the galaxy. Most portentous of all, they show at the very center a bizarre object. It appears to be no larger than ten times the distance from the sun to the earth and to have a mass of 50 million suns.

What is it? The center of speculation, if not of the galaxy

itself, is a gigantic black hole. As almost everyone knows, a black hole is a kind of cosmic vacuum cleaner: a center of gravity so intense that not even light can escape from it. Since a black hole could not emit any light, the radiation we detect from the object at the center of the galaxy would have to come from stars being torn apart before they disappeared into the hole's awful maw.

The Dangerous Charm of Black Holes

This is a good point to dwell a bit on black holes. The attractiveness of the idea of a black hole lies mainly in the fact that it is a logical extension of the general theory of relativity. One of the main predictions of the theory was that a light ray passing close to a massive body such as the sun would be bent toward that body, and the prediction has been confirmed. Another way of putting it is to say that in the vicinity of a massive body the curvature of space increases, so that light quanta follow a more curved path. If the body is massive enough and its gravitational field is concentrated enough, the curvature is so great that the light quanta spiral inward and cannot escape from the body at all.

I have the impression that most astronomers and physicists believe black holes really exist. Some, however, do not. Among them is Philip Morrison, whose opinion on any subject I have learned not to take lightly. He says: "I'll believe in black holes when I see one." This is a joke; since a black hole swallows up light rather than emits it, you could not see it even if it existed. The skeptical position is that there is no real observational evidence for the existence of black holes, only presumed effects and theoretical speculations. It is a classic positivist position: it is philosophically unsound to argue that because a successful theory predicts something, that something *must* exist.

After all, it is not the theory that is reality. If the theory predicts that something exists and the something cannot be found, so much the worse for the theory. Extending the general theory of relativity to a fantastic extreme might well expose the incompleteness of the theory, even as Einstein's theory of gravity (the general theory of relativity) exposed the incompleteness of Newton's theory of gravity. It might turn out that at that extreme there is something that would allow light to escape from a powerful center of gravitational force.

One might take into account another force: the force of words. The term "black hole" has a dangerous charm, perhaps even with depth-psychological connotations we need not go into here. Black holes have caught the fancy of many people who had never paid any attention to astronomy and physics, and astronomers themselves are only human.

I remember going to an astronomical meeting in the early days of black holes. Several of the talks at the meeting were about them. As is often the case, the program of talks had to be laid out without full knowledge of what the talkers were going to say. Someone had got the idea that a certain astrophysicist was interested in "white holes," and he was asked to give a talk on them. When the man got to the meeting, he asked: "What the hell *is* a white hole?" The sheer power of the term, at least at that time, had gone beyond theoretical speculation into literary symmetry.

Black holes have been a godsend to astronomers seeking to explain funny things going on in the universe. As a case in point, the particularly intense X rays and gamma rays emitted by certain exotic celestial objects call for highly energetic processes. A black hole might fill the bill in the following way.

You have a double star, one member of which is a normal star and the other is a black hole. If the two bodies are close enough together, the black hole might suck material out of the normal star. Since the system is rotating, the matter would not plunge straight into the black hole. It would zip around it a few times before falling over the "horizon" beyond which nothing can return. In so doing it would form what is called an accretion disk. It is the matter in the accretion disk, energized by the violent forces being exerted on it by the black hole, that would radiate X rays or gamma rays.

Many astronomers have wondered if black holes might not also explain quasars, the brightest objects in the universe. All in all, however, this particular spectator is playing it cool with black holes. It would be nice if they exist, but if they don't, the universe will be no less interesting.

Fireworks in the Froth

Whether or not they are energized by black holes, quasars are not extensions of theory but are spectacular observable objects. Although they are tiny in comparison with a galaxy, they can emit 1,000 times more energy than an entire galaxy of 100 billion stars. Moreover, some of them are receding at 90 percent of the speed of light. Therefore, in accordance with Hubble's law, they are some 10 billion light-years away. A few are even more distant.

If an object is 10 billion light-years away, we are seeing it not as it is now but as it was 10 billion years ago. Since the universe may not have begun much earlier than that, quasars may be characteristic of an early stage in the evolution of galaxies. There are apparently no quasars much closer to our galaxy than 3 billion light-years, but there *are* galaxies that show activity reminiscent of quasars. In such a galaxy there is violent activity in the center, not as violent as a quasar but pretty violent. Then there is our own galaxy, with its own cryptic signs of violence at the center.

There is obviously a lot more than we know to the celestial machine we call a galaxy. Furthermore, although it is clear that the primordial gas did condense into galaxies and stars, it is not at all clear why it did so. If the universe began in a stupendous flash of energy and matter, what kept the matter from simply expanding? Why, among other questions, should the stuff have formed clumps that could condense into galaxies and stars?

The answer may lie in the randomness of events at the fundamental quantum level. As I mentioned in the preceding piece, subatomic events such as when an electron in an atom will drop from a higher energy state to a lower one are unpredictable. There is a similar randomness in when, given the appropriate amount of energy, particles of matter can materialize out of a vacuum. It may well be that such random fluctuations in the first second of the big bang gave rise to an essential clumpiness in the gas that bred the galaxies and stars.

Moreover, until recently it was not at all clear how the universe we observe could have originated in events earlier than 10^{-30} second after the big bang. The trouble was that standard big-bang theory predicts for this fleeting epoch an enormous overproduction of the particles called magnetic monopoles. Such particles have not, in fact, been shown to exist at all. Standard cosmological theory also requires that the universe begin under certain stringent conditions. Those conditions are simply assumed, not explained.

These problems have been overcome by a modification of standard theory named the inflationary universe. After 10^{-30} second standard theory and the inflationary-universe theory agree.

Before that time the inflationary-universe theory has the primordial universe suddenly expanding by a factor of 10^{50}. It is only after that time that the three forces of nature separate and particles of matter freeze out. One consequence of such a stupendous expansion would be that the observable universe is embedded in a much larger region of space.

Both theory and observation suggest that the clumps of gas out of which clusters of galaxies formed were not roundish. They may well have been as flat as a pancake. If the clumps had tended to be round, clusters and superclusters of galaxies would also tend to be. Three-dimensional maps of the distribution of galaxies may be showing that they are arrayed in immense sheets and filaments perhaps 100 million light-years across. The voids that separate the sheets and filaments may be as much as 400 million light-years across. In fact, the universe of galaxies may resemble nothing so much as a vast froth.

Windows in the Swimming Pool

Such observations are a reminder that among the sciences astronomy is the one most powerfully shaped by instruments. Indeed, since Galileo and the early seventeenth century the history of astronomy has run almost perfectly parallel to the history of the telescope.

Galileo's little telescopes revealed for the first time that the moon has mountains, that Venus has phases like the moon, that Jupiter has moons of its own, that the sun has spots and that the Milky Way consists of stars. His telescopes, the largest of which was 33 power, were refractors, with two lenses like those of eyeglasses. Newton built the first reflecting telescope, in which the main lens is replaced by a concave mirror.

Newton also observed that when sunlight passes through a

prism, the colors that make up the light are dispersed into what he named a spectrum. In 1814 Joseph von Fraunhofer put a narrow slit in front of the prism and observed that the spectrum of the sun is crossed by hundreds of parallel dark lines. The spectrum of a flame in the laboratory showed bright lines at similar positions, and since the elements present in the flame were known, the way was opened to studying the constitution of stars and other celestial objects. Today the spectra of stars and other celestial objects are made mostly with the diffraction grating: glass scored with ultrafine parallel lines that disperse the colors of light much more than a prism can.

Refracting and reflecting telescopes evolved throughout the eighteenth and nineteenth centuries, revealing, among other things, that the stars (including the sun) move, that double stars revolve around each other and that the system of stars to which the sun belongs is flattened. Modern astronomy might be said to date from the completion in 1908 of the 60-inch reflector on Mount Wilson outside Los Angeles. With that instrument, for example, Harlow Shapley began his study of the distribution of globular clusters.

The 60-inch reflector was joined on Mount Wilson in 1918 by the 100-inch. With that instrument Edwin Hubble studied the red shifts of galaxies outside our own and established that the universe is expanding. The next major advance was the 200-inch reflector on Palomar Mountain, which went into operation in 1948. With it Hubble did his last work, confirming the expansion of the universe out to 2 billion light-years.

The 200-inch was joined on Palomar by a notably felicitous instrument. It was the 48-inch Schmidt telescope. A Schmidt telescope is a reflector with a thin refracting "correcting plate" at its front end. This combination of optics gives the telescope an unusually large and sharp field of view. Telescopes such as the 200-inch suffer from tunnel vision, so that with them it is difficult to study the distribution of objects in the sky. The 48-inch Schmidt has done yeoman work, for example, in revealing the distribution of galaxies. It also made the picture of the Andromeda galaxy that gives me a prickling sensation at the back of the neck.

Telescopes can gather not only light but also other kinds of electromagnetic radiation. It happens, however, that the earth's atmosphere is largely opaque to them. In fact, until the 1930s the only band of the electromagnetic spectrum that was visible to astronomers was light (and narrow bands of the adjacent spectrum in the ultraviolet and the infrared). To the long-wavelength side of the light spectrum was a vast realm of unseen infrared and radio waves, and to the short-wavelength side an equally vast one of unseen ultraviolet, X and gamma rays.

At that time it was discovered that the earth receives radio waves from space. Radio telescopes were built, and after the Second World War tremendous discoveries were made with them. It was found that the atoms and molecules in interstellar space emit and absorb radio waves; that made it possible to map the distribution of the atoms and molecules in our galaxy and other galaxies. It was also found that certain starlike objects are emitting prodigious amounts of radio energy. They were later seen to be an entirely new kind of celestial object: quasars. And it was radio astronomers who discovered pulsars.

The earth's atmosphere is not transparent to radio waves of all lengths. Fortunately there are "windows" in the atmosphere at enough wavelengths to make radio astronomy eminently feasible. For a long time it was not so for infrared astronomy, ultraviolet astronomy, X-ray astronomy and gamma-ray astronomy. There are only very small windows for the infrared and the ultraviolet, and none for X rays and gamma rays. Astronomers working at those wavelengths had to be satisfied with observations made with instruments carried aloft in rockets and high-altitude balloons.

All that has been transformed by artificial satellites of the earth. Instruments boosted into orbit above the earth's atmosphere have revealed the universe in, so to speak, full color. Maps of the sky made with infrared detectors borne on satellites clearly show stars forming in clouds of dust opaque to light. They also show inside the dust-shrouded core of the galaxy the glow of events that so far cannot be explained.

It is satellite-borne X-ray and gamma-ray detectors that show the powerful sources that look as though they might be neutron stars or black holes. In addition they show that the entire sky is suffused with an X-ray glow. A leading guess as to the source of the glow is that it is the combined X-ray output of the most distant quasars.

Light-gathering telescopes too can benefit from being above the earth's atmosphere. After all, observing celestial objects from the ground is rather like observing them from the bottom of a swimming pool. The atmospheric swimming pool is never still; it is what makes stars twinkle. Moreover, light-gathering telescopes on the ground (except for telescopes designed for observing the sun) can operate only at night and in good clear weather. None of those handicaps hold for a telescope in space.

The most ambitious of all astronomical efforts in space is the Hubble Space Telescope. When it is placed in orbit, its 94-inch mirror should be able to gather light from objects ten times fainter than those that can now be detected by the largest ground-based telescopes. Moreover, its resolution—its ability to detect detail—will be ten times greater.

Here a point needs to be clarified. I mentioned that the largest light-gathering telescope now in regular operation, the 200-inch on Palomar, could detect galaxies out to 2 billion light-years. Yet quasars are detected at a distance of 10 billion light-years. What is going on?

The apparent contradiction is explained by the fact that galaxies are not nearly as bright as quasars. When we speak of a telescope's being able to gather light from objects ten times fainter than those that can be detected by other telescopes, what is meant is that the more powerful telescope will be able to detect both galaxies that are ten times fainter and quasars that are ten times fainter. One result will be that we will be detecting galaxies lying between the most distant galaxies now detectable and the nearest quasars.

In spite of the advantages of having a telescope in space, the earth is still the best platform for a telescope, and other spectacular instruments are in the wind. Among them is the Very Long Baseline Array, consisting of ten radio telescopes (or arrays of radio telescopes) distributed from one coast of the United States to the other. Such an array has a resolution—a sharpness—equivalent to a single telescope 3,000 miles in diameter.

A twenty-first-century Vatican of telescopes will be the great Hawaiian volcano Mauna Kea, which rises nearly 14,000 feet above the sea. Eight observatories are already operating there, and the mountain has been chosen as the site for giant Japanese and American "national telescopes." Under construction is the W. M. Keck Telescope, which should be able to detect objects seventeen times fainter than those that will be detected by the Space Telescope. Scheduled for completion in 1992, the instrument will consist of thirty-six hexagonal mirrors, each six feet across. The mirrors will be aimed at a common focus, so that in effect they will be a single huge mirror 394 inches in diameter. All this has to be done to tolerances of better than a quarter of a wavelength of light. The U.S. National New Technology Telescope will be even bigger: four mirrors adding up to a diameter of 600 inches.

Which Way Is North?

The twenty-first century is bound to be an exciting one for astronomy. If history is any guide, it will be surprising if the Space Telescope, the Keck Telescope and other instruments do not produce surprises. Even if they do not, they may make it possible to solve one of the main riddles of the universe. Is the expanding universe going to continue expanding for all time? In other words, is the fundamental geometry of space either "flat" or "open"? Or is the universe going to stop expanding and eventually collapse back to the point at which it began? In other words, is the geometry of the universe "closed"?

Astronomers who study the red shifts of the most distant objects in the universe have looked hard for evidence that the shifts are departing from Hubble's law that the speed of recession increases with distance. If the most distant objects showed any sign of slowing down, it would be an indication that the universe is closed. The universe would be like one of those early rockets that could not attain a high enough velocity to escape from the gravitational pull of the earth; the rocket rose in a parabola and then fell back. If the universe is open, it would be like a rocket that had attained escape velocity and could keep going indefinitely.

So far no one has found any conclusive evidence of a slowing down. In fact, the inflationary model of the universe suggests that it may be even more difficult to detect the slowing down than anyone thought. Still, the question retains its philosophical interest. If the universe is open, it will die. Its stars will eventually use up all their nuclear fuel, radiate all their remaining energy and cool off to dark cinders. In accord with the second law of thermodynamics, which demands that energy run only downhill, the universe will end in heat death. Calculations indicate that this "big chill" could come in 10^{90} billion years.

That is a comfortably long time, but it would be nice to know if there is some reason to expect that the universe we observe will eventually live or die. One alternative to the big chill was put forward some forty years ago by Fred Hoyle and his colleagues. In their "steady state" cosmology a permanently expanding universe could be fundamentally unchanging, if only a modest amount of hydrogen were continuously materializing out of the cosmic vacuum. The rival cosmology was the big bang (a term, incidentally, that Hoyle himself introduced in derision).

At that time the big-bang cosmology, mostly in the hands of George Gamow, required that the elements heavier than hydrogen and helium be created in the big bang itself. Gamow was a most interesting man, a Russian physicist who had come to this country by way of Niels Bohr's institute in Copenhagen in the 1930s. He wrote many wonderful popular books and articles about physics, including several articles in *Scientific American*. When the articles arrived in our offices, they were elaborately printed and illustrated by hand, so that we sometimes felt we should reproduce them in facsimile. They miraculously incorporated Gamow's Russian accent; the word "law," for example, was consistently written "low." He maintained that even though he wrote beautifully he was illiterate in any language.

Gamow was an inveterate prankster. His main work on the creation of the heavier elements in the big bang was done in collaboration with Ralph Alpher. It occurred to him that the names Alpher and Gamow (pronounced Gamoff) sounded almost exactly like "alpha" and "gamma." All that was missing was the "beta." But wait a minute. He had a good friend, the eminent physicist Hans Bethe, whose name exactly fit the specification. He asked Bethe if he would join him and Alpher in signing a scientific paper. So it was that the main early publication on the subject was by Alpher, Bethe and Gamow.

Hoyle and others, mainly William Fowler at Cal Tech, worked long and hard to show that the heavier elements were cooked up not in the big bang but in the interior of stars. They succeeded, and the big-bang model had to be modified accordingly. What finally gave the steady-state model its deathblow was the discovery of the 3-degree radiation left over from the big bang.

There is a moral to this tale. Scientists originally motivated by a theory that turns out to be wrong often discover things that are right. Basically what Fowler and his colleagues did was to test virtually all the reactions between atomic nuclei to determine if they would "go" at the temperatures that would be encountered in the core of stars. In so doing they amassed an enormous amount of information about nuclear reactions in general. Their tool for banging the nuclei together was the electrostatic generator, a medium-energy particle accelerator.

I noted in the first piece in this book that one of the things scientists do is teach. Once when I was visiting Fowler I noticed on his bookshelf an array of what appeared to be notebooks, some loose-leaf and others bound. They were the Ph.D. theses of his graduate students, and there were more than fifty of them. Among the names on the theses were some of the best-known ones in a generation of physicists younger than Fowler's. Many of these men and women had cut their teeth on a problem that had originally been set by the steady-state theory.

If the universe were not open but closed, would it not also die? After all, if it were like a rocket that fell back instead of attaining escape velocity, it would stop expanding and start contracting. Eventually, in a reversal of the big bang, it would arrive at a "big crunch." Such a universe could, however, still live on:

it could start all over again in another big bang. Indeed, it could pulsate between the bang and the crunch, like a single-cylinder gasoline engine.

An immortal universe does not quite answer two questions asked by the child: What is on the outside of the universe? What was there before the universe began? I must confess that the child in me has not been able to rid his mind of those questions, but I can also see that they are pointless. The fifteenth-century scholar Nicholas of Cusa said: "The fabric of the universe has its center everywhere and its circumference nowhere." The theorist Stephen Hawking observed that asking "What came before the beginning of the universe?" is like standing at the North Pole and asking "Which way is north?" In short, the child's view of the universe fits only a small flat world and not the larger real one.

Many people are troubled by the question: Why did the universe begin? Not getting a ready answer from scientists, they seem to conclude that the entire effort to understand the universe is pointless. I myself have never been able to understand this. It implies that human beings are somehow entitled to an early explanation of everything. They have not been working at the exploration of the universe very long, and at the very least they should be patient. I can see nothing wrong with the position that human beings will learn quite a lot about the universe but that quite a lot will always remain to be learned.

There is an apposite story, one with many versions. One is that a college freshman elects a course in philosophy, and one day the professor says: "Today I'd like to take up cosmology— theories of the nature of the universe. There are many cosmologies, ancient and modern. A cosmology of which I am particularly fond is an ancient Indian one, in which the world rests on the backs of three huge elephants, which in turn stand on the shell of an enormous turtle."

At the end of the term the student approaches the professor.

"This is a wonderful course, and I am going to go right on with it. But you know, one thing you said bothers me. It's that business about the world resting on the backs of three huge elephants standing on the shell of an enormous turtle. What is the turtle standing on?"

The professor responds: "It's a good question. As a matter of fact, it is standing on the back of *another* enormous turtle."

At the end of the next term the student says: "But I don't get it. What is *that* turtle standing on?" and receives the same answer. He decides to major in philosophy, and whenever he gets a chance he repeats the question, with the same result. Finally he repeats it as he is getting his Ph.D. with the same professor. At that point the professor puts his hand on the student's shoulder in a fatherly manner and says: "Charles, it's turtles *all the way*."

Well, that's how it is with science. It's questions all the way.

GEOLOGY FEELS FOR
THE PULSES OF THE EARTH

I have been arguing in these pieces that the key to understanding modern science is the context provided by evolution and history. The heroes of history are geologists. It was they who discovered it. An educated European in the second half of the eighteenth century—let us say the heyday of Samuel Johnson—had a keen sense of history, but it was a history that went back only to Rome, Greece and the myths of the Old Testament. Many accepted what the Irish archbishop James Ussher had proved in the preceding century on the basis of Scripture: that the world began in 4004 B.C.

The geologists of the late eighteenth century and the early nineteenth, notably James Hutton and Charles Lyell, perceived that the earth couldn't possibly be that young. Looking at rock formations with reasonable eyes, they could see that the emplacement of the rocks called for a lot more than a few thousand years. Above all, some of the rocks contained the remains of unfamiliar plants and animals, evidence that a living world of the past had been different from the living world of the present. It is no coincidence that Charles Darwin began his career as a geologist.

Human beings have two main conceptions of time. One, perhaps suggested by the progression from birth to death, is that time is like an arrow. The other, perhaps suggested by the rote of the days and the seasons, is that time is a repeating cycle. Interestingly enough, both Hutton and Lyell regarded geologic time as being cyclic; Lyell thought it would see the return of the dinosaurs. Even so Hutton and Lyell regarded time as being far deeper than what was indicated by the Bible.

Of how old the world really is, however, the early geologists had little idea. In fact, when in the 1840s the physicist William Thomson, later Lord Kelvin, argued that the earth might be as much as 400 million years old, some leading geologists disagreed with him sternly. The earth is now known to be 4.6 billion years old.

The Intelligent Amphibians

The modern revision of the epic tale of geology began with the recognition that the continents are drifting across the surface of the earth like so many huge ice floes. This brings up what is meant by the term "geology." The concept of continental drift was proposed in the nineteenth century, but it was not confirmed until the 1960s. The scientists who confirmed it were mostly not geologists but oceanographers and geophysicists. The differences among these scientific tribes are not trivial. Lyell once said that someone studying the earth should behave like an intelligent amphibian. Historically, however, geologists have been less interested in the sea than in the land.

The great tradition of geology is the painstaking exploration and ordering of the vast jumble of rocks on the surface of the earth. The classic exercise is the piecing out of the underlying structure of a landscape from a few outcroppings. Since for earlier geologists the rocks of the sea bottom were largely inaccessible, a bias toward the land was understandable.

In addition to this bias there is a strain of geologists who have always been skeptical of theories about the earth. In the two centuries of the science most geological observations have survived but many theories have come and gone. People who spend much of their life clambering around in rugged terrain are proud of what they do and can have a certain disdain for people who have never done it. John McPhee, who has written first-rate articles about geology for *The New Yorker*, quotes a hard-rock geologist, Anita Harris, as saying: "There are a lot of people out there in the profession like me who don't believe much of [plate tectonics]. But we can't altogether complain. Plate tectonics has turned people on. It has brought a lot of new people into geology."

Plate tectonics is the theory that emerged from the confirmation of continental drift. The exploration of the depths of the ocean had begun with the global expedition of HMS *Challenger* from 1872 to 1876, but the ocean floor was not really laid bare until after the Second World War. During the war the U.S. Navy needed to know more about what lay beneath the surface of the ocean, and after the war it continued to finance ambitious surveys of the ocean floor.

From such explorations emerged all kinds of wonders. For one thing, it was discovered that running down the middle of the bottom of the Atlantic is a rugged ridge bisected by a deep rift. The same kind of rifted mid-ocean ridge was found in other oceans. For another thing, the rifts are full of freshly extruded lava. For a third, whereas rocks on the land go back nearly 4 billion years, none of the rocks dredged up from the bottom *anywhere* in the oceans are older than 200 million years. For a fourth, running parallel to the ridges on the bottom are broad "stripes" in which the north and south poles of magnetic minerals reverse from one stripe to the next.

Another wonder was also magnetic. Before the magnetic stripes were discovered on the ocean bottom physicists were studying the magnetism of certain volcanic rocks on land. The rocks had been deposited one after the other in orderly layers by volcanic eruptions in different parts of the world. At the time of their deposition certain minerals in them had lined up with the earth's magnetic field like so many tiny compass needles. The remarkable thing was that the needles in different layers point in different directions.

There seemed to be two possible explanations. One was that as the layers of volcanic rock were being laid down the magnetic poles of the earth had wandered. The other was that the land where the rocks were being laid down had wandered with respect to the magnetic poles. It turned out that the magnetic poles do wander to a certain extent. The continents, however, wander a great deal more.

It is common for children to notice on a map of the world that the east coast of North and South America and the west coast of Europe and Africa roughly match each other like two parts of a jigsaw puzzle. The fit is not, however, good enough to have lent much credence to the idea that the two land masses were once in contact. What breathed life into the idea was again the exploration of the ocean floor.

At the edges of continents is a submerged shelf that in places extends out hundreds of miles. After the Second World War the continental shelves were for the first time accurately mapped. Then it could be seen that the shelves of the continents on opposite sides of the Atlantic fit each other quite closely. Moreover, layered rock formations on opposite sides of the Atlantic—

notably in West Africa and Brazil—matched up beautifully. It was as though the formations had been pulled apart.

They had been. The meaning of the magnetic stripes and the youth of the rocks on the ocean floor began to come into focus. What is happening is that molten rock is welling up from the mid-ocean rift and cooling into new ocean floor. As it does so it pushes the rock of the floor outward from the rift and drives apart the continents that border the Atlantic.

As the rock cools into new ocean floor, the compass needles of its magnetic minerals freeze in the direction of the earth's magnetic field. It happens that the earlier studies of rock magnetism had not only shown that the compass needles point in different directions at different times but also revealed one of the damndest things you ever heard. From time to time the earth's magnetic field flops: the north magnetic pole becomes the south magnetic pole and vice versa. The reversals come at irregular intervals, but there have been nine of them in the past 3.6 million years.

The compass needles in two adjacent magnetic stripes on the ocean floor thus point in opposite directions. Therefore when the reversals of the magnetic poles had been accurately timed, it was possible to use them to establish the age of the stripes. The results showed that new ocean floor is growing out from mid-ocean rifts at rates measured in inches per year—about as fast as a growing fingernail. At such rates the entire floor of any ocean in the world would have been manufactured in less than 200 million years. The youth of the ocean-floor rocks was explained.

Ultimately it was seen that the mid-ocean rifts divide the crust of the earth into seven major plates and several minor ones. These are the plates of plate tectonics. Tectonics is defined as the structural deformation of the earth's crust, and the movement of the plates deforms the crust in dramatic ways.

Long Live Planetary Science

When these ideas began to emerge, many geologists found them hard to swallow. In fact, some geologists, such as the one quoted by McPhee, still don't really swallow them. The objections seem to have less to do with the theory as a whole than with details. Some enthusiastic plate tectonicists have explained the geology of large areas in terms of plate tectonics, and geologists have pointed out that their explanations do not fit the rocks. As the years go by, however, the plate-tectonic explanations get better.

The fact remains that for the first time geology has a real theory, and geologists were not in the forefront of creating it. The study of the earth has seen a shift, so to speak, in its center of gravity. Where once the subject was reserved almost entirely to geologists, it is now shared not only by the oceanographers and geophysicists who pioneered plate tectonics but also by geochemists, seismologists, meteorologists and, most significantly, astronomers.

One scholar recently went so far as to write: "Geology is dead. Long live the earth sciences." He was overstating the case, since there are still plenty of hardworking geologists, but many departments of geology have changed their name to department of the earth sciences. Indeed, some departments have broadened it to planetary science.

The past thirty years have been the golden age of planetary science. The reason, of course, is the intelligence sent back by spacecraft that have now landed on the moon, Mars and Venus and have passed close to or orbited all of the other planets except the outermost two: Neptune and Pluto. The stimulus of this marvelous achievement cannot pass without comment.

Astronomers have always dreamed of getting away from the earth, or at least above the earth's atmosphere, in order to see celestial objects more clearly. Before 1957, however, such efforts were limited to brief forays with a few special high-altitude balloons and early rockets, including salvaged German V-2s. What happened in 1957 was that the Russians launched the first artificial satellite—Sputnik. It was not until then that the U.S. government, shocked by the Russian achievement, invested the funds necessary to develop large rockets, land men on the moon and join in the exploration of space.

In short, the funding of the U.S. space program, like the funding of large accelerators in physics, was motivated by considerations other than the acquisition of knowledge. Knowledge was, to be sure, brilliantly acquired, and perhaps one should not look gift horses in the mouth. One yearns, however, for the day when the pursuit of such knowledge will be supported for the right reasons. One reason is geology.

Carnage in the Disk

Geology cannot really be understood without referring to the origin of the earth and the rest of the solar system. As we saw in the preceding piece, the sun and its planets materialized out of a cloud of hydrogen and helium containing, like sparse snowflakes, grains incorporating heavier elements that had been cooked in older stars. As the cloud spun down to a thin disk like a miniature galaxy, the sun lit up. Simultaneously the disk was the scene of subtle physics and chemistry.

First of all, the disk itself was an exquisite dynamical system. A good analogy is the rings of Saturn. The rings are not a continuous disk like a phonograph record. Gravity has marshaled them into a complex series, some rings wider, some narrower, some undulating in waves, some made up of coarser stuff, some of finer. It was probably like that in the disk around the brightening sun.

Second, as the sun brightened it heated the inner part of the disk more than it did the outer part. This heating had fateful consequences for the later evolution of the solar system. The more volatile material in the inner disk evaporated or could not condense in the first place. Examples are molecules and snow crystals of water and methane (CH_4). What was left was the more refractory stuff. Examples are grains rich in iron or in silicates: multifarious compounds of silicon, oxygen and other elements.

In addition the new sun probably flared up before it settled down to the amiable star we see today. This behavior was first noted in a young star in the constellation Taurus, T Tauri, and it has been observed in many other young stars since. The wind from a T Tauri star is far more intense than the solar wind, and if the young sun did blow the more intense wind, it would have tended to drive out the lighter material in the inner disk. That not only would have augmented the effects of evaporation but also would have blown farther out in the disk the gases present in the original cloud: hydrogen and helium.

In short, soon after the sun began to shine, the rings in the inner part of the disk were rich in heavy and refractory material and the rings farther out were rich in light and volatile material. That segregation is reflected in the fact that the four inner planets—Mercury, Venus, the earth and Mars—are balls consisting almost entirely of rock. By the same token the giant outer planets—Jupiter, Saturn, Uranus and Neptune—are balls with a rocky core but consisting mostly of hydrogen and helium. On Jupiter and Saturn the hydrogen and helium are liquefied; on the less massive Uranus and Neptune the hydrogen is combined with oxygen (water), carbon (methane) and nitrogen (ammonia). Pluto, the small outermost planet, is a maverick. Like the inner planets, it is a rock (with a thin atmosphere of methane, some of which is frozen in polar caps).

There are other dramatic manifestations of the segregation.

Many of the moons from those of Jupiter on out consist largely of ice. Titan, one of the moons of Saturn, has an ocean of liquid methane. Conversely, the only three satellites of the four inner planets—the earth's moon and Mars's tiny Deimos and Phobos —are rocks.

The best evidence that the planets and their moons did coalesce out of a disk rotating around the sun is that they lie very nearly in the same plane: the plane of the ecliptic. (An exception, again, is Pluto, whose orbit is substantially tilted from the plane of the ecliptic.) Moreover, the planets and their moons move around the sun or around a planet in the same direction. (An exception is Neptune's large moon Triton, which moves in the opposite direction.)

Finally, the planets and their moons *spin* in the same direction. (Exceptions are Venus, which spins very slowly in the opposite direction, and Uranus and its moons, which spin nearly at right angles to the plane of the ecliptic. The moons and rings of Uranus also orbit the planet at right angles to the plane of the ecliptic. The entire Uranian system may have been knocked over 90 degrees by a massive collision early in the history of the solar system.)

An interesting fact is that there are bodies in the solar system with orbits that are not confined to the plane of the ecliptic. They are comets, whose orbital planes are random. Comets may therefore be analogous to the galaxy's globular star clusters, a remnant of the time before the round cloud of dust and gas that bore the sun and the planets spun down to a disk.

Vast numbers of comets orbit the sun at distances far beyond Pluto. Occasionally the orbit of such a comet is perturbed and the comet plunges close to the sun, growing a tail and exciting wonder on the earth. Consisting of ice and particles of dust, comets may be samples of the material in the outer part of the cloud that spun down into a thin disk and then coalesced into the planets and their moons. Early in the process comets may have been far more abundant in the inner solar system. If they were, they would have been swept up by the growing rocky planets. Since they consist largely of ice, they may have endowed the earth with its oceans.

However that may be, the dust particles in the ring that gave rise to the planets tended to stick together, forming larger and larger aggregates. In a fairly short period, astronomically speaking, the aggregates grew large enough for the encounters between them to be violent. It was a time of mighty bashing and whacking, a cosmic Punch and Judy show. A familiar picture of what it was like half a billion years after the planets formed is the frozen face of the earth's moon, splattered with the craters left by bodies large and small that crashed into it.

The earth does not look like the moon because its evolution erased its craters. Still, the bashing continues to this day, though at a far lower rate. The solar system is full of flying debris, some of it crumbly meteorites—carbonaceous chondrites—that look like samples of material in the primordial disk. Some of it is bodies the size of small asteroids that orbit far out of the normal asteroid belt, which lies between Mars and Jupiter. It is estimated that such a body crashes into the earth about once every 250,000 years, and the collision must have formidable effects. For example, if the body hit in the middle of the Atlantic, it could propel a wall of water hundreds of feet high onto the adjacent continents.

Such collisions have been a boon to earth scientists seeking to explain dramatic events in earth history, as black holes have been a boon to astrophysicists seeking to explain dramatic processes in the universe. A major collision has been invoked to account for the extinction of dinosaurs and many other forms of life at the end of the Mesozoic era 63 million years ago. The hypothesis has received much public attention; dinosaurs, like

black holes, have a dangerous charm. Many earth scientists still
find the idea attractive, but it is by no means generally accepted.

Once an artist who worked for *Scientific American* told me
that he had a curious difficulty with drawing dinosaurs: from the
carnivorous *Tyrannosaurus* to the herbivorous *Brontosaurus*, they
always seemed to be smiling. I think I know why they are smiling.
They realized that their successors would have a terrible time
explaining how they became lords of the earth and then vanished.

The Terrestrial Cream Separator

The bashing that gave rise to the earth was so violent that patches
on the growing planet glowed dull red. A particularly energetic
collision with a body the size of Mars may have sprayed out
enough material to form a massive ring. A current hypothesis is
that it was the material in such a ring that gave the earth its
moon. The material would have coalesced into the moon quickly,
leaving the moon subject to the later stages of the bashing.

The heating of the planets, like the heating of the disk
around the young sun, had fateful consequences for their later
evolution. The heat was generated not only by collisions but also
by the nuclear energy of tiny quantities of radioactive elements
in the planetary material, mainly uranium, thorium and an iso-
tope of potassium. It is the radioactive decay of such elements
that heats the earth today.

The smaller bodies in the solar system lost their heat fairly
quickly. That is why most of them, like the earth's moon, are
frozen and dead. A fascinating exception is Jupiter's moon Io.
Subject to the powerful gravitational attractions of Jupiter and its
other moons, Io is flexed like a tennis ball being squeezed in the
hand. The tidal flexing generates so much heat that volatile

elements and compounds have been lost in volcanic eruptions that continue to this day. What is left behind gives the planet the appearance of a sulfurous pizza.

The larger bodies in the solar system retain much of their heat. That is why they are still alive. The colorful turbulence of Jupiter's atmosphere, revealed in such exquisite detail by space-craft, is driven both by the sun's heat and the planet's internal heat. And internal heat is what energizes the tectonic activity of the earth.

When I was a boy, milk was not homogenized and sold in a cardboard carton. It came in a glass bottle, and you could see the cream that had risen to the top. The earth too is a kind of cream separator. The heavy stuff sinks to the bottom and the light stuff rises to the top.

The heaviest material in any abundance is metallic iron. Iron was abundant in the rocky bodies that came together to form the earth; in fact, the larger bodies probably had a core of metallic iron. Since the impact of such bodies heated the growing earth, the heat may have been sufficient to melt their core material. Alternatively (or simultaneously) metallic iron may have been smelted out of rocky material.

Another alternative favored by some planetary scientists is that the first bodies to coalesce into the earth were substantially metallic and the later bodies were substantially rocky. In that case the first bodies might have given the earth a metallic core. However that may be, the metallic iron in the growing earth was heavier than the rocky material, and it would have tended to sink. And since the rocky material was lighter, it would have floated on the iron and given the earth a rocky mantle.

The distance from the earth's center to its surface is 3,960 miles. The first 2,160 miles is core, the inner part of it solid and the outer part fluid. The iron of the core may be alloyed with other elements, such as nickel, sulfur and oxygen. The rest of the earth is the rocky mantle, except for the thin outer layer that includes the earth's crust, the oceans and the atmosphere.

Rock is silicate: to repeat, compounds of silicon, oxygen and other elements. At the surface of the earth the silicates are rigid, as any rock attests. About sixty miles down, however, the temperature and pressure are high enough for silicate to flow. The flow is more like a creep, but it is a flow nonetheless. The rigid upper sixty miles of the mantle is the lithosphere, from the Greek *lithos*, rock. Immediately under it is a less rigid layer, the asthenosphere, from *asthenos*, weak.

The fluid of the mantle is obviously warmer at the bottom than it is at the top. When such is the case, the warmer fluid rises and the cooler fluid sinks. These flows tend to form closed vertical loops: convection cells. Where the loops in the convection cells meet each other the flow is in the same direction. Adjacent loops therefore rotate in opposite directions.

The convection cells in the mantle are large: hundreds and perhaps thousands of miles across. The cells rotate very slowly indeed, perhaps as slowly as once every 200 million years. Most of the earth scientists interested in such flows believe the mantle convection cells are arrayed in two layers, one toward the bottom of the mantle and the other toward the top.

Very well. You have slow, powerful convection cells rotating under a rigid lithosphere. It is the lithosphere that constitutes the earth's plates. The lithosphere is cracked at the mid-ocean rifts. As new ocean floor spreads outward from the rifts, it either pushes other plates ahead of it or plunges under them. The plunging is called subduction. Where the ocean floor is subducted it returns to the fluid mantle and completes the cycle of sea-floor spreading. It is the rotation of the convection cells in the mantle that drives the cycle.

It is tempting to suppose that under each plate is a single

convection cell, with the hotter rising current at the mid-ocean rift and the cooler sinking current at the subduction zone where the plate plunges under another plate. Many illustrations show it that way. It seems not to be the case: the convection cells are smaller. In fact, the entire process of the earth's slow boiling is complex.

As an example, in addition to the upward flows of fluid rock at mid-ocean rifts there are upward flows at a single point. Such flows are called hot spots, and among the thirty-odd hot spots are one under Yellowstone National Park and another under the Hawaiian Islands. The Hawaiian hot spot drives a jet of fluid mantle material through the oceanic plate above it to raise volcanoes: the Hawaiian Islands themselves.

The Hawaiian hot spot, like other hot spots, does not move along with the plate. Therefore as the plate has moved, the hot spot has built a series of volcanic islands in a chain. Hot spots may exist on other planets. One may account for the Great Red Spot at the top of Jupiter's atmosphere. Another may underlie Mars's great volcano Olympus Mons, far larger than any on the earth.

As a second example of the complexity of the earth's boiling, in a few places around the world mantle material may have simply exploded through the crust. The shaft of rock left in the crust by such an eruption is called a kimberlite pipe, and kimberlite is the closest thing we have to a sample of the mantle. The kimberlite must come from at least eighty miles down. Why? Because it contains diamonds, and diamonds cannot form at depths any shallower. If the kimberlite did explode through the crust, it must have fired diamonds into the air like buckshot.

As a third example, the fluid material that oozes out at mid-ocean rifts and volcanoes is not simply the convecting fluid of the mantle. It comes from what are called magma chambers: bubbles of much thinner fluid perhaps a couple of miles across and a mile down. The magma chamber is a kind of cream separator too. In it various minerals of the mantle are being reconstituted, with the heavier ones tending to sink and the lighter ones to rise.

This raises a question. If the cream separator of the earth caused the heavier elements such as iron to sink, why do we find such elements in the earth's crust? The answer is that the heavier elements in the crust are chemically combined with lighter ones in minerals. Moreover, some of the combinations are lighter than others because, when they crystallize, their atoms are less tightly packed. The cream separator has its way.

(The packing of atoms in crystals has another profound effect on the nature of the earth. When most liquids freeze, their atoms pack densely and the crystals sink; the liquid freezes from the bottom up. When water freezes, its molecules pack in a rather open structure. As a result ice floats and water freezes from the top down. If it froze from the bottom up, the oceans, with their ice insulated by the ice above it, would never thaw.)

The Scum of the Earth

Since the earth is a sphere, the cream separator gives rise to layers like those, to mix the metaphor, of an onion. Apart from its outer film of water and air the planet has a metallic core and a silicate mantle. At the top of the mantle are the asthenosphere and the lithosphere. At the top of the lithosphere is a further thin layer: the crust. Whereas the thickness of the lithosphere is some sixty miles, the thickness of the crust varies between three and forty miles. Seventy percent of the crust's area is ocean bottom; the rest is land. Most of the land, of course, is continents. Why do the continents stand higher than the ocean bottom?

First of all, oceanic crust is different from continental crust.

Apart from sediment that has sifted down from the ocean, it is basalt, a dense black rock most familiar to us as volcanic lava. The oceanic crust is also thin, averaging three and a half miles in depth. In fact, it is simply the material moving upward and outward at the mid-ocean rifts. At the top the material is lava that has flowed out and solidified on the ocean floor; at the bottom it is a series of vertical sheets that have been pushed outward from the mid-ocean rifts and have solidified more slowly.

Continental crust has only a little basalt in it. It is a great mélange of rock types, but a common one will serve as a key example. It is granite. There are many different kinds of granite, but they are all characterized by crystalline grains so coarse they can be seen with the unaided eye.

The important thing here is that granite is some 3 percent lighter than basalt. It floats on basalt. The same is true of the other continental rocks. The continents float on the heavier underlying rock like icebergs. By the same token they push down into the heavier rock. As a result continental crust is much thicker than oceanic crust, averaging some thirty miles in depth.

Where does this lighter rock come from? Let us return to granite. Granite does not flow out of volcanoes, but its crystallinity clearly indicates that it solidified out of a fluid. Its physics and chemistry indicate that it does so deep in the continental crust. At the same time its lightness thrusts it upward. Where the rocks above it are removed, the granite is exposed to the corrosive effects of air and water. It is broken down, and one of the breakdown products of granite is sand.

Transported by air and water, the sand collects as a sediment in depressions, including the great depression of the sea around the continent. The process is not steady but pulsed, so that new sediment is added in layers. In time the layers pile up to the degree that their sheer weight can push the underlying rock down thousands of feet. Then the deeper layers of sediment are transformed by heat, pressure, dissolution and chemistry into rock, in this case sandstone.

When a sandstone descends even deeper, it too is transformed, for example into the type of rock called gneiss. At the depths where such metamorphosis occurs, rocks are plastic. They flow, and the flows can be fantastically contorted. Gneiss is a layered rock, and when it is exposed at the surface by later geological processes, its original layers are still visible but may look like the waves in a stormy sea. Like all rocks exposed at the surface, gneisses are frozen frames in a movie being shot deep in the earth's crust.

The evolution from granite to sandstone to gneiss defines the three main types of rock. The granite is igneous rock, the sandstone is sedimentary rock, the gneiss is metamorphic rock. Basalt, like granite in having solidified out of a fluid, is igneous. Among the more common sedimentary rocks are shale, which originates with mud, and limestone, which originates with the precipitation of calcium carbonate in sea water. Most of the carbonate is the shells of tiny marine organisms.

Where did the granite and the other light rocks of the continental crust come from? The answer will bring us back to plate tectonics, but it has a simple, if not entirely explicit, basis. In the slow boiling of the mantle the mantle minerals are constantly being re-formed, and the cream separator brings the lighter ones to the top. Seen this way, the mantle is a deep slag at the surface of the core and the light continental rocks are a thin scum at the surface of the mantle.

The Enduring Continents

The oldest continental rocks that have been found are gneisses in Greenland. They are 3.8 billion years old, only 800 million years younger than the earth itself. Thus the continental crust is much older than the oceanic crust. It is not hard to see why. Since the ocean floor spreads outward from the mid-ocean rifts and sinks back into the mantle on a cycle of not more than 200 million years, none of the oceanic crust is any older.

The continents, floating like rafts on the plates of the earth's crust, do not participate in the cycle but are profoundly influenced by it. Plate tectonics exerts powerful forces on them. The land can bend, tear, crumple or break. Great sheets of continental rock can be pushed over or under other sheets. It is such activity that contorts the continental crust and presents geologists with the fiendishly difficult rock puzzles they delight in solving.

The oceanic crust is not, on the whole, as rugged as the land. An exception is the great trenches where one plate is subducted under another; they are deeper than Everest is high. The oceanic crust is largely a flat layer of basalt on which is superimposed the sediment that has settled or precipitated out of the ocean. Close to the mid-ocean ridges, where the ocean floor is new and sediment has not had time to collect, the basalt is bare. With increasing distance from the ridges the layer of sediment gets thicker.

What happens to a plate and its load of sediment when the plate plunges under another plate with a continent at its edge? As the plunging plate moves downward into the mantle the sediments can be scraped off by the overriding continental crust and plastered onto its edge. The rock of the plunging crust is quite wet because ocean water has percolated into fissures in it. It is also heated by friction between the plunging plate and the mantle above it. At a depth of perhaps 350 miles the leading edge of the plate melts and blends into the mantle.

At the upper edge of the plunging plate much is happening. The minerals of the subducted crust are being re-formed by water and heat. They boil off the top of the plate and rise to the surface.

There they form magma chambers and flow out in volcanoes. If the subducting crust is offshore, the volcanoes rise from the ocean bottom. If they rise high enough, they emerge above the surface of the sea and manufacture new land. Such land is exemplified by "island arcs" such as Japan and the Philippines.

If the subducting crust plunges directly under the land, the magma in the magma chambers can rise through breaks in the continental crust and pour out on the surface. The amount of material added to continental crust in this way can be prodigious; in the state of Washington there are layered volcanic formations thousands of feet deep. The volcanoes that produced them are part of the chain that runs almost continuously along the west coast of North, Central and South America.

If the plate that is being subducted has a continent riding on it, there can be a spectacular collision between two continents. Some 45 million years ago India and Asia collided in this way. The geological carnage lifted the Himalayas.

Actually it is such collisions, most of them smaller in scale and less violent, that have built the continents. A case in point is what has happened over the past 200 million years to the western side of North America. In that time the conveyor belt of the spreading Pacific floor has brought to the continent scores of small bits of land. As a result the West Coast is a geological collage. The small land masses cemented into the collage have been named terranes. The San Francisco area alone consists of three terranes that docked one after the other.

The convection currents of the mantle can break a plate of lithosphere not only under an ocean but also under a continent. When that happens the continent rifts apart and a new ocean comes into being where the new lithosphere is being generated. Just that is happening in the Red Sea, where a new ocean is opening between Africa and Western Asia.

An extraordinary episode of plate tectonics came six million years ago in the Mediterranean. The Mediterranean had once been a broad seaway connecting the Indian Ocean and the Atlantic. Then Africa drifted north and, colliding with Asia, closed the seaway at its eastern end. Continuing to move north, Africa then collided with Europe and closed the seaway at its western end. When that happened, the closed sea totally dried up! Its bottom was a scorching desert 10,000 feet below sea level. (The Dead Sea is only 1,300 feet below sea level.) Some 500,000 years later the Atlantic broke through again at the Strait of Gibraltar, creating a waterfall with 1,000 times the flow of Niagara. In a century or so the Mediterranean was refilled.

The powerful forces of plate tectonics literally shake the earth. Where the crust is fractured by such forces, it moves along the fracture—a fault such as the San Andreas in California—by stick and slip. When it slips, there is an earthquake, and then it sticks until the next slip. Where a plate plunges under a continent at a subduction zone, it too generates earthquakes. Such quakes can be as deep as 350 miles, where the subducting plate is blending back into the mantle.

It is the waves generated by earthquakes that have enabled seismologists to peer into the earth and determine such things as the size of the earth's metallic core. Some earthquake waves are resonances of the entire earth. A strong earthquake can make the entire earth ring like a superbass gong!

Einstein stories have been so assiduously collected that there is even one about seismology. When Einstein lived in Germany, one of his closest friends was the seismologist Beno Gutenberg. During the Hitler period they both came to America, but then they did not see each other for quite a while. One reason was that Einstein was in Princeton and Gutenberg was at Cal Tech in Pasadena.

Cal Tech has a large seismological laboratory because California is rich in earthquakes. After Gutenberg arrived he eagerly awaited the first substantial earthquake, but for a frustratingly long time none was forthcoming. Then one morning Einstein arrived for a long-awaited visit. As lunchtime approached the two men started a long walk from the seismological laboratory to the Athenaeum, the Cal Tech faculty club. Deep in conversation, they did not notice that people around them were in a state of high excitement and agitation. When they arrived at the Athenaeum, their friend Richard Tolman was standing on the steps. "Well," he said, "now you've had firsthand experience with a real earthquake." Einstein and Gutenberg said in unison: "There was an *earthquake*?"

Water and Air

The continents, then, are constantly being pushed, compressed, crumpled, added to and pulled apart by the slow boiling of the underlying mantle. Being lighter than mantle stuff, they persist. So too do the oceans and the atmosphere. How did those two intimately linked fluids come into being?

As we have seen, most of the water in the disk around the burgeoning sun was driven into the outer disk. Still, there was enough of it left in the young earth, or enough was added by the fall of comets, to account for the tiny fraction of the earth's volume represented by the oceans. Sometime in the first 800 million of the earth's 4.6 billion years the surface of the waters was broken by the first continents. In the rest of earth history the composition of the ocean changed in interesting ways, for example in the uptake of soluble minerals and atmospheric oxygen and carbon dioxide. The ocean nonetheless remained more than 97 percent water.

The history of the atmosphere is quite different. The bodies that formed the earth had no atmosphere; being small, they did not have enough gravity to hold one. The atmosphere of the earth originated largely with outgassing: the earth's fizzing and farting. It is not at all clear what gases were present in the primordial atmosphere, but it is quite clear that the composition of the atmosphere we know is quite different.

Today the earth's atmosphere, apart from its content of water vapor, is more than 99 percent oxygen and nitrogen, with the oxygen accounting for a fifth and the nitrogen for four-fifths. The nitrogen is there because nitrogen is chemically not very reactive. When it is released by any process, it tends not to recombine with other elements. Therefore over the history of the earth it has simply accumulated in the atmosphere and remained in place.

The oxygen is there because of life. When living organisms arose on the earth some 3.5 billion years ago, they did not release oxygen. Later organisms evolved the gift of photosynthesis: the ability to make themselves by harnessing the energy of sunlight. A waste product of photosynthesis is gaseous oxygen, and that is where the oxygen in the atmosphere comes from. Of equal significance for the history of the earth and of life is that one of the two raw materials of photosynthesis is carbon dioxide. (The other is water.) Therefore photosynthetic organisms pump oxygen into the atmosphere and suck carbon dioxide out of it.

Photosynthesis had profound effects on the geology of the earth. Oxygen is notoriously reactive, and it combines readily with many minerals. Therefore it participates in the breakdown of rocks and accelerates the grand-scale cycle of erosion that transforms the igneous rocks of the continents into sedimentary rocks, the sedimentary rocks into metamorphic rocks and the metamorphic rocks back into igneous rocks.

In fact, minerals that have been oxidized date the arrival of photosynthetic organisms. In many parts of the world are "red beds": layers of rock that originated with iron-rich sediments that oxygen had rusted. The oldest of these rocks date back 2.5 billion years.

Both oxygen and carbon dioxide readily dissolve in water. One consequence is that they nourish the tiny floating photosynthetic organisms of the sea: the sea's grass. Such organisms "fix" the carbon from carbon dioxide in more complex compounds. Those compounds steadily precipitate out of the ocean and ultimately participate in the formation of carbonate rocks such as limestone. As a result of such processes virtually all of the earth's carbon dioxide is stored in the ocean and in rocks; only a tiny fraction remains in the atmosphere.

The discovery that carbon dioxide dissolves in water is one of the most engaging in the history of science. Joseph Priestley, the discoverer of oxygen, lived for a time near a brewery. In 1767 he observed that above the brewing vats there was a lot of "fixed air" (later identified as carbon dioxide). He found that when he held two glasses above a vat and poured water back and forth between them, the water rapidly became charged with bubbles of the gas. He had invented soda water!

Rain and Snow

The oceans and the atmosphere interact in many other ways. Warmed by the sun, ocean water evaporates into the atmosphere and becomes part of it. The water vapor condenses into clouds, and the clouds shed rain. The geological effects of rain are everywhere to be seen on the land. Water is a strong solvent that readily dissolves many minerals, notably salts. It is the solution for most of the chemical reactions that help to break down rock. It is also a low-viscosity fluid, so that it readily penetrates into crevices in the rock.

This last has pervasive effects. The water that penetrates crevices in rock can freeze, and ice is less dense than water. What this means is that when a given volume of water freezes, it occupies a larger volume: it expands. In expanding, as every householder who worries about the freezing of pipes knows, it can exert powerful forces, and if the freezing water is in rock crevices, those forces can break the hardest rock. The repetitive freezing of water in rock crevices is one of the main agents of erosion.

The clouds also shed snow, which has its own profound geological effects. In parts of the earth where snow does not entirely melt, such as the polar areas and high mountains, it builds up into ice. Ice flows, and in time it can flow in the great river of a glacier. The ice of a glacier is dirty with rocks and rock particles that have fallen onto it from the crags above it or have been picked up from the rock under it, and when the glacier flows, the rock in it grinds at the rock under it.

There have been long periods in the earth's history when glaciers were absent. Ancient rocks show, however, that in the deep past there were at least three glacial epochs. Why the ice should come and go over long periods of time is a mystery. Many explanations have been offered, including the drifting of the continents over the earth's surface. For example, if most of the land were near the warm Equator, conditions for ice sheets to grow would not be as favorable as they would be if most of the land were nearer the cold poles.

People often refer to "the ice age" as though it were a time of the geological past. Actually we are still living in the ice age, although it is not at its height. Glaciers still flow down from high mountains and spread in huge ice sheets over Greenland and Antarctica. The current glacial epoch has lasted about a million years, and in that span the ice has advanced and retreated numerous times. Here again many explanations of why it should have done so have been offered. One that may give part of the answer is the Milankovitch hypothesis, developed in the 1920s and 1930s by Milutin Milankovitch of Yugoslavia.

The earth's orbit around the sun is slightly elliptical, and on cycles of 95,000, 123,000 and 413,000 years the ellipse flexes: at times the orbit is more elliptical and at other times it is less so. Secondly, the earth's axis of rotation is tilted with respect to the plane of the orbit, and the angle of tilt changes on a cycle of 41,000 years. Thirdly, the direction in which the axis points changes on a cycle of 21,000 years. According to the Milankovitch hypothesis, when such factors all pull, as it were, in the same direction, they reduce the amount of sunlight received by the earth at high latitudes in the Northern Hemisphere. When that happens, summers are cooler, snow accumulates and glaciers flow.

At the height of the current glacial epoch ice as deep as two miles blanketed North America almost as far south as St. Louis and blanketed Europe as far south as France. The water that froze into the glaciers was drawn from the world ocean. In fact, so much of the earth's water was stored in the ice sheets that the level of the ocean dropped some 400 feet. Continental shelves were exposed, and rivers running down to the more distant sea cut deep canyons in them. The material washed out from the edge of the ice sheet by streams built broad plains of sand, gravel and boulders. A remnant of such a plain is the row of lovely strands off the northeast coast of the United States: Long Island, Block Island, Martha's Vineyard, Nantucket and Cape Cod.

The mass of the ice was so great that it pressed the underlying crust deeper into the mantle. To this day the slow rebound of the crust in North America, inching up like a ratchet, generates small earthquakes. The ice sheets also worked the crust like a mighty planing machine. They ground down exposed bedrock and carried soil and big boulders along with them. When they finally melted and retreated, they dumped their load, creating entire landscapes such as the one that today runs from Maine west to the Dakotas.

They also left thousands of freshwater lakes, including the largest in North America, Europe and Asia today. In many places the lakes grew behind insubstantial dams of earth and ice. When the dams broke, the result was some of the most spectacular catastrophes in earth history.

One such event scoured a rugged landscape of 1,500 square miles in eastern Washington named the Channeled Scablands. Part of this landscape is the Grand Coulee, a canyon 900 feet deep and 50 miles long. Some 18,000 years ago an ice dam in Idaho created a lake extending deep into Montana and holding half as much water as Lake Michigan. When the dam let go, a wall of water more than 600 feet high rushed down to the Pacific, stripping away virtually all of the loose material in its path.

The Flows of the Earth

The water vapor that condenses into rain and freezes into snow is transported around the world by the circulation of the atmosphere. The circulation of the water vapor is, however, uneven. For example, near the Equator warm air laden with water vapor rises, cools and sheds copious rain. That is why rain forests are in equatorial regions. When the cooled air flows north and sinks at latitudes between 10 and 35 degrees, it is dry. That is why the world's great deserts are in those latitudes.

North of 35 degrees the atmosphere flows mostly from west to east. It moves in great eddies that interact to manufacture winds, clouds, storms, rain and snow, fair weather and foul. These are all manifestations of the overall action of the atmosphere: to distribute the heat of the sun over the globe. The amount of heat the earth receives from the sun is 5,000 times the amount flowing up from the mantle. Sunlight is strongest, of course, at the Equator and weakest at the poles. If its energy were not carried away from the Equator by the atmosphere, the Equator would be a lot hotter, the poles a lot colder and the earth quite a different place.

The circulation of the atmosphere also drives the circulation of the ocean. Convection does enter in: cold waters near the poles sink and flow toward the Equator along the bottom, and they are replaced by warm waters flowing away from the Equator at the surface. Still, they tend to remain at the bottom. If it were not for the wind tugging at its surface, the ocean would be rather stagnant. As it is, the wind-driven currents force the upwelling of the cold deep waters. Such waters are rich in nutrients for the organisms of the surface, and so where they well up, as they do off the coast of Peru, they have a high biological productivity: they nourish plankton, which nourish small invertebrates, which nourish fish, which nourish birds.

The ocean waves generated by the wind have multifarious effects. Waves large and small increase the friction between the wind and the water, so that the water is driven faster. When waves break, either when they come ashore or when they are swept by a strong wind at sea, they churn up the burst of air bubbles called a whitecap. When the bubbles collapse, they fire droplets of salt water into the air. And when the droplets evaporate, they leave suspended in the air tiny particles of salt. Such particles can now act as nuclei on which new droplets can condense. In this way whitecaps accelerate the condensation of water vapor into rain.

Breaking waves gnaw at the land, leaving cliffs, building beaches and dumping more sediment onto the continental shelves. I cannot leave the subject of beaches without mentioning a practical lesson I learned from the earth sciences. It is that there is no such thing as an undertow: a powerful current that extends along a beach and can pull bathers out to sea. What does exist is rip currents, narrow flows where the water brought in by waves breaking on the beach runs out again. The distinction may seem trivial, but making it can save a swimmer's life. If one is caught in a rip current, one can become exhausted swimming against it toward the shore. What one must do is swim a short distance parallel to the shore until one is out of the rip.

If the land on which the waves are breaking is an island, the waves may plane the whole thing down to wave base: the deepest level in the water at which the largest surface waves are felt. The geologist in Charles Darwin saw how this process could contribute to the making of a coral atoll. First an undersea volcano rises above the sea surface. Then waves chew at the flanks of the volcano and plane it down to a flat-topped "seamount." While this is happening corals are growing in the shallow sunlit waters provided by the volcano. In the end they form over the seamount a cap of coral limestone and a ring of sandspits: an atoll.

The water of the ocean and the land—lakes, streams, glaciers and ground water—is collectively the hydrosphere. It is clear that the circulating fluid of the atmosphere and the circulating fluid of the hydrosphere are closely coupled. *The remarkable fact is that except for the solid center of the earth's core the entire earth is a system of coupled circulating fluids.* The rates at which the fluids circulate differ enormously, but the flows are coupled nonetheless.

The fluid outer part of the core, like the rest of the earth, is heated by the decay of radioactive elements in it. It is losing that heat to the mantle above it, largely through ponderous convection flows. Since it is iron, it is a good conductor of electricity. The combination of its flows and the spin of the earth make it act as a dynamo that generates the earth's magnetic field.

Extending into space, the lines of force in the magnetic

field bend the paths of the electrically charged particles of the solar wind so that they spill into the earth's upper atmosphere. There they generate the pale multicolored light of the aurora. In other words, flows of molten metal far below the earth's surface direct the flow of charged particles high above the surface.

The rocky material of the earth's mantle, as we have seen, also flows by convection. The flows create new lithosphere and move the continents. They add to the continents by volcanic eruption and raise mountains by plate tectonics. The flows of the atmosphere and the hydrosphere, energized by absorbed sunlight, wear down the mountains and further shape the earth.

Life Too Is a Flow

The most remarkable of all terrestrial flows are those of the biosphere: the totality of all life on the planet. Embedded in the atmosphere, the hydrosphere and the lithosphere, the biosphere massively influences them all. As we have seen, life created the oxygen-rich atmosphere that oxidizes rocks and nourishes higher plants and animals, including ourselves. Life in the hydrosphere created oil and carbonate rocks such as limestone. Life in and on the lithosphere, to say nothing at all of its overwhelming presence in our own environment, created soils and coal and participated in the erosion of the land. At the same time life, in the form of trees and other vegetation, helped preserve the land by shielding it against erosion.

Since living things reproduce themselves, life too is a flow. From the global point of view, however, the flows of life are the flows of energy, water, oxygen, carbon, nitrogen, and numerous minerals such as phosphorus and sulfur. All of these things flow in closed cycles: they are taken up by living organisms, returned to the environment and taken up again.

It is here that one finds the earth's own great chain of being. The cyclic flows of the earth, including the flows of life, mesh like gears of different sizes and speeds in some fantastically complex piece of machinery. Some fifty years ago an eminent Dutch geologist, J. H. F. Umbgrove, wrote a book evocatively titled *The Pulse of the Earth*. He was largely referring to the cycle in which mountains rise and are worn down and rise again. In actuality the earth has many pulses.

In spite of all this activity the earth does not change very much over hundreds of millions of years. It is in a steady state. Mountains rise and fall, continents drift, oceans grow and shrink, but overall the planet remains much the same.

Color pictures of the earth from space, which reveal no trace of human activities, show the earth as it has been for perhaps two billion years. It is a uniquely blue planet. Its blueness is the blue of its waters. Its atmosphere, except for its white clouds, is transparent to the small band of wavelengths—light—that are felicitous for life: they are energetic enough to drive an efficient photosynthesis and yet are not so energetic that they would disrupt complex molecules before they could be built into living organisms. The more energetic wavelengths, such as ultraviolet and X rays, are filtered out.

In his book *Gaia, a New Look at Life on Earth*, J. E. Lovelock goes so far as to suggest that life orchestrates the steady state of the atmosphere to its own advantage. For example, the atmospheric shield against ultraviolet is ozone, and ozone is a form (O_3) of the oxygen pumped into the atmosphere by life.

What is more, life removes carbon dioxide from the atmosphere. If it did not, the carbon dioxide would have a greater "greenhouse effect." In its steady-state energy cycle the earth receives energy from the sun in the form of light and radiates it back into space in the form of infrared. On its way back into space some of the infrared is absorbed by carbon dioxide, making the earth warmer. If the concentration of carbon dioxide in the atmosphere increased, it would make the earth warmer still. The planet Venus has an atmosphere of carbon dioxide, which makes the surface of the planet hot enough to melt lead.

Currently the earth's steady-state energy cycle is being perturbed by a single living species—human beings. In burning ever larger quantities of coal and oil they have accelerated the cycles with which coal and oil are created and destroyed. Regarded in the sweep of earth history, coal and oil are temporary repositories of carbon in the crust of the earth. Coal is plant material that was submerged in swamps before its carbon had a chance to be fully oxidized into carbon dioxide. Oil is bacterial material that escaped oxidation by being buried in sediment. In the fullness of time, however, both coal and oil are either exposed at the surface and oxidized to carbon dioxide or sunk to greater depths and metamorphosed into other minerals.

Human beings accelerate the carbon cycle by bringing coal and oil to the surface and oxidizing them—that is, burning them—in a hurry. In so doing they increase the concentration of carbon dioxide in the atmosphere. As we read almost daily, the increase in the concentration of carbon dioxide bids fair to enhance the greenhouse effect and start a warming trend as early as the 1990s.

The results would not necessarily be all bad for human beings. We might, however, have to cope with such effects as the rise in the sea level brought about by the disintegration of the West Antarctic ice sheet, which is believed to be unstable. If the ice sheet did break up and melt, the sea level would rise some twenty feet. That would not only flood most coastal cities but also, among other things, submerge half the state of Florida.

A more immediate threat is the effects of a possible all-out nuclear war. Although no one knows exactly what those effects would be, efforts to calculate them are convincing enough to indicate that for human life they would be catastrophic. It seems unlikely that *Homo sapiens* would cease to exist, but even if it did, the geological effects would be trivial. The earth would maintain its steady state, although there would be no one around to marvel at it.

BIOLOGY, HAVING FOUND ITS
HOLY GRAIL, DRINKS FROM IT

In *The Third Policeman* Flann O'Brien's universal scholar de Selby reflects on Irish policemen and bicycles. It is well known to physicists that if you take two different metals, say lead and gold, and place them in close contact, after a period of time you will find some lead atoms in the gold and some gold atoms in the lead. This is testimony to the fact that at ordinary temperatures the atoms in the two metals are in a constant state of vibration, and some of them even break loose from the metal altogether. Thinking on such phenomena, de Selby came up with the following.

In Ireland at the time of *The Third Policeman* all policemen rode bicycles. In fact, some of them rode bicycles so much that, according to de Selby, Policeman Gilhaney was on his bicycle 48 percent of the time. Therefore, as you can plainly see, atoms of the bicycle slowly migrated into Gilhaney and atoms of Gilhaney slowly migrated into the bicycle. De Selby thought it was an explanation of why Irish policemen, like bicycles, could be leaned up against a wall, and why bicycles were often found in kitchens where there had been a mysterious disappearance of pie.

De Selby was closer to the mark than you might think.

Believe it or not, the molecules of most of the tissues in the human body have a half-life of less than two weeks. Even the calcium in bone has a half-life of less than four years. When you consider that a human being can live some twenty times that long, it gives you a new perspective on human beings and other living organisms. Instead of being a mere object, a living organism is a vortex of matter and energy.

Susan Roberts of the Massachusetts Institute of Technology (who happens to be my daughter-in-law) has taken the trouble to work this out for my benefit. The half-life of a molecule in the body is the time it takes for half the molecules of that kind to be replaced by other molecules of the same kind. Half-life can be extended to larger fractions, and Dr. Roberts has extended it to 95-percent-life: the time it takes for 95 percent of the molecules to be replaced.

One of the main types of molecule in living matter is protein. The estimated 95-percent-lives of protein molecules in a few sample tissues are as follows. For protein in muscle and brain the 95-percent-life is 86 days. For protein in lung the figure is 43 days. For protein in intestine it is 12 days. For calcium in bone, which is held in crystals of the mineral hydroxyapatite, the 95-percent-life is 14.7 years. In a healthy body all the other materials are similarly replaced. As an example, three million red blood cells die and are replaced every *second*.

There is the same kind of turnover, of course, in all other living organisms. Viewed in this way a living organism is rather like a flame. A flame maintains its form as fuel and oxygen flow through it. Within the flame the fuel and oxygen combine, releasing energy and the waste products carbon dioxide and water. For human beings and other animals the overall chemical equation is the same.

The flame of a living organism burns at a low temperature. It does so by means of the catalysts called enzymes. A catalyst is defined as a substance that changes the rate of a chemical reaction without itself being changed. If it were not for the catalytic action of enzymes, the chemical reactions of life would proceed so slowly that life could scarcely exist. A single cell in the human body has been estimated to contain 100,000 enzyme molecules to catalyze between 1,000 and 2,000 kinds of chemical reactions.

The fuel of the living flame is mostly carbohydrate and fat. The fuel does not directly combine with the oxygen of the atmosphere to release energy and the waste products carbon dioxide and water. It is transformed through a series of enzymatic reactions into a fuel of, so to speak, higher octane. That fuel is adenosine triphosphate, or ATP. It is ATP that drives the biochemical reactions that require energy.

The chemical regime I have been describing is respiration. It is one of the two principal energy-transforming regimes of life. The other is photosynthesis, in which a plant harnesses sunlight to make itself out of carbon dioxide, water and a pinch of minerals. Plants, like animals, respire. Animals, of course, cannot photosynthesize; their energy and substance come from plants. The situation was neatly characterized by Eugene Rabinowitch in a *Scientific American* article on photosynthesis: "If plants could express themselves, they would probably have the same low opinion of animals as we have of fleas and tapeworms—organisms that must lazily depend on others for survival."

The Molecular Machine

One of the most significant advances in the entire history of human knowledge has been the visualization of living matter at the molecular level. It is as though a mighty microscope has been trained on living tissue and the very fabric and machinery of that tissue have come into focus. In some respects the microscope is a real one: many things have been made apparent by the light microscope and the electron microscope. But for the most part the microscope that has revealed the fabric and machinery of living matter has been the microscope of the mind.

Working with a pioneering light microscope of his own design, Robert Hooke saw in 1665 that woody tissue is made up of cells. It was not until 1838, however, that Matthias Jakob Schleiden and Theodor Schwann perceived that *all* living tissue is made up of cells. Throughout the nineteenth century living matter was also being examined by chemists. It was they who were approaching the subject not by what they could see but by what they could figure out by logic and experiment. In this way they could go below the level of the cell and its visible contents to the level of molecules.

By the twentieth century it had been well established that living matter consists mainly of, in addition to water, four kinds of compounds: carbohydrates, fats, proteins and nucleic acids. This is not to suggest that the other kinds of compounds in living matter are unimportant. Among them are minerals (as in bone), pigments (such as chlorophyll) and alkaloids (such as quinine and nicotine). The fact remains that the four major kinds of compounds occupy the center of the stage.

Carbohydrates are compounds of carbon, hydrogen and oxygen. Simple sugar molecules consist of those atoms arranged in a ring. Starch molecules are sugar rings linked in a chain, straight or branched. Sugars are not only fuel for the living machine but also structural material. Chains of sugars make up cellulose—the tough outer wall of plant cells and the main structural material of plants.

Fats belong to the class of molecules called lipids. The molecules of the fat with which we are familiar in a steak or in our own midsection consist mostly of chains of carbon atoms with two hydrogen atoms attached to each carbon. Lipids, however, have many other molecular configurations. The molecule of cholesterol, for example, consists of four rings of atoms with a short chain of atoms attached. Lipids play an important structural role in forming a membrane around the living cell.

Proteins were something of a mystery until the late 1940s. It was known that they are composed not only of carbon, hydrogen and oxygen but also of a substantial amount of nitrogen. It was also known that their molecules are gigantic. As an example, a single molecule of the milk protein lactoglobulin consists of some 6,000 atoms and has the formula $C_{1864}H_{3012}O_{576}N_{468}S_{21}$. Finally it was known that protein molecules are made up of smaller molecules linked in a chain.

The smaller molecules are twenty different amino acids, each consisting of between ten and twenty-seven atoms. In each amino acid is a group of atoms that can link up with the same group of atoms in another amino acid. That is how the amino acids form the protein chain. The rest of each amino acid in the chain sticks out to the side. By taking protein chains apart chemists were able to determine the sequence of amino acids in several proteins and to show that each protein has a unique sequence.

But how are the atoms of a protein arranged in three dimensions? That fundamental biological problem too was solved not by biologists but by both chemists and physicists. This is not to take anything away from biologists but to reiterate that between any two departments of knowledge there is no real seam. To the Canterbury of living matter there was not one road but many.

One road was the basic study of molecules. The young chemist Linus Pauling was on the scene in Germany at the time quantum mechanics was first electrifying the scientific world. Pauling quickly absorbed the new knowledge and made his own contributions to it. He also saw its applications to chemistry, in that it explained the forces that held atoms together in molecules. He published a classic treatise, *The Nature of the Chemical Bond*.

Pauling also had a strong sense of the geometry of molecules. Pondering the nature of proteins in the 1940s, he and his colleague Robert Corey worked out the three-dimensional structure of amino-acid molecules in order to see how they might fit together in a chain. One of their discoveries was that when amino acids are linked, they can form a corkscrew. They named the structure the alpha helix (not to be confused with the double helix of DNA).

At the same time a different kind of mind and a different tradition were following a different road. A crystal is a regular array of atoms, sometimes likened to the array of trees in a regularly planted orchard. When you drive past an orchard in a car, you can see, one after the other, a series of straight lanes through the trees. If a crystal were enormously magnified, you could see similar lanes through its atoms in three dimensions.

In 1913 it was discovered that when a beam of X rays is trained on a crystal such as a diamond, the lanes of atoms in the crystal reflect the X rays like mirrors set at a low angle. When the reflected X rays fall on a photographic film, they expose the film in a regular pattern. The pattern can then be analyzed— not without considerable difficulty—to determine the arrangement of atoms in the crystal. The method is called X-ray crystallography, and its practitioners are physicists.

In living matter protein molecules do not usually form crystals, but in the laboratory they can be made to do so. In such a crystal the giant protein molecules are regularly stacked so that the lanes of atoms are repeated over and over again. The regular array of molecules and their constituent atoms can then be subjected to X-ray analysis. With this approach John Kendrew in 1957 first worked out the three-dimensional structure of a protein molecule. The protein was myoglobin, which stores oxygen in muscle.

The actual model of the structure was a forest of vertical

rods to which were attached smaller models of the amino acids in the protein chain. Translated into a drawing for *Scientific American*, it looked rather like a mass of crumpled chicken wire. Nevertheless it was one of the great visions of the century, revealing for the first time the true complexity of a protein molecule. In the model it could be seen that the protein chain, including stretches of alpha helix, was folded back on itself several times, so that the molecule was roughly globular.

Many proteins are not globular but fibrous; their molecules are long and skinny rather than round. Fibrous proteins appropriately lend themselves to the fabric of living matter. In the human body the fibrous protein collagen is one of the main constituents of skin, bone, cartilage and tendon; the fibrous protein myosin is one of the main constituents of muscle; the fibrous protein keratin is one of the main constituents of skin, fingernail and hair. Globular proteins, functioning as enzymes, lend themselves to being the machine tools in the factory of living matter.

How does an enzyme perform its remarkable feat of engineering the chemical reactions of life? Since an enzyme is a protein and a typical protein consists of thousands of atoms, there is plenty of room in the enzyme molecule for a complex cleft into which a smaller molecule can fit as a key fits into a lock. When the smaller molecule enters the cleft, the particular arrangement of atoms in the cleft exerts forces on it that can snap it apart. By the same token, when two molecules that can combine lie in the same cleft, the enzyme molecule can snap them together.

The Information Machine

Carbohydrates, fats, proteins—that leaves nucleic acids. The tale goes back to Gregor Mendel, who was taking another road to the

Canterbury of living matter. In 1865 Mendel presented his evidence that characteristics of pea plants, such as the height of the plant or the color of its flowers, are determined by distinct entities that can be inherited. Those entities were later named genes. At the same time Friedrich Miescher was taking the road of biochemistry: the chemical study of living matter.

In 1869 Miescher discovered the class of compounds later called nucleic acids, although he did not know they had anything to do with genes. In fact, nobody had any idea what genes were. The concept of the gene was nonetheless so powerful that it gave rise to genetics, a rich and productive science concerned with the transmission of characteristics from living organisms to their descendants and with the expression of those characteristics in the descendants.

In the 1940s Oswald Avery and his colleagues Colin MacLeod and Maclyn McCarty were on the road of microbiology: the study of microorganisms. It was known that if material extracted from one strain of the pneumococcus bacterium was added to another strain, an important hereditary characteristic of the first strain— an outer capsule of sugar—could be transferred to the second. Avery, MacLeod and McCarty found that the essential constituent of the extracted material was nucleic acid. In other words, the nucleic acid was acting as a gene.

Soon afterward George Beadle and Edward Tatum, on the road of genetics, arrived at the "one gene—one enzyme" concept. They proposed that for each protein there is a corresponding gene. The actual mechanism of genetics, however, remained what electrical engineers call a black box: a device of known function but unknown components.

In the same years other scientists were taking yet another road: the study of viruses. A virus is at the borderline between living matter and nonliving matter; it is not a cell but a tiny particle; it can reproduce but only inside a cell. The viruses these scientists were studying were viruses that infect bacteria. Such a virus is a particle consisting of nucleic acid wrapped in protein. It was found that when a virus infects a bacterial cell, it leaves its protein jacket at the surface of the cell and inserts its nucleic acid into the cell. The cell is then tricked, so to speak, into manufacturing not only its own substance but also new virus particles. Hence viruses offered a further clue that the stuff of genes is nucleic acid.

The travelers were now joined by two young strangers: James Watson, a biologist who had started out in ornithology, and Francis Crick, a physicist mainly interested in X-ray crystallography. When they came along in the early 1950s, a long and hard road had already been traveled by biochemists. They had shown that nucleic acid molecules, like protein molecules, are long chains made from smaller molecules. The links in the chain are not amino acids but nucleotides. In the chemistry of the nucleotides was a clue, albeit a dark one, to how they might serve the purposes of genes.

The question was: Do nucleic acids have a structure that might throw some light on what genes are and how they work? Watson and Crick were looking at the nucleic acid that later became a household word: DNA (for deoxyribonucleic acid). As had happened with the effort to determine the three-dimensional structure of proteins, two roads had come together: X-ray crystallography and the geometry of the smaller molecules that make up the DNA chain.

Watson and Crick worked with—in one case, according to Watson, virtually stole—X-ray pictures of DNA made by others. It was already clear that the DNA consisted of long, thin fibers. Watson and Crick perceived in the X-ray pictures that at the molecular level the fibers had a corkscrew twist. They also suspected that the fibers consisted of two corkscrews wound around each other.

Here the dark clue from biochemistry entered in. The atoms of a nucleotide—one of the links in the DNA chain—are organized in a sugar, a phosphate and one of four nitrogen-containing bases: adenine, guanine, thymine and cytosine, abbreviated A, G, T, C. The order of the bases in the DNA chain is irregular. The biochemist Erwin Chargaff had discovered, however, that in DNA the ratios of A to G and of T to C are close to 1:1. Watson and Crick wondered: if the DNA chain is a double one, perhaps Chargaff's ratios were an indication that an A on one chain is always paired with a T on the other chain, and that a G is always paired with a C.

They set to work making models of A, G, T and C and seeing how the models fitted together. They quickly found that A fitted T and G fitted C! It leapt to their delighted eyes, and to the eyes of everyone else who read their 1953 paper in the journal *Nature*, that DNA is a double corkscrew with the two chains held together by bonds between the paired nucleotides—the now famous double helix.

One of the significant things about the helix's being double, as Watson and Crick wrote at the end of their paper, was that it provided a means for the chains to duplicate themselves. Since the As and Gs of one chain were always paired with the Ts and Cs of the other, each chain was a kind of mirror image of the other. The two chains in the double helix could come apart and a new chain could be assembled, one nucleotide after another, on each chain in the complementary sequence. The result would be another double helix. In this way the living cell could pass copies of its DNA on to its descendants.

But if DNA was the stuff of genes, how was the sequence of nucleotides in DNA translated into the sequence of amino acids in protein? There could not be a one-to-one correspondence between the amino acids and the nucleotides: the four nucleotides of DNA were much too few to code for the twenty amino acids of protein. How about taking the nucleotides two at a time, which would give sixteen possible combinations? That would still not be enough for coding twenty amino acids. How about taking them three at a time, which would give sixty-four possible combinations? That would do it. Certain biological experiments supported the idea, but it was still not clear what triplets of nucleotides would code for what amino acids.

A remarkably simple experiment by Marshall Nirenberg in 1961 showed how to find out. Traveling the biochemical road, Nirenberg made a synthetic nucleic acid in which the same nucleotide was repeated over and over again. He then added the nucleic acid to a test-tube mixture of substances extracted from living cells that was known to be capable of manufacturing protein. The repetitive nucleic acid caused the mixture to manufacture a repetitive protein.

The nitrogen-containing base of the nucleotide in Nirenberg's repetitive nucleic acid was uracil, or U, not A, T, G or C. Uracil is found not in DNA but in another nucleic acid: RNA. The links in the RNA chain are A, U, G and C; the T of DNA is replaced by U. Therefore Nirenberg's repetitive synthetic nucleic acid was an RNA represented as UUUUUUUUUUUUUUU . . . The repetitive protein chain manufactured in the test tube consisted exclusively of the amino acid phenylalanine, designated Phe, so that the chain was Phe-Phe-Phe-Phe-Phe- . . . In other words, the nucleotide code for phenylalanine was the triplet UUU! In a remarkably short time biochemists worked out the triplets coding for the rest of the amino acids.

In the same year that Nirenberg did his experiment François Jacob and Jacques Monod, also following the biochemical road, proposed that RNA was a messenger between DNA and protein. Today the picture is like this: A gene is a long stretch of nucleotides in DNA—typically 300—that incorporates all the information needed for the spinning of a long chain of amino acids —typically 100. The gene may therefore be likened to a section of computer tape. Messenger RNA is a molecule in which the information on the section of DNA tape has been transcribed.

The messenger-RNA tape is engaged by a minuscule tape player: the kind of particle in the living cell called the ribosome. Individual amino acids are ferried to the ribosome by another kind of RNA: transfer RNA. In the ribosome the sequence of nucleotides in the messenger RNA is translated into a sequence of amino acids that emerges, one amino acid after another, as a protein chain. Thereafter the chain coils and folds itself up into the complex configuration of the protein molecule.

But how does the chain coil and fold itself up? I mentioned that in a protein chain the amino acids are linked by the same group of atoms and that the rest of each amino-acid molecule sticks out to the side. These side groups have diverse chemical and physical characteristics. For example, some form a strong chemical bond with another side group of the same kind, so that they can tie part of the protein chain into a loop.

Some side groups are repelled by water and some are attracted to it. Since water is the environment of the protein chain, such attraction and repulsion can fold the chain by pushing and pulling at it. In a globular protein the amino acids repelled by water tend to end up on the inside of the molecule and those attracted by water tend to end up on the outside. It is the amino-acid side groups that endow each kind of protein molecule with its unique character and enable it to do its work.

Visions of the Living Cell

This extraordinary series of discoveries has been recognized by some seventy Nobel prizes over the past thirty years. Even as

those discoveries were being made, however, different kinds of
scientists were opening up other visions of living matter. Modern
physics has shown that electrons are both particles and waves,
and electron waves are shorter than light waves. Therefore a
microscope that illuminates a specimen with electrons can resolve
details finer than those that can be resolved by a microscope that
illuminates a specimen with light.

Electrons cannot travel far through air, and so the path of
the electron beam in the electron microscope must be a vacuum.
This is unfortunate for the examination of living matter, which
in a vacuum dries up or explodes. Moreover, the electron beam
itself tends to destroy the tissue. What to do? In the 1950s Keith
Porter and Albert Claude came up with the solution: transform
living tissue into a tough material that can withstand both the
vacuum and the electron beam.

Such material can be made with the aid of a plastic: poly-
methyl methacrylate, or Lucite. The molecules of the plastic are
long chains of smaller molecules, which can be dissolved in a
solvent. When a catalyst is added to the solution, the smaller
molecules link up in the chains of the solid plastic. To make a
tissue specimen for electron microscopy one soaks the tissue in
the solution and then adds the catalyst. The tissue, permeated
with the solution, is then part and parcel of a piece of plastic.
Moreover, a compound of a heavy metal can be added to the
solution, so that the structures in the tissue are stained with atoms
that to electrons are denser, and therefore more visible, than the
atoms of the tissue itself.

The problem remained of making the plastic thin enough
for the electrons to go through it and form an image. The metal
knives of the microtomes that generations of microscopists had
used to slice tissues are not sharp enough. What finally worked
was the keen edge of broken glass. With such a knife in the

microtome the plastic can be cut into gossamer slices the electrons can traverse.

I mention this technique because it will suggest how biology, like astronomy, is profoundly influenced by advances in methods of observation. As a matter of fact, during this same period advances in several other techniques played a critical role in the understanding of living matter. Notable among them were three methods of separating molecules—amino acids, proteins and many others—that are chemically very much alike. They are ultra-centrifugation (where the molecules are spun at high speed and separate because of small differences in their size and density), chromatography (where the molecules are passed through a chemically inert medium and separate because of small differences in their tendency to stick to the medium) and electrophoresis (where the molecules are placed in an electric field and separate because of small differences in their electric charge and size). Since that time far more refined techniques have evolved.

A ubiquitous instrument in biological laboratories is humbler. It is none other than the kitchen blender. When you want to disrupt a tissue—liver, say—into its constituent cells, you drop it into the blender and turn on the switch. If you want to analyze the chemical constituents of an entire organism, you can even make a mousse of an entire mouse! (Predeceased, of course.) Strange to relate, the original blender was developed by a well-known dance-band leader: Fred Waring, of Fred Waring and His Pennsylvanians.

The pictures that emerged from the electron microscope opened up an entire new world of living matter. The light microscope had shown that inside the cell are distinct bodies, among them the cell nucleus, the small particles called mitochondria and chloroplasts and the flattened sacs of the Golgi apparatus. The general picture of the cell yielded by the light microscope, however, was that the cell is a bag of fluid with the other bodies floating inside it.

The picture of the cell yielded by the electron microscope was quite different. It showed that the cell, far from being merely a bag of fluid, is a small universe of highly organized semisolid matter. For example, certain kinds of cells are almost entirely filled with a fantastically convoluted membrane system called the endoplasmic reticulum.

The bodies inside the cell are seen to be universes in themselves. Consider mitochondria and chloroplasts. It was already known that these particles are energy transformers. The mitochondrion is a site of one of the two main types of energy transformation in cells: respiration. In the electron micrographs it could now be seen that it is an object rather like a tiny peanut with an outer membrane and a folded inner membrane. Embedded in the inner membrane are enzymes, arrayed like machines in an assembly line, that run a complex series of chemical reactions that transform the energy of carbohydrate into the energy of the universal cellular fuel ATP.

Mitochondria are found in both animal and plant cells; chloroplasts are found only in plant cells. The chloroplast is a site of the other main type of energy transformation in cells: photosynthesis. Electron micrographs revealed that it too has an outer membrane enclosing a folded inner membrane. The form of the inner membrane, however, is different from that of the membrane in mitochondria. The chloroplast membrane is draped in an array resembling stacks of coins. Embedded in it are molecules of the pigment chlorophyll, which absorb the solar energy that drives photosynthesis. The pigment is green because it is tuned to wavelengths in the red and blue parts of the spectrum; the green is what is reflected rather than absorbed.

The new microscopic visions captured the imagination of scientists who were taking other roads to the Canterbury of the living cell. Biochemists, for example, had been accustomed to thinking of the reactions catalyzed by enzymes as taking place in a solution rather like the one in their test tube. Now they could see that many of the enzymes are part of an elaborate larger architecture that organizes their function.

The Diversity of Cells

There is no such thing as a cell that is typical of all cells. This was brought home to me one time when my colleagues and I were preparing an issue of *Scientific American* titled "The Living Cell." We wanted to start the issue with a picture of a representative cell, but what kind of cell would be truly representative? Plant cells and animal cells are so different that one could not be representative of the other. Moreover, the cell of a single-celled organism would be representative of neither. We finally had to settle for a drawing that combined the features of most, but by no means all, animal cells.

Such a cell has a nucleus and several other tiny organs: organelles. Within the nucleus is chromatin, the threadlike material that incorporates DNA. When the cell prepares to divide, the chromatin is reorganized into the sausagelike bodies called chromosomes. Outside the nucleus are two organelles called centrosomes, each consisting of two tiny parallel rods surrounded by nine others. At the time of cell division the centrosomes lie at the poles of the apparatus that pulls apart the two duplicate sets of chromosomes, one for each daughter cell.

Also outside the nucleus are the convoluted folds of the endoplasmic reticulum. Along the surfaces of the reticulum and elsewhere in the cell are myriads of ribosomes, little more than dots even in an electron micrograph. Since virtually all of the cell's DNA is in the nucleus, and since it is the ribosomes that link amino acids into the chains of protein, the RNA that carries the message of the DNA to the ribosome must migrate out of the nucleus. Separate from the endoplasmic reticulum are the sacs of the Golgi apparatus, which among other things serves the function of packaging a cell product—an enzyme, say—for export from the cell.

Scattered throughout the cell outside the nucleus are mitochondria. Of similar size are the organelles called lysosomes, which act as a Disposall containing enzymes that break down large molecules such as nucleic acids and proteins by cutting their chains. If these enzymes were not segregated from the rest of the cell, they would digest it as well.

At the surface of the cell is a thin membrane consisting of a double layer of fatty molecules. Thin though it is, the membrane effectively maintains the cell's integrity. Still, things need to get into cells and out of them. Some small molecules, such as those of water, pass through the cell membrane passively. Others, such as ions—electrically charged atoms—of sodium and potassium must be actively transported across the membrane. This function is served by protein molecules attached to the membrane or embedded in it.

The protein molecules of the cell membrane are also a universe in themselves. Some form rafts; others form pores. Many are receptors that are highly specific for some other molecule. As an example, on the surface of certain T cells that activate the immune system of the body to resist a virus infection are protein molecules that can "recognize" a viral antigen: a characteristic protein molecule of the virus. When they do so, the T cells multiply and signal B cells to manufacture antibodies: protein molecules that can combine with the virus protein and inactivate the virus.

Other protein molecules within the cell can join up in long fibers. Some of the fibers are stiff and serve to maintain the shape of the cell. Others have the ability to contract and relax; they can either move things around in the cell or change the shape of the cell. The most prominent fibers of this type are muscle fibers, which consist largely of two proteins: actin and myosin.

Motion and Information

Muscle cells well illustrate how cells are so specialized that no one kind is typical of the rest. A muscle cell is specialized for contraction and relaxation. It is a spindle-shaped cell almost entirely made up of actin, myosin and their associated proteins, with mitochondria to fuel contraction with ATP. Actin forms thin filaments, myosin thick ones. The filaments lie parallel to one another, with short bridges extending from the myosin to the actin.

The bridges act as a kind of ratchet mechanism. When the muscle cell is signaled to contract, the bridges pull the actin filaments past the myosin filaments and cause the entire cell to shorten. Large arrays of such cells can perform mighty feats such as lifting the leg of an elephant or bending the 100-foot body of a blue whale.

A muscle cell is signaled to contract by another specialized cell: the nerve cell. A nerve cell is specialized for making myriad contacts with other cells, particularly muscle cells, gland cells and other nerve cells. It branches out into fine fibers. One fiber of each cell—the axon—can be much longer than the others; in the human nervous system its length can be three feet. The axon has the ability to conduct coded impulses rather like the dots in an old-fashioned telegraph code.

A dot signal travels down the axon to the point where the axon almost—but not quite—touches another cell. There the axon delivers across the narrow gap between it and the other cell tiny squirts of a specialized chemical: a neurotransmitter. If the other cell is a muscle cell, the neurotransmitter can cause it to contract. If the other cell is a gland cell, the neurotransmitter can cause it to release a hormone. If the other cell is a nerve cell, which is most often the case, the neurotransmitter can activate it. Nerve cells can also, however, do other things, for example inhibit another nerve cell from being activated.

The discovery of neurotransmitters is a lovely example of the role that can be played in science by imagination. A nerve signal is a traveling wave of electrical excitation, and for a long time many physiologists believed that what conveyed the signal from one cell to another was electricity. The pharmacologist Otto Loewi was one of those who believed it was not electricity but a chemical. How to devise an experiment to demonstrate it? He found a way—the experiment came to him in a dream. In fact, he dreamed it twice.

One morning in 1921 Loewi awoke to discover that in the middle of the night he had made some notes on a tiny piece of paper. He knew they were about something important, but he couldn't remember what, and they were indecipherable. The next night he awoke at 3 a.m. with the perfect experiment clearly in his mind. Not trusting his memory, he immediately went to the laboratory. By 5 a.m. he had completed the experiment.

The experiment called for two frog hearts. If an isolated frog heart is filled with a salt solution, it can be kept beating for hours. Attached to one of the two beating hearts were two major nerves: the vagus nerve and the sympathetic nerve. When the vagus nerve of that heart was stimulated, the heartbeat slowed down, and when the sympathetic nerve was stimulated, the heartbeat speeded up.

What Loewi did was to stimulate the vagus nerve of the one heart, remove salt solution from it with a thin glass tube and insert the solution into the other heart. The beating of the other heart slowed down! When he did the same with the sympathetic nerve, the beating of the other heart speeded up. There was no way these effects could have been caused by electricity; they had to be caused by some chemical in the solution. For this discovery Loewi received a Nobel prize.

Nerve cells are organized into networks like the circuits of a computer. Such networks exist not only in the brain but also in animals as simple as jellyfish. In the progression of complexity upward from jellyfish to mammals, nerve cells are marshaled first in isolated clusters—ganglia—and then consolidated in spinal cord and brain. Sigmund Freud saw the human mind (in *Civilization and Its Discontents*) as being like the city of Rome, with the modern metropolis underlain and shaped by all its antecedents. It is like that with the human nervous system, except that the antecedents are all alive and functioning.

The human brain, weight two and a half pounds, is the most complicated object known. In contemplating itself it has not yet made much progress in understanding such complex functions as thought and language. All the same, the brain has learned a fair amount about itself. For example, much of brain function is seen to be highly localized. Impulses from nerve endings in the skin go to highly specific addresses in the cerebrum. In fact, if the addresses are mapped on the surface of the human cerebrum, they trace out a "homunculus": a distorted image of the body.

The distortion of the homunculus is related to the concentration of the nerve endings in the skin. The hands, feet and lips are grotesquely enlarged; the limbs and the trunk are shrunken. The same kind of homunculus is traced out by the areas of the brain that dispatch impulses that command the muscles to contract.

Other brain functions are similarly localized, but many brain functions are not. For example, there is no evidence for

the localization of a function seemingly as simple as eye movement. The functions of the brain are served by the intercon-
nectedness of hundreds of billions of nerve cells, and it is hardly
surprising that it is taking time to work out the circuits. Moreover,
the circuits may be organized in ways that go far beyond the
imagination of a computer architect. How the brain works is the
deepest problem confronting modern biology.

(One of the most illuminating stories I have ever heard about
the subtlety of the nervous system was told to me by W. K.
Livingston, a surgeon who was also a leading investigator of pain.
Livingston had served his surgical internship at Massachusetts
General Hospital just after the First World War. One day one
of the staff surgeons asked him to open the colon of an elderly
male patient whose lower bowel was blocked by a tumor. Livingston knew that the procedure called for fishing a loop of colon
out through an open incision in the abdomen, holding the loop
in place with a glass rod and making a hole in the colon wall.
He did not, however, know how the hole was made.

He sought the advice of one of the older interns, who told
him he should get a blowtorch and a soldering iron from the
hospital plumber, heat the soldering iron red hot and then burn
a hole in the colon with it. Thinking he was the victim of a
practical joke, Livingston insisted that the other intern show him
how it was done. Somewhat testily the other intern agreed. They
acquired the blowtorch and soldering iron and took them to the
patient's room. The other intern got the blowtorch going, and
while the soldering iron was heating up the fully conscious patient
looked on in horror. Paying no attention, the other intern fished
out the loop of colon and applied the soldering iron to it. At that
point the patient sank back on his pillow with a blissful smile of
relief. He had felt no pain at all!

Livingston said to himself: "What is going on here? People
get bellyaches. Why is there no pain when the same organ is

burned?" The answer, which started Livingston on a lifelong career of studying pain, is that the alimentary tract feels only certain kinds of pain, as when it is inflated.)

One of the other deep problems confronting modern biology is how a single cell can give rise to an entire many-celled organism. The single cell is the egg cell. After the egg cell has been fertilized by a sperm cell, its DNA contains all the information needed for the construction of the entire organism. In other words, the cell contains a complete set of the genes for the organism. What is more, *with a few minor exceptions the cells descended from that single cell—in the case of an animal, skin cells, liver cells, nerve cells and what have you—receive the same complete set of genes.*

On the face of it this seems paradoxical: if DNA makes RNA and RNA makes protein, how is it that the cell is not constantly flooded with all the proteins for which the DNA codes? One answer has been found in bacteria: certain genes—the stretches of DNA that code for protein—have on them a molecular clamp. The clamp is a specialized protein molecule that physically blocks the transcription of the DNA into RNA. Then, under the appropriate circumstances, another kind of molecule comes along and signals the clamp to separate from the stretch of DNA representing the gene. When that happens, the DNA of the gene is free to be transcribed into RNA and the RNA can be translated into protein. How the expression of DNA is controlled in the cells of organisms more complex than bacteria, however, is subtler and still something of a mystery.

The processes that operate in the development of the fertilized egg into an entire organism are subtler still. The sequence in which the genes are turned on is regulated by a complex program, the nature of which is not yet known. Moreover, the embryonic cells descended from the egg cell have properties that cause them to interact in highly specific ways. For example, embryonic nerve cells send out feelers with a lifetime of only a few minutes. When such a feeler encounters another nerve cell of the appropriate kind, it gives rise to a fiber that connects the two cells in the nervous system. In such ways do the cells of the embryo weave the complex pattern of the entire organism.

The Rise of Cells

How did life begin? A detailed answer is not yet possible, but there is a general answer. Certain conditions on the primitive earth—heat, lightning and ultraviolet radiation from the sun—might well have favored the formation of molecules such as amino acids and nucleotides. Certain other conditions could have enabled these molecules to link up in chains and replicate themselves.

Which came first, the chicken or the egg, that is, the chain of amino acids (proteins) or the chain of nucleotides (nucleic acids)? Interestingly enough, if it was the chain of nucleotides, it may have been not DNA but RNA. It has been found that certain RNAs act as enzymes, so that they can catalyze their own formation. It is therefore possible that the first world of life on the earth was an RNA world, and that DNA and proteins came later.

In any case, the chains could have come to be enclosed in a tiny envelope of fatty molecules, where they would be still more likely to persist and replicate. Suffice it to say that today the simplest free-living organisms are bacteria, which are a collection of self-reproducing molecules enclosed in a tiny envelope. It seems probable the first living organisms were much like them.

The simplest bacteria live by browsing on inorganic material such as sulfur. By reducing (adding hydrogen to) or oxidizing these gritty substances they get the energy they need to build and maintain themselves. The oxidation is not, however, accomplished with oxygen from the atmosphere. Indeed, the free gaseous oxygen of today's atmosphere is lethal to such bacteria; they can exist only where they are sequestered from the oxygen in the air or dissolved in the water, say by being buried in mud.

Then, about half a billion years after the origin of life, there arose new kinds of bacteria. They were cells capable of obtaining their energy not from inorganic substances but from sunlight. This was the advent of photosynthesis, in which the energy of sunlight is absorbed by molecules of pigment. For example, in blue-green bacteria the blue-green pigment absorbs certain wavelengths of sunlight and energizes the removal of hydrogen from water and the transfer of the hydrogen to carbon dioxide. The product, as we have seen, is carbohydrates, substances that provide the energy for the rest of the cell's activities.

Note that when hydrogen is removed from H_2O, only O is left. The O is the source of the oxygen in the earth's atmosphere. *It brought about a change in the environment of living things that was, apart from the origin of life, the most significant single event in the history of life.* It enabled new kinds of organisms to arise that could take advantage of the great energy of oxidations that proceed directly from free oxygen. Among them, in due course, were animals.

When I was a high-school and college student in the 1930s all living things were listed in one or the other of two "kingdoms": the plant kingdom and the animal kingdom. The bacteria that were not capable of photosynthesis were an awkward exception, and they were usually placed arbitrarily in the plant kingdom. Now all that is changed.

The up-to-date classification of living things—so up-to-date that it is still the subject of debate—is as follows. There are three kingdoms: the archaebacteria, the eubacteria and the eukaryotes. The archaebacteria are the simple bacteria that feed on inorganic substances. The eubacteria are more complex and include the bacteria capable of photosynthesis. The eukaryotes include all the many-celled organisms, including animals and many-celled plants.

When Molière's M. Jourdain first learned the meaning of the word "prose," he realized it was what he had been speaking all his life. We human beings should realize we have been eukaryotes for most of our evolutionary lives. The "eu" is from the Greek *eus*, good. The "karyo" is from the Greek *karuon*, kernel or nut; it refers to the cell nucleus. When new words are coined from more than one root in old words, it is good form for them to be coined uniformly from old words in the same language. Since modern science often calls for new words for newly discovered things, the following brief tale may be pertinent.

It is said that when Johann Wolfgang von Goethe was a very old man, his literary assistant Eckermann came to him one day in great excitement. Eckermann said he had just seen a demonstration of an amazing new machine. It was a carriage driven by a steam engine, so that it needed no horses. He added that the machine was called automobile. Goethe retired to his study to think about it, and after a while he came out all smiles. "Eckermann," he said, "you are having another of your little jokes. If somebody *had* invented such a machine, they would never have mixed their Greek and Latin roots. The machine would have been called either the autokineticon or the ipsomobile."

Eukaryote and Prokaryote

The eukaryotes, then, are cells (and organisms made up of such cells) with a good nucleus, meaning a well-defined one. Their

DNA is woven into strands with protein, and at the time of cell division the strands are marshaled into chromosomes. They also have organelles such as mitochondria and chloroplasts. The archaebacteria and eubacteria, the two other great divisions of life, are prokaryotes: they do not have a well-defined nucleus, chromosomes or organelles.

Prokaryotes, however, might *be* organelles—at least some organelles. Most of the DNA in a eukaryotic cell is in the nucleus. A small amount of it, however, is in the mitochondria and chloroplasts, the organelles where respiration and photosynthesis take place.

How did the DNA come to be in the mitochondrion and the chloroplast? It is not clear, but it is suggestive. If the mitochondrion and the chloroplast had originally been independent organisms, they might well contain a vestige of their own original DNA. It is now believed, though by no means proven, that the mitochondrion was originally a purple bacterium or something pretty close to it, and that the chloroplast was originally a blue-green bacterium.

Seen in this light, the eukaryotic cell originated as a kind of colony of prokaryotic cells. Colonies of cells, in fact, are one of the great themes of life. Plants and animals may be considered such colonies. Much simpler colonies are instructive. Consider lichens, the scaly crust that grows on rocks and tree trunks.

A lichen is a colony of two entirely different types of cell. One is an alga, a cell with the capability of photosynthesis. The other is a fungus, a cell without that capability. The carbohydrates manufactured by the algae nourish the fungus; the fungus provides a mat on which the algae can live.

A different kind of colony is represented by the organisms called cellular slime molds. For most of its life a cellular slime mold is a free-living single cell, an amoeba hitching itself through the soil as it feeds on bacteria. Then when the time comes for the amoeba to reproduce, it and many other amoebae like it stream toward a common center.

When the amoebae come together, they form a slug perhaps a sixteenth of an inch long. The little slug creeps through the soil until it finds a place suitable for a remarkable performance. Some of the amoebae rise up into a tiny stalk that sticks up from the soil. At the top of the stalk is a small ball of cells that ultimately bursts and liberates spores of the amoeba. When a spore finds itself near a feed of bacteria, it splits open and frees an amoeba that participates in a repetition of the cycle.

The interesting thing is that while the amoebae are separate, they are unspecialized. Then when they come together, they differentiate into specialized cells: stalk cells and spore cells. In this regard the free-living amoeba resembles the egg cell of a many-celled organism. Like the slime-mold amoeba the egg cell differentiates into different cell types, creating a highly complex aggregation of cells such as a pine tree or a grizzly bear.

The streaming together of the slime-mold amoebae raises an obvious question: What makes them stream together? It is a substance the amoebae liberate into the soil when the time comes for them to reproduce. John Tyler Bonner, who has spent much of his life studying cellular slime molds, named it acrasin, after the family of slime molds he studies: the Acrasiales. But what is acrasin? In some species of slime mold it turns out to be cyclic AMP, a substance that plays an important role in many-celled organisms.

Cyclic AMP is a relatively small molecule that in many-celled organisms acts as a "second messenger." The first messenger can be a hormone: a substance secreted by a cell that influences the activity of another cell. When the hormone molecule arrives at the outer membrane of a cell, it does not need to enter the cell. Instead it can signal the cell to make and release cyclic AMP, which then carries the message to the cell machinery. Such chemical messengers are one of the two ways the activity of cells in a many-celled organism are integrated. The other way is the nervous system, which, of course, is found only in animals.

The presence of cyclic AMP in organisms as different as cellular slime molds and ourselves illustrates the universality of the basic mechanisms of life. In the archaebacteria—the simplest living organisms—DNA makes RNA and RNA makes protein, just as they do in many-celled organisms. The triplet code of the DNA in archaebacteria is the same as the triplet code in human beings. Moreover, much of the biochemistry in archaebacteria is the same as that in the cells of human beings.

Soft Bodies and Hard

An amoeba is a single-celled animal: a protozoan. Protozoa are animals in the sense that they are not capable of feeding on inorganic matter as archaebacteria and photosynthetic bacteria are. The first many-celled animals came into existence perhaps 800 million years ago, 2.7 billion years after the origin of life on the earth. They were soft-bodied organisms like modern jellyfish. Some 500 million years ago animals appeared that had hard parts, such as teeth and a skeleton, either external or internal.

Typical of the animals with an external skeleton was the ubiquitous trilobite, a creature somewhat resembling a large beetle that crawled along the bottom of shallow seas. The first animals with external skeletons gave rise to the entire zoo of modern animals with the same architecture, such as crustaceans, insects and spiders. The animals with internal skeletons were the vertebrates—animals with a backbone. The first vertebrates were fishes; they were followed by amphibians (350 million years ago), reptiles (275 million years ago) and mammals (180 million years ago). Human beings like ourselves arose no more than 200,000 years ago and perhaps as recently as 35,000 years ago, in either case a snap of the fingers in the 3.5 billion years of life.

Since all animals are basically sustained by plants, it is natural to assume that plants arose before animals. This is true for single-celled photosynthetic organisms but not for what we commonly regard as plants—grasses, shrubs, trees. The first many-celled plants arose at about the same time as the first many-celled animals. In fact, the first plants we would recognize as such appeared some 400 million years ago. They were the vascular plants: plants with a circulatory system that could carry water up from roots and carbohydrates down from leaves.

The first plants with flowers—the angiosperms—arrived much later: 135 million years ago, or even later than the mammals. Thereby hangs a tale of the fine-spun interactions between plants and animals. Vascular plants reproduce sexually: pollen shed by such a plant fertilizes the egg cells either of the same plant or of other plants of the same species. For nonflowering plants the pollen is distributed mostly by gravity and the wind. For flowering plants the pollen is distributed mostly by insects. The flowers are therefore specialized to attract a certain kind of insect and the insects are specialized to visit a certain kind of flower. Flowers and the insects that visit them are therefore a kind of fugue—two contrapuntal themes in the organ music of biological evolution.

The Facts of Life

Three and a half billion years ago life on the earth consisted of simple forms such as bacteria and today it consists of complex forms such as human beings. It is hard to avoid the conclusion that the simpler forms gave rise to the more complex. In fact, it seems as plain as day, and yet school boards in some parts of the United States require that evolution be labeled a theory.

Part of the trouble lies with the word "theory." In my discussion of theories in physics I mentioned that the everyday meaning of "theory" is speculation and that the scientific meaning of the word is a substantial body of reasoning. It is like that with the Darwinian theory of evolution. *Evolution itself is not a theory; it is an inescapable fact.* Charles Darwin did much to call attention to that fact. Modern Darwinian theory, however, is an effort to explain *how* life evolves.

It is a theory based on two simple premises. The first is that when living organisms reproduce, offspring are not precisely the same as their parents. The second is that the variations introduced by the offspring are tested in the laboratory of the environment for their effectiveness in enabling the offspring to give rise to new offspring.

A point of central importance is that the variations themselves are not in some way directed: they are purely random. Those variations that give rise to more offspring, however, tend to be preserved, and those that give rise to fewer offspring tend to disappear. A very long series of successful variations can give rise to a new species. Hence the title of Darwin's blockbuster of 1859: *On the Origin of Species*.

Darwin knew nothing about the sources of variation. They came into view only with the rise of genetics and modern molecular biology. It turns out that at the molecular level there is a great deal more variation than can be squared with the simple picture that successful variations survive and unsuccessful ones do not. That presents problems to modern Darwinian theorists —problems of the kind that confront all of the sciences.

The testing of variations in the laboratory of the environment is what is called natural selection. It too presents problems to modern Darwinian theorists. From time to time scholarly meetings on the problems of Darwinism give rise to newspaper stories suggesting that something is basically wrong with the Darwinian theory of evolution. The fact is that no one (except those who believe in the literal interpretation of Scripture) has offered any alternative.

New variations in living organisms can be observed from one generation to the next, but normally evolution cannot be observed. Although the engine of evolutionary change is the successful reproduction of variant organisms, the *effect* of selection can be observed only in populations and over a substantial period of time. In fact, one of the central themes of modern Darwinism is the study of populations. A population is either all the currently living members of one species or those members of the species that are isolated from the rest.

A classic example of population biology is what happens when a species—let us say a species of bird—somehow arrives on an isolated island. If conditions on the island are favorable to the immigrant birds, the members of the species multiply. As they do so variations among them are passed on to their descendants, so that in the island population as a whole variations accumulate. Simultaneously variations are accumulating in the population from which the island population originated. In time so many variations have accumulated in both populations that a member of one is somewhat different from a member of the other.

Let us now say that we mate birds of the island population with birds of the original population. Even if the birds of one population are somewhat different from the birds of the other, the matings may very well yield offspring. If matings of the *off-*

spring do not yield offspring, however, it is evidence that the genes of the two populations have changed so much that at the molecular level they no longer match up well.

When that is the case, the cell divisions that produce sperm and egg cells are faulty and new offspring cannot result. The definition of a living species (the definition of an extinct species is harder) is a population in which the males and females have fertile offspring. Therefore if matings of the island population and the original population cannot produce fertile offspring, the island population has become a new species.

The changes in the island population have been both random and selected. All the variations were random, but some of the variations that survived made the members of the population better able to reproduce in the new island environment. That kind of change is what is called adaptation.

Most characteristics of living things are adaptations of one kind or another. That includes animal behavior. An engaging behavioral adaptation I encountered recently is observed in the sloth. The sloth is the proverbially slow-moving mammal that lives in the dense treetops of the South American rain forest. There it hangs upside down from the branches and feeds on leaves. It rarely comes down to the ground; if it did it would be vulnerable to predators and pretty soon there would be no more sloths. Moreover, it does not defecate while it is in the treetops; if it did, a predator might be signaled that there is a sloth overhead.

About once a week, however, the sloth does come down to the ground. It does so to defecate. What it does is dig a hole with its spadelike tail at the base of the tree and deposit its fecal pellets in it. In this way the animal returns to the tree half of the nitrogen it has removed from the tree by eating its leaves!

This pattern of behavior must be largely, if not entirely, inherited, not learned. Therefore it must be explained by variations in behavior ultimately controlled by genes. Such variations must have taken a long time to accumulate in sloths' pattern of behavior, but accumulate they did. The only explanation for their survival is that each variation made the sloth that evinced it better able to reproduce.

If the evolutionary origin of such behavior seems hard to accept, consider a journalistic experience I once had. I was visiting the laboratory of Theodosius Dobzhansky, a leading geneticist and evolutionist who worked with fruit flies. There I saw a strange object: some kind of vertical maze made of transparent plastic. At one side of the vertical maze was a single tube. It forked into two tubes, each of which forked into two more tubes and so on. After four forks there were sixteen tubes at the other side of the maze.

What Dobzhansky and his colleagues were doing was putting single fruit flies into the single tube at one side of the maze. When the fly came to the first vertical fork, it went either up or down. If its tendency to go up, say, had been strong enough, it would have continued making the same choice at each fork and would have emerged at the top tube at the other side of the maze.

In actual experiments wild fruit flies went either up or down at each fork randomly, so that they usually emerged from neither the top tube nor the bottom one but from one or another of the middle tubes. The experimenters then mated male and female flies that had emerged from the uppermost of the middle tubes. They continued the matings on the same basis. In an experiment with one strain of wild fruit flies, at the end of twenty generations 84 percent of the flies chose on the average to go up rather than down!

The same was true of flies bred for going down rather than up. Clearly the flies' tendency to go up or down is under genetic control. If under natural conditions a tendency to go up rather than down makes a fruit fly more likely to survive and reproduce, the upward-going members of the fruit-fly population would out-number the downward-going ones in very short order. Fruit flies reproduce in ten days, so that twenty generations would take less than seven months.

Most variations are the result of the shuffling of genes in the population. In organisms that reproduce sexually some of the shuffling occurs at the cell level. Such an organism has two sets of genes, one from each of its parents. Moreover, when the genes are marshaled into chromosomes at the time of cell division, they form two sets of chromosomes, one from each parent. Human beings, for example, have forty-six chromosomes, twenty-three from each parent.

When the organism produces sperm cells or egg cells, the two sets of chromosomes line up in pairs. At that time two chromosomes can break and exchange parts. Furthermore, the chromosomes are reassorted so that the sperm or egg cell contains a mixture of chromosomes from the two parents. The number of possible new gene combinations is astronomical.

Mating itself is a shuffling of genes. Since the parents are not normally identical twins, their genes are not identical. Therefore the offspring represent a new combination of genes. The offspring are different from their parents, and each is a new random experiment in the laboratory of the environment. Sexual reproduction vastly increases variation, and organisms with more variation have been the ones to introduce more experiments. Seen this way, sexual passion in human beings is a cosmic joke played on us by evolution.

(A friend of mine, Walter Modell of the Cornell University Medical College, once had another kind of joke played on him by the biology of sex. As a medical student he undertook to do an experiment that called for a substantial number of white rats. When he went to the school's animal department, he was presented with a good-sized cardboard box half full of rats. As he was lugging the box back to his laboratory it occurred to him that for the purposes of his experiment he was going to have to separate the male rats from the female, and that he didn't have the foggiest idea of how to tell one from the other.

When he opened the box, what he saw gave him an inspiration. Many of the rats had mounted other rats; clearly males and females had already paired off. All he had to do was to pull off the top rat in each pair and put it in a second box, so that in due course the two sexes would be separated. That he did, putting the top rats in a box labeled "Males." Then he stepped out of the lab for a few minutes. When he came back, many of the rats in the second box had mounted other rats again!)

A small number of variations are the result not of gene shuffling but of mutation. A mutation is a random change in a gene that results in a change in the sequence of nucleotides and therefore a change in the protein for which the gene codes. In the overwhelming number of instances the experiment is a failure, even a lethal one. In some instances, however, it is a new biochemical invention that enables the mutant organism to produce more offspring than nonmutants. Mutation, then, is the source of new genes and the ultimate source of all variation.

The Living Film

As we have seen, the totality of life on the earth is the biosphere. When you stop to think about it, the biosphere is a mere film —a kind of oil slick—on the surface of the planet. Even allowing for its extension into the atmosphere and the ooze of the deepest ocean deeps it is no more than twenty miles thick. Of the earth's 4,000-mile radius that is half a percent.

Thin though it is, the film of life is furiously active. It is almost like a single spherical organism that harnesses the energy of sunlight to build and maintain itself by cycling carbon dioxide, water, oxygen, nitrogen and comparatively small quantities of minerals. The cycles mesh like the gears of clockwork and run with extraordinary steadiness.

The cycles spin a web of interactions so fine that it is beyond the current level of human understanding. The study of this web is ecology. As a layman I have always found ecology one of the most attractive sciences. Where sciences such as physics—and even much of biology—seek to reduce the world to its simplest constituents, ecology seeks to understand how the simplest constituents interact to give rise to the living world we actually perceive with our senses.

The word "ecology" has been somewhat debased by recent usage. It is sometimes used to describe the modern movement to conserve the natural environment. An acquaintance of mine, a man of means who had retired, once said to me: "You know what I am doing now? I'm an ecologist." What he meant was that he was working with a conservation group. Recently I even saw a garbage truck emblazoned "Ecology Carting Co."

Another acquaintance gave me a better definition. As a student at Oxford some years ago he attended a course of lectures given by one of the founders of modern ecology, Charles Elton. Elton began his first lecture with the sentence: "These lectures are about the universe." So it is with true ecology. It is about all the interrelations of the biosphere, including those between living matter and the nonliving matter that gives rise to it.

A small sample will suggest what ecologists do and how complex the interrelations of the biosphere are. When an animal dies under natural conditions, its tissues do not simply break down into their nonliving constituents. They support an entire community of other organisms. How large is that community? Jerry A. Payne, an ecologist at the Oak Ridge National Laboratory, undertook to find out.

Payne got the carcasses of small pigs that had died of natural causes and put them on the ground in a Tennessee woods. After eight days all that remained of the carcasses were dry skin, cartilage, teeth and bones. Over the eight days Payne regularly sampled the carcasses for the organisms that had come to them (not including himself). He identified a total of 522 species, representing 3 phyla, 9 classes, 31 orders, 151 families and 359 genera. Of the 522 species, 422 were insects.

Life on Other Worlds

The sheer pullulating richness of the biosphere is one of many reasons to believe that, given the right conditions, life is inevitable. It simply arises through random processes. Moreover, given the right conditions, random processes give rise to ever more complex forms of life. At the same time the richness of the biosphere makes many people skeptical that life and complex organisms can have arisen through random processes. Is there not a need for some kind of organizing force or principle?

Such skepticism often cites the second law of thermodynamics. The second law states in effect that energy can run only downhill, that higher forms of energy are degraded into lower ones and that more complex organizations of matter are degraded into less complex ones. In the end the entire universe dies a "heat death," in which all energy has reached its lowest level and all matter its least organized state. Is there not a need for some kind of force or principle to counter the effects of the second law?

There can be no doubt that the second law is correct, but there are many places in the universe where the flow of energy from a higher form to a lower one is harnessed to create more complex forms of matter. One need look no farther than the household refrigerator, where energy from the electric-power station transforms the disordered molecules of water into the ordered crystalline structure of ice. Another such place is a star, where simple atomic nuclei are built into more complex ones. Another is the earth's biosphere. One need only consider a green leaf's absorbing sunlight to build carbon dioxide and water into carbohydrate.

To be sure, the sunlight absorbed by the leaf is ultimately degraded into heat, in accord with the second law. In the end, also in accord with the second law, the sun and the other stars will stop shining and the universe will die its heat death. The date, as I mentioned in an earlier piece in this book, is calculated to be 10^{90} billion years hence. Meanwhile the downhill flow of energy will be able to build more complex forms of matter by random processes.

If, given the right conditions, life is inevitable, it would seem that life in the universe must be rather common. The catch, of course, is having the right conditions. The conditions on the earth have given rise to a kind of life based on the transformation of carbon compounds in water solution. A chemist can imagine life based on other compounds in other mediums. A requirement that would seem to have no alternative, however, is the right temperature.

If it is too cold, the molecules move about so slowly that they do not encounter one another often enough to allow any kind of chemistry that could be described as life. If it is too hot, the molecules rattle around and bang into one another so frequently and with such violence that complex compounds break down even as they are forming. Here again, however, a chemist can imagine life based on compounds that are stabler than carbon compounds at higher temperatures. Still, it is hard to imagine any form of life at a range of temperatures much different from the range in which life exists at the surface of the earth.

To take the modern Copernican view, namely that there is

nothing privileged about our position in the universe, it seems impossible that life does not exist somewhere else in the universe. There are at least 100 million stars in our galaxy and at least 100 billion galaxies. There simply have to be other stars like the sun and other planets with conditions not too unlike those on the earth. And if there are, there simply has to be life on them.

So the argument goes. But if there is life elsewhere in the universe, how could it be known to us? In recent years there have been ingenious proposals about how we might detect it. There have been programs of listening with radio telescopes for the kind of signals that intelligent life might broadcast, and signals have even been broadcast from the earth.

Even if contact is established, it will be for all practical purposes a monologue. Since the nearest star is some four light-years away, a round-trip exchange of signals between it and the solar system would take eight years. It is much more likely that such communication, if it is ever achieved, would be at a distance of hundreds or thousands of light-years. All the same, receiving a signal from another civilization would be the most electrifying event in human history.

Philip Morrison, who has had much to do with the programs to establish contact with other civilizations, has another argument. If there *is* intelligent life elsewhere in the universe, presumably some of it is less evolved than life on the earth and some of it is more evolved. The members of a highly evolved civilization would have their own methods of detecting life on the earth. Once they had detected it, they might well decide to study it as ecologists. Since that would be difficult to do at a distance, they would do it at close range on the earth.

With their mastery of biotechnology, the engineers of the advanced civilization would create a population of self-reproducing human beings and unobtrusively land them on the earth. The members of the population would then undertake their refined studies and transmit the results back to the home planet. These synthetic human beings would of course be interesting in themselves. They would be a *very* good imitation of a human being, but it is unlikely they would be a perfect imitation. They would look a bit strange, and they would certainly be smarter than human beings. In spite of efforts to avoid giving themselves away they would be overrepresented in activities such as mathematics, physics and music. Moreover, since they would tend to get bored with their assignment, they would be overrepresented in fun activities such as moviemaking. In short, they are Hungarians.

The notion of creating a synthetic human being is almost too close to the bone in these days of nascent genetic engineering. Biology has more interesting pursuits. A curious thing about biology is that its fundamental problem is already solved. This statement by a nonbiologist is almost certain to make biologists pale with rage. But consider. The Holy Grail of physics—to find a unifying principle of the entire subject—is not yet attained, but the Holy Grail of biology *is* attained. The unifying principle is natural selection operating on the information content of DNA. There is no "mystery of life."

This is not to say that biology is not faced with plenty of nonfundamental problems. The fantastic intricacy of the machinery of living matter might well take even more than the twenty-first century to work out. Furthermore, profound principles—less fundamental than the fundamental one but nonetheless profound—may yet emerge. Three good candidates for areas where they will emerge are the functioning of the human brain, the development of the fertilized egg cell into an entire many-celled organism and the sequence of events in the origin of life on the earth. Those three problems should generate enough questions for the practitioners of any science.

THE HUMAN SPECIES
CREATES ITSELF

This piece is about technology. Like everything else, technology is best understood as an evolutionary and historical process. The interesting thing about the evolution of technology, in the sweep of human history, is that it is so much faster than biological evolution. Technology evolves so fast that in less than one human generation it can even outmode funny stories.

When I was growing up in the 1920s and 1930s, the commuter railroad between my parents' neighborhood in Bucks County, Pennsylvania, and Philadelphia was still operating with steam locomotives. At that time, for reasons I cannot explain, I enjoyed scanning the long columns of social notes in the Doylestown *Daily Intelligencer*. They typically read in their entirety: "Mr. and Mrs. Norman Kratz, Chalfont, spent Sunday evening with Mr. and Mrs. Elmer Clymer." One such note included the inadvertent sentence: "After the ceremony the bride and groom were driven to Hatboro, where they made connections by steam." I wonder if a teenager of today, accustomed to newer modes of transport, would get the joke.

These days technology is sometimes discussed as though it

were something that had come along recently and that human beings might be better off without. It is hard to see how the concepts "human being" and "technology" can be disentangled. The history of the human species would seem to be the history of technology.

It is not that the human species invented tools; chimpanzees wield clubs, crack nuts with stones and manipulate twigs to fish termites out of their nest and eat them. It is not that the human species invented agriculture and animal husbandry; certain ants are masterly at cultivating fungi or tending flocks of aphids. It is not that the human species invented a complex form of communication; rabbits, to choose only one example out of many, have glands under their chin and around their anus that enable them to create diverse perfumed messages: "Joe is top rabbit around here," "You are encroaching on the turf of another gang" or "Celeste's nursing young are in this burrow and keep out."

It may not even be that the human species has a monopoly on refined mental abilities such as the appreciation of beauty. Adriaan Kortlandt is a Dutch biologist who studies the behavior of chimpanzees in the wild. Once he was in his observation blind at sundown on a clear day, watching a group of chimpanzees gathering papaws for their evening meal. A male in the group looked up and caught sight of the setting sun. The chimpanzee stopped dead in his tracks and watched the glowing red ball for a full fifteen minutes. By then it had got so dark he had to retire into the forest without gathering a papaw.

Nevertheless the key to the evolutionary adaptation called technology is somewhere to be found in human biology. What is unusual about the human animal? Some have cited its high ratio of brain size to body size, even though the ratio is higher in a few other animals. Some have cited the human animal's erect posture, which enables it to walk long distances with a low expenditure of energy, gives its visual system a broader sweep of the environment and frees its forelimbs for the manipulation of tools. Some have cited its extended period from birth to sexual maturity, which keeps the animal in a plastic behavioral state longer than other animals and gives it more time to absorb new information.

What is unusual about the human species might be all of those characteristics and others as well. *When all is said and done, the unique thing about the human animal is its ability not only to transmit information from one generation to the next but also to store and transmit information over many generations by means of culture.* In all organisms information is transmitted from one generation to the next in the genes, and in all animals the living generation can acquire information by learning. Furthermore, in many animals learned information can be transmitted from one generation to the next. What culture does is to enormously amplify the quantity of information that can be transmitted.

Culture is everything human beings know, including technology. The rate of cultural evolution with respect to biological evolution may be gauged by the fact that, judging by the fossil bones, human beings have not changed anatomically in at least 35,000 years. Yet it is only in the past 10,000 of those years that human beings have taken up such activities as agriculture and animal husbandry, living in cities, writing, extracting metals from ores, harnessing sources of energy other than their own muscles, communicating with one another around the world and manipulating information at rates far beyond the capacity of the brain.

It is clear that cultural evolution is an entirely new kind of evolution. This is not to say that it operates outside Darwinian evolution. Culture can be adaptive, and human groups that have better cultural adaptations do better than groups that do not have them. Moreover, *the cultural evolution of the human species powerfully molds its biological evolution.*

Predecessors of human beings started using stone tools at least two million years ago. These hominids walked erect, but their brains were small. As they evolved, their brain size increased. What may well have been responsible is their manipulation of tools, favoring variations in brain size that resulted in better hand-eye coordination. A larger brain might also have been favored by the adaptive success of an advanced form of animal communication: speech. A leading archaeologist, V. Gordon Childe, once encapsulated the process in the title of a book: *Man Makes Himself.*

By the time anatomically modern human beings arrived, perhaps 100,000 years ago, hominids were already successful tool-using hunters, gatherers and scavengers. Then, 10,000 years ago, came the first of the three great technological revolutions that utterly transformed human life. That was the agricultural revolution, which caused human beings to live in settled communities, to greatly intensify the division of labor and to develop technologies for the safe storage of food (pottery) and the recording of commercial activities (writing).

The Energy River Flows Down to the Sea

The second technological revolution was the industrial revolution of the eighteenth and nineteenth centuries, which through the steam engine gave human beings access to the energy stored in the chemical compounds of fossil fuels (coal, oil and gas). The third revolution was the information revolution of the nineteenth and twentieth centuries, which qualitatively changed human capacities for communication and information handling. All three revolutions are still very much in progress.

Basic human needs are traditionally defined as food, clothing and shelter. Today they might better be described as energy, materials and information. Let us start with energy.

The second law of thermodynamics states that higher forms of energy can be transformed only into lower forms. All the forms of energy currently exploited by human beings start out with the nuclear energy of stars. In the core of our star, the sun, nuclear energy is transformed into electromagnetic energy, including the sunlight that bathes the earth. The wood burned by the human beings who first maintained fires was stellar energy stored in the chemical compounds of plant tissue. Fossil fuels are stellar energy stored in carbon compounds. Wind power and water power are transformed stellar energy. Nuclear fuels—fissionable elements built up in stars other than the sun and later incorporated in the primitive earth—are stellar energy stored in heavy atomic nuclei.

Since the internal heat of the earth is generated by the radioactive decay of elements manufactured in stars and incorporated in the primitive earth, even geothermal power is stored stellar energy. One exception should be mentioned. Tidal power does not originate with stellar energy; it is gravitational energy stored in rotational momentum going back to the origin of the earth. But then tidal power is not much exploited by human beings, and it seems unlikely to be an important factor in the future. (If it were a large factor over a long period of time, the earth would eventually stop rotating!)

Much of the energy transformed by industrial societies is direct stellar energy, in that solar energy powers the growth of crop plants (including not only food plants but also materials plants such as cotton and trees). The myriad transformations of indirect—that is, stored—stellar energy can be regarded as a river. It is, however, an unusual kind of river, resembling one of those braided streams that flow across a desert: even after the river has been formed by tributaries it repeatedly branches and the branches come back together again.

In the United States the tributaries from the stored-energy highlands and their contribution to the overall flow, in order of their importance as of 1985, are oil (38.5 percent), gas (27.8 percent), coal (23.6 percent), nuclear fuels (5.7 percent), hydroelectric reservoirs (4.1 percent) and other fuels, for example wood (0.3 percent). When the tributaries come to their first major confluence, they form two broad streams: energy transformed directly into end uses (64.1 percent) and energy transformed into electricity (35.9 percent).

Both streams then branch into three end-use streams: industrial uses (21.5 percent, with the largest share of energy going to the smelting of metals), household and commercial uses (16 percent, with the largest share going to the heating of houses and buildings) and transportation uses (7 percent, mostly the fueling of automobiles, trucks and airplanes). But note that these last three percentages fall far short of adding up to 100. More than half of the energy in the original tributaries is lost as waste heat. Indeed, even the energy that is transformed for useful purposes ends up as heat. Thus in accordance with the second law of thermodynamics the human energy river empties into a lukewarm energy sea.

In discussions of energy the 35.9 percent of the stored energy that is transformed into electricity gets a large share of the attention. The tributaries to the generation of electric power are coal (56.7 percent), nuclear fuels (15.6 percent), gas (11.8 percent), hydroelectric reservoirs (11.4 percent), oil (4.1 percent) and other fuels (0.4 percent). Over the next fifty years the flows of these streams are going to change radically. Oil and gas are currently plentiful and comparatively cheap, but they are doomed to become scarce and expensive within decades. The reason is not so much that existing oil and gas fields are being depleted, although they are, but that the rate of discovery of new fields is sharply decreasing.

What, then, will replace the oil and gas? Coal is a leading candidate; coal reserves are much larger than oil and gas reserves. The burning of coal, however, generates large quantities of solid waste. It also has the same drawback as the burning of oil and gas: it generates large quantities of sulfur oxides, nitrogen oxides and carbon dioxide. The sulfur and nitrogen oxides not only pollute the air but also make rain more acid, which is hard on the ecosystem; the carbon dioxide may be making the surface of the earth warmer and less hospitable to the human species.

Nuclear power does not have such waste products but it does have its own. Whatever the problems of reactor safety and the disposal of radioactive waste may be, there are nearly 400 nuclear power reactors around the world and more are being built. This is not true of the United States, which has more than 100 nuclear power plants but because of public opposition seems unlikely to build any new ones for some time to come.

What will be interesting is how the worldwide record of nuclear power looks by the arrival of the twenty-first century. At that time France, which as of 1986 was already getting 65 percent of its electricity from forty nuclear reactors, will be getting virtually all of it from nuclear reactors. If some nations are freed from dependence on coal, oil and gas for the generation of electric power, and if their reactor-safety record is good, the body politic of the United States will have hard decisions to make.

One of the advantages of nuclear power is that nuclear fuel can be "bred": the fission of the rare uranium 235 can make reactor fuel out of the abundant uranium 238 and thorium 232. As a result fission fuels could in principle meet human energy needs almost indefinitely. The same is true of fusion fuels: deuterium (hydrogen 2) and tritium (hydrogen 3). In a fusion reactor such fuels would react as they do in stars. Progress toward a fusion reactor is slow, but many good physicists believe one can be achieved in time. The question for planners is: How much time? The predictions, whenever they are made, seem to remain steady at about twenty years.

What about electric power from "free" sources: water power, geothermal power, solar power, wind power and the like? Hydroelectric power plays an important role, but dams have already been built at most of the good sites, and at other sites there is strong public sentiment for maintaining the river valley as it is. Good sources of geothermal power are scarce. Solar power and wind power are everybody's darling, but they present a bitter lesson in economics. The main drawback of solar power is that it is intermittent, and people need electricity at night and on overcast days. The solution is power storage: a giant array of batteries, say, or an artificial lake that can be filled by pumping when power is available and then allowed to run into water turbines when power is needed. Such storage also runs into money.

Moreover, solar energy is dilute, so that a large area is needed to collect it. It has been calculated that if the collectors were in a desert area (which is of course rich in sunlight) and if they were 20 percent efficient (which is a good deal more efficient than commercial collectors are at present), a standard 1,000-megawatt electric-power plant would call for 13.5 square miles of them. That amount of land anywhere near a city would clearly be expensive.

I recently saw a photograph of a forest of avant-garde windmills in California that were said to be feeding their electric output into the state power grid, thereby taking up a tiny part of the grid's overall demand. Such a grid interconnects communities by means of long power lines, so that the communities' fluctuating power demands are evened out.

As a matter of fact, a single power grid now covers almost

the entire United States. In principle, then, a part of the country where the air was calm could get power from a part where it was windy, or a part of the country that was overcast could get power from a part that was sunny. If such a system were to make any substantial contribution to the demand, however, power storage would still be needed. Winds and clouds are capricious, and the rotation of the earth guarantees that for about a third of the day none of the forty-eight contiguous states are getting any sunlight at all.

The economic disadvantages of such "alternative" sources of energy have been known for a long time, yet the United States has invested large sums of money in investigating their possibilities. This is testimony to another form of power: the power of an electorate and its representatives that have not been fully informed on some obvious realities. In the long run, however, the same electorate will make rational decisions: scarcely anyone wants to pay a larger electric bill for sentimental reasons.

Transformers

My friend John Purcell has written a charming book: *From Hand Ax to Laser*. As you can see, it is a book about tools and human history, and Purcell stresses the point that tools are energy transformers. A hand ax transforms the chemical energy of human muscle metabolism into mechanical energy in such a way that the object to be struck is given a sharp and focused blow. A laser transforms electrical energy into light energy in such a way that the light waves are all in step and can, for example, be modulated to transmit information through a thin glass fiber.

Technology not only transforms one kind of energy into

another but also increases the efficiency with which different kinds of energy are transformed. When the hominid predecessors of the genus *Homo* devised tools for hunting, gathering and scavenging, they increased the efficiency of their obtaining food.

In particular, their use of tools for hunting enabled them to augment plant foods with animal foods, which pound for pound are some twenty times richer in energy than plant foods. As early as 500,000 years ago members of the species *Home erectus*, the immediate ancestors of *Homo sapiens*, knew how to maintain a fire. In so doing they too increased their energetic efficiency, mainly by keeping warm, by partially predigesting their food (with cooking) and by prolonging their working day (with firelight).

By 60,000 years ago *Homo sapiens* not only had fire and advanced stone tools but also had clothing and artificial shelter, both made of animal skins. With these technologies human beings conserved heat energy in unfavorable weather, further increased the efficiency of their obtaining food, and extended their geographic range. By 35,000 years ago they had added a host of other energy transformers; spear-throwing sticks, harpoons, hafted axes, grinding stones, bone awls and needles, fishhooks and fishnets, dugout canoes, paddles, baskets and oil lamps. Then with the agricultural revolution of 10,000 years ago they put in train a long sequence of advances in energetic efficiency that overshadowed all that had gone before.

A remarkable thing about the cultivation of plants is that some of the very first plants to be cultivated are still the mainstays of human nutrition: rice, wheat and corn. What is more, the rest of the plants that play a substantial role in human nutrition were first cultivated in prehistoric times: potatoes, sweet potatoes, cassava, barley, oats, sorghum, millet, soybeans, grapes and sunflowers. One can only assume that the long experimentation in plant cultivation that preceded the agricultural revolution selected out the wild plants best suited to this human adaptation.

A remarkable thing about agriculture in general is that in a developed economy it calls for so few people. As I mentioned in a preceding piece, in the United States the fraction of the labor force actually working on the land is now only 1.8 percent. This is the result of the 10,000-year technological evolution from the digging stick to irrigation to the ox-drawn plow to the powerful agricultural machines, fertilizers, herbicides and pesticides of today. Along the way strains of domesticated plants that yielded more product than other strains were steadily selected.

The most spectacular developments of this kind have come in the past fifty years. Hybrid corn was developed in the 1920s and 1930s; by 1950 it had typically increased corn yields per acre by 500 percent. The "green revolution" starting in the 1960s is associated with wheat varieties that were paradoxically not larger than older varieties but smaller. Tall wheat is susceptible to "lodging," the beating down of the plants by a storm. A Rockefeller Foundation program in Mexico developed short wheats that are resistant to lodging and have high yields and other good characteristics. When such wheats were introduced around the world (together with the increased application of fertilizers, herbicides and pesticides and improvements in tillage), yields per acre were increased as much as 1,000 percent.

Fully as important to agriculture as advances in mechanical, chemical and biological technology have been advances in processing and distribution. A case in point is the tomato. Once *Scientific American* published an article about modern tomato production. Soon thereafter a friend of mine accosted me in high dudgeon: "Not one word in that bloody article about the fact that the tomatoes are not as good as they used to be."

Many other people feel the same way. If they live in an area such as the northeastern United States, what they may be overlooking is that the tomatoes they find wanting are available in the dead of winter. They may have been shipped from as far away as southern California.

Such tomatoes are bred for their shippability; a big, red, juicy tomato would not last the trip. The tomatoes of yesteryear have not, however, disappeared. They are still as available as they ever were when they are growing locally, which may be only a few weeks in late summer. At other times of the year the consumer can either wait for the tomato-growing season or buy smaller, less red, less juicy tomatoes. Most people who buy tomatoes choose the latter alternative; the consumption of tomatoes in the United States (including, to be sure, tomatoes in various preserved forms) has tripled in the past sixty years.

No less momentous for human life than the domestication of plants was the domestication of animals. Human beings have deep feelings about other animals, even when they exploit them. The cave paintings of the pre-agricultural period are evidence that it has always been so. The first animals to be domesticated would seem to have been immature ones that were kept as pets. Dog bones in association with human ones date back 14,000 years. The extraordinary diversification of dog breeds, which goes back to prehistory, testifies to the fact that dogs early served as companions, as helpers in the hunt, as beasts of burden and even as a source of food.

As with plants, the experimentation that led to the domestication of animals seems to have exhausted the animals suitable for the purpose quite early. The main domesticated food animals of today were domesticated between 9,000 and 4,000 years ago:

cattle, pigs (both in the Middle East) and chickens (probably in Southeast Asia). Today the three animals act as large-scale energy transformers: they transform plant protein into the more concentrated animal protein. Chickens are the most efficient in this transformation (from feed into meat and eggs). Pigs are second and cattle (for both meat and milk) are third.

Milk is a most interesting link between early technology and ultramodern technology. Milk is fermented by bacteria, and prehistoric peoples learned that what is left after the milk has fermented (cheese) can be even more useful than the milk itself: it can keep much longer and is a more concentrated food. Today we know that it is richer in protein, since the bacteria have converted some of the carbohydrate and fat in the milk into protein of their own.

Prehistoric peoples also learned that plant foods (grapes and grain) are fermented by yeast. It is practically impossible to keep grape juice from fermenting into wine because the waxy gray "bloom" on the skin of the grape traps yeast spores floating in the air. A mash of grain ferments into beer. Both fluids are somewhat nutritious and have the unusual property that they make the drinker feel better about life (up to a point). When yeast is added to bread dough, it predigests part of the wheat carbohydrate. The waste product is carbon dioxide, which inflates the dough and makes the bread still more digestible. *In short, at the dawn of history human beings were already master biotechnologists.*

Microbial Machines

"Biotechnology" is a broad term, but to most people these days it means genetic engineering: creating "superbugs" to do things microorganisms never did before. A new gene is inserted into a microorganism so that the microorganism makes a new protein. The microorganism can then be used in an industrial process, for example manufacturing a human protein hormone.

Even before such manipulations became possible in the 1970s industrial microbiology was a flourishing technology, with products valued in the United States alone at tens of billions of dollars per year. Many of the products were an integral part of human life long before the industrial revolution: in addition to cheese, wine, beer and bread there were vinegar, yogurt, pickles, sauerkraut, bean curd, soy sauce, sake (from fermented rice), brandy (distilled wine) and whiskey (distilled beer). Added to the list in this century were many things other than food or drink: acetone, industrial alcohols, industrial enzymes, amino acids, citric acid, vitamins and antibiotics and other pharmaceuticals.

A typical story is one about the microbiological production of the solvent acetone. In the First World War the British were short of the solvent, which was needed for the making of munitions. A Russian-born chemist, Chaim Weizmann, developed a process in which the bacterium *Clostridium acetobutylicum* fermented carbohydrate into acetone and an alcohol. Weizmann later was one of the founders of the state of Israel and became its first president. His microbiological process served well not only during the war but also for many years afterward, until it was economically displaced by processes based not on microorganism feed but on petroleum. Never forget that in technology what is technically possible is always secondary to what is economically feasible.

During the Second World War industrial microbiology had another signal triumph. In the 1920s Alexander Fleming had observed that the mold *Penicillium* exuded a substance that was toxic to bacteria, but he did not pursue his discovery. Then in 1941 Howard Florey, Ernst Chain and their colleagues at Oxford isolated the substance and showed that it could cure bacterial infections.

(According to Norman Heatley, a member of the Florey group, the link between Fleming and his successors was so tenuous that when Florey told Chain one day that Fleming would be visiting the Oxford laboratory, Chain said: "My God, I thought he was dead." A curious example of Fleming's apotheosis I once encountered is that outside the bullring in Madrid there is a heroic statue of him, because he is considered the man who saved bullfighters from the infections that inevitably followed their being gored. For the same reason in Cordoba there is an Avenida Alexander Fleming.)

Penicillin was immediately in great demand to treat and prevent infections in war wounds. In the beginning the mold was grown on the surface of a nutrient broth in glass bottles, and the yield of penicillin was tiny. The Oxford workers turned to laboratories and companies in the United States, particularly for experience with fermentation in tanks. At the same time the mold *Penicillium chrysogenum* was exposed to X rays and other agents that cause random mutations, and mutants were screened for strains with a higher yield. Today such strains, routinely grown in 25,000-gallon tanks, have a yield greater than that of the original strain by a factor of 10,000.

The point is that even before it was possible to artificially insert new genes into microorganisms, it was possible to change genes by artificial mutation and selection. That is the basis of the current multibillion-dollar microbiological industry. Still, the insertion of new genes into microorganisms is the wave of the future. So far particular successes have been few but impressive: microbial processes for the manufacture of interferons, human growth hormone, human insulin (as opposed to insulin from other animals) and somatostatin (a hormone secreted by the hypothalamus of the brain that stimulates the secretion of other hormones by the pituitary).

The principal microorganism that has been programmed for such processes is the bacterium *Escherichia coli*. It is also possible to program animal cells and grow them in tanks like bacteria. In fact, animal cells can manufacture useful substances that bacteria, molds and yeasts cannot. For some years cells from the kidney of the baby hamster have been cultured on a large scale to make vaccines for the prevention of foot-and-mouth disease in cattle and pigs. Certain human cells too can be grown in tanks. They have the advantage that they do not produce substances toxic to human beings. Such substances must be laboriously removed from products manufactured by *E. coli*.

A hybrid between two types of animal cell has notable promise. Cells in the immune system of the human body are capable of making more than a million different kinds of antibodies, the protein molecules that can combine with antigens: molecules of substances foreign to the body. Each kind of antibody is manufactured by one clone—one strain—of cell. It would be a good thing if such a clone could be isolated and grown in a culture medium, so that that one kind of antibody could be produced in large quantities. The monoclonal antibody could then be used, say, to diagnose an obscure infection with high precision or to treat or prevent an infection with high specificity.

A normal cell that makes antibody cannot be maintained in a culture medium. There is, however, an abnormal cell that makes large quantities of abnormal antibody and that can be so maintained. It is the cell of the malignancy named multiple myeloma. Since by definition cancer cells divide and proliferate indefinitely, the multiple myeloma cell does the same in a culture medium.

Georges Köhler and Cesar Milstein came up with an ingenious idea: hybridize a multiple myeloma cell with a normal antibody-making cell. The result is the kind of cell called a hybridoma. In a culture medium the hybrid cell both multiplies indefinitely and manufactures a monoclonal antibody. Such antibodies are already in wide service for the precision identification of antigens.

Ever since the concept of genetic engineering emerged many people have viewed it with alarm. In fact, biologists themselves called attention, notably at the Asilomar conference in 1975, to the possibility that engineered microorganisms might escape the bounds of their application and cause big trouble. There were reminders of ecological disasters such as the introduction of rabbits into Australia. It also seemed as if biologists were saying: "You physicists sprang the atomic bomb on the rest of us without warning, but we biologists are going to be more responsible."

The effects of the warning were good and bad. The good news was that reasonable measures were taken for someone other than the genetic engineer to reflect on and regulate what the engineer wants to do. The bad news was that several communities where universities are located tried to outlaw research in which the genes of bacteria are manipulated. The effort came to nothing, but town-and-gown tensions, which are always present in such communities, were exacerbated. All in all, the consensus of informed opinion seems to be that there is not much danger from genetic engineering. Nature itself performs so many experiments with the genetics of microorganisms that it seems unlikely that human experimenters will come up with anything genuinely new.

The Chemical Economy

Biotechnology is chemical technology, but it is only a modest part of the chemical industry. To most people the term "chemical industry" is clear enough but what goes on inside that industry is dark. Like other industries, the chemical industry takes raw materials and converts them into products. But consider the following.

A nonexhaustive list of the raw materials of the chemical industry is: coal, petroleum, natural gas, cellulose, limestone, sulfur, phosphorus, salt, clays, air, water, lead, zinc, copper, iron, boron, chromium, manganese, lithium and aluminum. Such raw materials are converted into intermediate products, such as: chlorine, sulfuric acid and the hydrocarbons ethylene, toluene, propylene, xylene, butadiene and benzene.

A partial list of the final products, in alphabetical order, is: adhesives, agricultural chemicals, bleaching compounds, cleaning and polishing compounds, cosmetic and toilet preparations, drugs and medicines, dyes, electronics-industry materials, electroplating compounds, explosives, hydraulic fluids, missile fuels, packaging films, paints and varnishes, paper chemicals, petroleum additives, photographic chemicals, plastics, refrigerants, rubber chemicals, soaps and detergents, solvents, synthetic fibers, synthetic rubbers, textile chemicals and water-purification agents.

For some of these intermediate and final products there is only one pathway from the raw material to the product. For many of them, however, there are alternative pathways. The pathway the chemical engineer must choose is sternly ruled by economics—sometimes even by politics.

Consider benzene, the famous molecule consisting of six carbon atoms in a ring with a hydrogen atom attached to each (C_6H_6). It is a major solvent and an intermediate essential for products ranging from synthetic rubber to pharmaceuticals. Benzene is a fraction of gasoline, but not all of it can be obtained from that source because it is a necessary constituent of the fuel. In the 1960s the most economic source for the rest of it was toluene and xylene from gasoline. Toluene can be made into benzene by removing from it a methyl group (CH_3); xylene, by removing from it two methyl groups.

At that time the octane-rating requirements of gasoline were largely being met by the addition of tetraethyl lead. Then the Clean Air Act of 1970 required that automobiles have catalytic converters to remove pollutants. It happens that tetraethyl lead poisons a catalytic converter so that it cannot function. How, then, to make high-octane gasoline? It happens, again, that the octane rating of gasoline is increased by its content of benzene, toluene and xylene. At that point the economic source of benzene dried up. The alternative source, which was somewhat more expensive but unavoidable, was a light oil produced by the cooking of coal into coke. There is clearly a lot more to chemical engineering than technology.

Modern chemical plants have their own fascination. What are those silvery towers and entire cities of piping and structural steel we see along the highway? Some of them are oil refineries, based on processes physical as well as chemical. Petroleum is a rich mixture of hydrocarbon fractions: molecules with a structure ranging from one carbon atom and four hydrogen atoms (methane) to chains to rings to multiple rings. The skinny towers in a refinery are stills where the petroleum is heated to boil off its lighter fractions; the lightest fractions are drawn off at the top and the heaviest at the bottom.

A heftier structure in a refinery is a "cat cracker," a big, heavy-walled steel vessel where less desirable heavy fractions are broken down—cracked—into more desirable light ones by heat, pressure and the presence of a catalyst. The catalyst is typically a powdered composite of silica and alumina, which is blown through the vessel to provide surfaces on which the reactions can proceed. The same kind of vessel can serve for "reforming," in which heat, pressure and a catalyst reconstruct less desirable molecules into more desirable ones.

Most of modern chemical technology can be divided into the realms of organic chemistry and inorganic chemistry. Organic chemistry is the chemistry of carbon compounds, so that the chemistry of other compounds is left to inorganic chemistry. Because organic chemistry arose only in the nineteenth century, inorganic chemistry was not even defined until then. Indeed, until then most of what was called chemistry was inorganic chemistry.

That chemistry dealt largely with acids and alkalies. Today chemicals in those categories are still the foundation of the chemical industry. The main acids are sulfuric, nitric, hydrochloric and phosphoric. The main alkalies are sodium carbonate and sodium hydroxide. Also classified as inorganic chemicals are the fertilizer chemicals ammonia, ammonium nitrate and ammonium sulfate (all sources of nitrogen for crop plants), the industrial gases chlorine, carbon dioxide, hydrogen, nitrogen and oxygen, and a long list of others.

Organic chemistry nonetheless remains the great branching tree of modern chemical technology. The tree has a curious rootstock. Early in the eighteenth century the charcoal traditionally burned to smelt iron was replaced by coke. When coke is made from coal, a residue is the awful gunk called coal tar. Late in the century cities began to make gas for illuminating purposes from the partial burning of coal, again with a residue of coal tar.

Coal is an even richer blend of chemical compounds than petroleum is; it is estimated that it consists of at least 200,000 of them. Coal tar is scarcely less rich. Nineteenth-century chemists were challenged to separate the constituents of the stuff; they put it in big iron stills and gathered the different compounds as they came out of the still drop by drop.

Some of the compounds lent themselves to being transformed into magnificent dyes. Chemists in those days had the habit of smelling and tasting things, sometimes at their peril; in this way they discovered compounds with physiological properties. Among the chemicals derived from coal tar were saccharin and acetylsalicylic acid, better known today as aspirin. It was mainly the efforts of the coal-tar pioneers that gave rise to a blend—modern chemical technology—almost as rich as its starting material.

From Stone to Steel

I mentioned near the outset of this piece that basic human needs could be described as energy, materials and information. Chemical technology is a bridge between energy and materials, since it not only produces fuels and substances that control the flow of energy in a thousand subtle ways but also creates materials themselves. Overall there are five kinds of materials: ceramics, glasses, metals, polymers and composite materials. All have been embedded in technology since human beings first emerged.

A ceramic is a combination of one or more metallic elements with a nonmetallic element, usually oxygen. Stone, which is basically an oxide of silicon, can be regarded as a ceramic. Early human beings were able to fracture and chip stone into excellent tools because it is hard, strong and brittle. Those are the main properties of most other ceramics.

A mud pie dried in the sun is a low-grade ceramic, and when the agricultural revolution caused human beings to live in settled communities, houses were built of sun-dried brick. It was also discovered that if clay was baked in a fire or a hot oven, it acquired properties akin to stone: hardness, strength, brittleness and also imperviousness to water and chemical attack. Another crucial property that was discovered early was the ability of burnt limestone to cement other materials on being wetted. Even today concrete far outweighs all other man-made structural materials put together.

Modern ceramics have a host of additional properties. Among the most significant is high resistance to heat, which makes it possible to build fire-brick furnaces that will melt the most re- fractory metals. The essence of modern ceramic technology, however, is that it is now possible to design ceramics for what seems like almost anything. I have even heard of an experimental automobile engine with an engine block and pistons made of ceramic.

Cyril Stanley Smith of MIT is a philosopher of materials, ancient and modern. He points out that the real difference be- tween ancient materials technology, which created some mate- rials that cannot be surpassed today, is that we now understand the microstructure of materials. In the case of ceramics it is seen that oxygen is a large atom that can form a vast number of different crystalline arrays with smaller metal atoms. Moreover, the chem- ical bonds between oxygen atoms and metal atoms are unusually strong—stronger, say, than the bonds between the atoms in a metal. Since more than two-thirds of the elements found in nature are metals, one begins to get an idea of the future pos- sibilities of ceramics.

Glasses too are ceramics, even though they are usually listed separately from them. The reason they are so listed is that ce- ramics are crystalline and glasses are not. A glass is a material halfway between a liquid and a crystal: its oxygen and metal atoms are frozen in a disorderly state. The glassy state has many useful properties, among them transparency and a relatively low melting point. It was the latter property that made glasses so useful for the glazing of pottery; a slurry of fine sand applied to the pot melted into glass when the pot was fired. Since like other ceramics glasses are combinations of oxygen atoms and metal atoms, their future possibilities too are spacious.

Yet another useful property of ceramics (including glasses) is that they do not readily conduct heat and electricity. Metals do. Metals are also lustrous, can be readily melted and cast, can be rolled or hammered into shape and can be alloyed and welded. All these things (except for the conduction of electricity) were known virtually from the beginning. The first metal technology, going back in the Middle East at least 9,000 years ago, was the cold hammering of copper, pieces of which are found in nature already separated from ore. The next metal technology, starting about 6,000 years ago, was smelting copper out of ore by heating the ore with charcoal.

Certain copper ores in the Middle East were also rich in the metals antimony and arsenic. The inadvertent alloy smelted from such ores had a lower melting point than copper and was better for casting. Some 5,000 years ago it was discovered that tin and copper—bronze—made a still better alloy. Cyril Smith observes that during the Bronze Age iron was known but until ways were found to improve its properties objects made out of it were inferior to those made out of bronze. Actually what brought the Iron Age was economics: tin ores are scarce and iron ores are plentiful.

To me as a layman there has always been something of a mystery about iron and steel. What exactly *is* steel? Is it simply iron to which other things have been added to give the material desirable properties? The answer is a good deal more interesting than that.

When iron ore was heated in the ancient charcoal-burning furnaces, the iron separated out in a spongy material. In that form the white-hot metal could be hammered into what is called wrought iron. Around 1200 B.C. it was discovered that when wrought iron was put back in the furnace for a while and then quenched in water, it became harder. The treated metal, which was particularly useful for knives and other tools, was steel. Repeatedly heated, hammered and quenched, the material later lent itself to the legendary swords of Damascus (the best made in Iran out of iron cast in India) and Japan (the best of all).

Today we know that the steel was harder than the wrought iron not only because it was heat-treated but also because as much as 1 percent of it was carbon picked up from the charcoal fuel of the furnace. When iron ore was heated longer in the furnace, the iron took up even more carbon. It then melted easily and could be cast. Cast iron is hard but also brittle, and in ancient times it was not much used except in China.

In Europe by the sixteenth century iron was being smelted in tall blast furnaces, where air was blown through a mixture of ore, charcoal (later coke) and limestone (which made the molten iron flow more easily). Most of the smelted iron was cast into "pigs," which were then remelted in furnaces to get a spongy mass that could be hammered or rolled into bars of a tough, malleable wrought iron. Such iron could be forged into beams, plates and other forms, and together with cast iron it was used to build the first iron bridges and iron ships. Where hardness was needed, steel was also made, rather laboriously, by processes that added carbon to the iron and by heat treatment.

By the 1860s there was great demand for cheaper metal with better properties, largely for railroad rails. Henry Bessemer invented a process in which air is blown through molten pig iron. The shower of sparks coming out of the top of the Bessemer converter, so beloved of photographers, is impurities being burned out of the metal. In the Bessemer converter, and soon afterward in the open-hearth furnace, the composition of the metal could be controlled to get different properties—for example more carbon for hardness, less carbon for workability.

Much of the metal, however, contained too little carbon for it to be hardened by heat treatment. Therefore it was not steel by the classic definition. The Bessemer salesmen nevertheless called it steel, and the debased term has stuck.

Today steel is largely made in electric furnaces and in furnaces where pure oxygen is blown into the molten metal. In those furnaces scrap steel and, in smaller quantities, pig iron from twenty-story blast furnaces are melted under conditions where the composition of the steel can be closely controlled. Impurities such as silicon, sulfur, phosphorus and excess carbon are burned off and alloying elements such as manganese, nickel, chromium and tungsten are added. In its diverse compositions steel is formed into slabs, sheets, bars, rails, structural beams, tubes, pipe, rod and wire. It is then fabricated into everything from paper clips to automobiles to bridges.

The cheap steel first made available by the Bessemer converter liberated the imagination of engineers and architects. They were already using wrought iron and cast iron for elaborate trusses, large ship hulls, suspension bridges and crystal palaces. Now they could proceed with far fewer constraints. A case in point is the design and construction of tall buildings.

In 1880 one of the tallest buildings in the world was the Monadnock Building in Chicago. It still stands sixteen stories tall. Its main load-bearing structure is its stone walls. The walls at the top are supported by the walls below them, so that from top to bottom the walls have to be progressively thicker. At the sidewalk level they are seven feet thick!

With the arrival of cheap steel architects could conceive tall buildings where the walls did not have to support the walls above them but were hung from a steel skeleton. The end result was the great crystal palaces of today. My friend James Marston Fitch, a penetrating architectural historian and critic, has eloquently described such developments and at the same time has pointed out how much they fail to exploit architectural knowledge that human beings gained by wit and trial and error over 10,000 years.

An example cited by Fitch is the energy economy of modern buildings. Where a skyscraper has a lot of glass in it, the well-known properties of the material cause the building to lose a lot of heat in the winter and gain a lot in the summer. In the winter, as a result, such a building requires a lot of heating, and in the summer it requires a lot of air conditioning. When fuel and electricity are cheap, nobody much cares, but fuel and electricity are not always cheap and are likely to be less so in the future.

Many cultures long ago discovered the energy-conserving properties of stone and brick. In many climates the days are hot and the nights are cool. Stone and brick, being like other ceramics poor conductors, are slow to absorb heat and slow to surrender it. If you happen to live in a heavy-walled building, you know that it stays relatively cool during the day and stays relatively warm at night. In effect the day-night temperature curve is flattened out, and energy is conserved. To be sure, no one charged with designing a skyscraper is going to go back to the Monadnock Building for energy reasons, but in an energy-conscious age, more attention could well be paid to the energy efficiency of architecture.

Chain Power

If steel liberated the imagination of engineers and architects in the nineteenth century, polymers and composite materials have done the same for human beings as far back as prehistory. What exactly is a polymer? The word is from the Greek *poly*, many, and *meros*, a part. A polymer is therefore defined as a molecule with many parts. There are natural polymers and synthetic polymers, and it was not until the middle of the twentieth century that the nature of either was understood. Then it was seen that a polymer is a long chain of repeating molecular units, even millions of them. The repeating units were named monomers.

Proteins are natural polymers, chains of amino-acid monomers. Therefore when early human beings were using animal skins, they were using polymeric materials. More imaginative was the use of hair protein (wool) for the spinning of yarn and the weaving of fabric. The cellulose of plants also is a polymer, a chain of sugar monomers. In the form of cotton it too was used early for spinning and weaving. The first synthetic fiber, introduced in 1889, was made from wood cellulose. It was rayon, which is made by breaking down the wood, chemically modifying the cellulose and extruding the stuff through fine holes.

Since then the textile industry has been steadily enriched by more strictly synthetic polymers: nylon, Orlon, Dacron, Acrilan, polyesters and many more. Of equal importance has been the emergence of plastics, starting in the 1860s with celluloid, like rayon made from cellulose. Today an army of plastics lend themselves to molded objects, sheets, films, rods, tubing and electrical insulation. And other polymers serve for rubbers, floor coverings, paints, textile coatings, adhesives, lubricants and chewing gum. All of these polymers are made from simple monomers, most of them originating with petroleum. Like modern ceramics, polymeric materials are a symphony of technological and economic possibilities.

Composite materials too are both new and old. Composites consist of two materials, each of which has a notable strength and a notable weakness. The strength of the one material makes up for the weakness of the other and vice versa. The natural composite material par excellence is wood, and although there is no direct evidence for it, the material must have been exploited by hominids as early as stone was. Considered as a material, wood has two components: cellulose and lignin. The effect of the lignin is to cement the cellulose fibers together and to isolate breaks in them that would weaken the wood. Wood is thus far stronger than it would be if it consisted only of cellulose.

A clearer example of the principle is provided by a man-made composite: fiberglass. Glass fibers are strong but notoriously brittle. If they are embedded in a plastic, they are protected from breakage and the plastic is made far stronger. Crystalline fibers of carbon are even stronger than glass fibers, and they too can be embedded in plastic. Such a composite is much more expensive than fiberglass, so that its uses are restricted to special purposes such as tennis rackets, golf clubs and components of military aircraft.

The man-made composite that dwarfs all others in importance and tonnage is reinforced concrete. Concrete is strong in compression and weak in tension: it is almost like rock when a load is put on it but tends to crack and crumble when it is pulled at. If the concrete is poured around a meshwork of steel rods, however, the steel's strength in tension compensates for the concrete's weakness. Moreover, embedding the steel in concrete compensates for a weakness of the steel: rust.

Reinforced concrete, like the other new materials, has been an imagination liberator. The oldest principle of building construction is the post and lintel, where a horizontal beam is laid across two verticals. Concrete is good for the posts but less good for the lintel. If reinforced concrete is called on for the lintel, it is often rather bulky for the needs of the design. An alternative is pre-stressed concrete, in which a concrete beam is poured around steel cables running its length. The cables, moored in steel plates at the ends of the beam, are tightened so that the weakness of the concrete in tension is countervailed by its being put in compression. In this way a strong, light concrete member can be made that can compete with a steel one.

The second-oldest principle of building construction is the arch, where the strength of stone, concrete or brick in compression is exploited by a two-dimensional geometry. The three-dimensional extension of the arch is the dome. With reinforced and pre-stressed concrete the designer can think of concrete domes of complex geometry and almost diaphanous lightness. The design of such shells calls for high mathematical skill, one of the engineer's most attractive abilities.

I mentioned in the first piece in this book that W. H. Auden was so taken with an article in *Scientific American* that he wrote a poem about it. An issue of the magazine devoted to materials had the same effect on John Updike. In response he wrote "The Dance of the Solids":

All things are Atoms: Earth and Water, Air
    And Fire, all, *Democritus* foretold.
    Swiss *Paracelsus*, in's alchemic lair,
    Saw Sulfur, Salt, and Mercury unfold
    Amid Millennial hopes of faking Gold.
    Lavoisier dethroned Phlogiston; then
    Molecular Analysis made bold
    Forays into the gases: Hydrogen
Stood naked in the dazzled sight of Learned Men.

The Solid State, however, kept its grains
    Of Microstructure coarsely veiled until
    X-ray diffraction pierced the Crystal Planes
    That roofed the giddy Dance, the taut Quadrille
    Where Silicon and Carbon Atoms will
    Link Valencies, four-figured, hand in hand
    With common Ions and Rare Earths to fill
    The lattices of Matter, Glass or Sand,
With tiny Excitations, quantitatively grand.

The *Metals*, lustrous Monarchs of the Cave,
    Are ductile and conductive and opaque
    Because each Atom generously gave
    Its own Electrons to a mutual Stake,
    A Pool that acts as a Bond. The Ions take

The stacking shape of Spheres, and slip and flow
When pressed or dented; thusly *Metals* make
A better Paper Clip than a Window,
Are vulnerable to Shear, and, heated, brightly glow.

Ceramic, muddy Queen of human Arts,
    First served as simple Stone. Feldspar supplied
Crude Clay; and Rubies, Porcelain, and Quartz
Came each to light. Aluminum Oxide
    Is typical—a Metal is allied
    With Oxygen ionically; no free
Electrons form a lubricating tide,
    Hence, Empresslike, *Ceramics* tend to be
Resistant, porous, brittle, and refractory.

Prince *Glass*, *Ceramic*'s son, though crystal-clear,
    Is no wise crystalline. The fond Voyeur
And Narcissist alike devoutly peer
Into Disorder, the Disorderer
    Being Covalent Bondings that prefer
    Prolonged Viscosity and spread loose nets
Photons slip through. The average *Polymer*
    Enjoys a Glassy state, but cools, forgets
To slump, and clouds in closely patterned Minuets.

The *Polymers*, those giant Molecules,
    Like Starch and Polyoxymethylene,
Flesh out, as protein serfs and plastic fools,
The Kingdom with Life's Stuff. Our time has seen
    The synthesis of Polyisoprene
    And many cross-linked Helixes unknown
To *Robert Hooke*; but each primordial Bean
    Knew Cellulose by heart: *Nature* alone
Of Collagen and Apatite compounded Bone.

What happens in these Lattices when *Heat*
   Transports Vibrations through a solid mass?
   $T = 3Nk$ is much too neat;
   A rigid Crystal's not a fluid Gas.
   Debye in 1912 proposed Elas-
   Tic Waves called *phonons* which obey *Max Planck's*
   Great Quantum Law. Although amorphous Glass,
   Umklapp Switchbacks, and Isotopes play pranks
Upon his Formulae, *Debye* deserves warm Thanks.

Electroconductivity depends
   On Free Electrons: in Germanium
   A touch of Arsenic liberates; in blends
   Like Nickel Oxide, *Ohms* thwart Current. From
   Pure Copper threads to wads of Chewing Gum
   Resistance varies hugely. Cold and Light
   As well as "doping" modify the sum
   Of *Fermi* levels, Ion scatter, site
Proximity, and other factors recondite.

Textbooks and Heaven only are Ideal;
   Solidity is an imperfect state.
   Within the cracked and dislocated Real
   Nonstoichiometric crystals dominate.
   Stray Atoms sully and precipitate;
   Strange holes, *excitons*, wander loose; because
   Of Dangling Bonds, a chemical Substrate
   Corrodes and catalyzes—surface Flaws
Help Epitaxial Growth to fix adsorptive claws.

White Sunlight, *Newton* saw, is not so pure;
   A Spectrum bared the Rainbow to his view.
   Each Element absorbs its signature:
   Go add a negative Electron to

Potassium Chloride; it turns deep blue,
And Chromium incarnadines Sapphire.
Wavelengths, absorbed, are reëmitted through
Fluorescence, Phosphorescence, and the higher
Intensities that deadly *Laser Beams* require.

Magnetic Atoms, such as Iron, keep
Unpaired Electrons in their middle shell,
Each one a spinning Magnet that would leap
The *Bloch* Walls whereat antiparallel
Domains converge. Diffuse Material
Becomes *Magnetic* when another Field
Aligns domains like Seaweed in a swell.
How nicely microscopic forces yield,
In Units growing Visible, the World we wield!

Tools Create Themselves

One of the deep themes of human history is the evolution of
mechanical devices for applying, transforming and controlling
energy. As John Purcell points out in his book, the first such
devices were simple tools, and early principles of altering materials still define the tool industry: hammering, chipping, cutting, sawing, grinding, polishing, shearing, scraping, filing,
chiseling, reaming, planing, forging, stamping, punching, roll-
ing, fiber spindling, weaving, molding, casting, extruding, boring
and turning. Early boring (the bow drill for making fire) and
turning (the pottery wheel) were perhaps the most influential
principles, since the large majority of later mechanical devices
incorporate rotary motion.

The keynote of the modern machine-tool industry is automatic operation. I remember being mesmerized as a child in the

1920s when I saw in Times Square a machine that made cigarettes from the tobacco and paper to the finished package without any human operator. Such a machine would not be considered automatic today. It was a kind of dinosaur that could do only one thing and lacked feedback: the ability of a device to control itself by sensing its output and taking corrective action when the output departs from the norm.

The term "feedback" was coined by electrical engineers who devised circuits that maintained their stability when part of their output was fed back to the input. The principle goes back at least to the Greeks, and James Watt applied it elegantly in the flyball governor that controlled his first steam engines late in the eighteenth century. Furthermore, feedback control abounds in the nervous system, in ecosystems and in economic systems. A homely modern example of feedback control is an electric blanket. The temperature of the blanket is held steady by a thermostat, but it has a human control as well. If a man is sleeping under an electric blanket and gets a little cold, he turns the blanket up. If he gets a little warm, he turns the blanket down. Normally he arrives at a setting where the temperature is just right.

This is properly called negative feedback, in that when the system departs from a certain desired state, the departure is decreased. There is also positive feedback. It can be explained with the aid of a man and his wife who have a dual-control electric blanket. When the bed was made, the blanket was inadvertently turned over, so that the man's control regulates his wife's side of the blanket and her control regulates his side. The man gets a little cold and turns up his control. His wife therefore gets a little warm, and turns *down* her control. To make a long story short, he ends up freezing and she ends up roasting. The system is out of control. You can see why in the design of self-controlling systems it is necessary to distinguish between negative feedback and positive.

Perhaps the best example of industrial feedback control is found in the chemical industry. In many chemical plants things are processed in batches; one step in the process is completed before the stuff being processed is passed along to the next step. It is much more economic if the stuff can be passed along continuously, and many large chemical plants are continuous. Such a plant is a metallic jungle of pipes, tanks and chemical reactors, and arranging matters so that all the flows come out even is a formidable task. Nevertheless it is routinely accomplished by having thousands of sensors throughout the plant feeding their information back to thousands of control devices.

It was done even before the advent of the modern computer, and so successfully that in a huge chemical plant the only workers you see are maintenance men. Such plants have become indispensable. A chemical engineer, Eugene Ayres, told us at *Scientific American* a story about a petroleum refinery his company was commissioned to build in India. The Indian officials observed that in India there was no shortage of labor, and that it would be better if the plant was controlled not by automatic devices but by people. The American engineers tried to design such a plant but finally had to give up. Too much would be happening too fast for human beings to be able to cope with it.

With modern feedback systems and modern computers for information handling it is entirely possible to build an automatic factory, and many factories around the world are automatic to a remarkable degree. A fully automatic factory, however, has a hard economic row to hoe. The heavy capital investment needed to build one demands that the factory operate continuously turning out its product. Yet the demand for any product is notoriously variable. That immediately militates against making a huge investment in an automatic factory to manufacture a complex product such as an automobile.

An automatic factory that manufactures a less complex

product, say a component of automobiles, is a better bet. Then you can build into the factory ways of shifting from one product to another when demands fluctuate. There are obvious limits, however, in the degree to which any factory can shift from one product to another. An automatic factory manufacturing automobile bodies from sheet steel could hardly be expected to be capable of shifting even to the manufacture of hot-water heaters from the same material.

The best bet currently is to have a factory with machine tools that are individually automatic. Such tools can be programmed to turn out many different products. An automatic milling machine, for example, can make almost anything that has to be cut out of a metal slab or block. A battery of automatic machine tools, coupled with automatic devices for handling parts and computers for handling information, enables a factory to flexibly shift its products. Among the automatic devices for handling parts are robots, which are defined as programmable machines with at least four independent degrees of freedom—in other words, joints.

Heat Transformers

If in doing their work tools transform one kind of energy into another, other well-known devices exist for that purpose alone. They go back to oars, sails and wheels, and signal roles in history have been played by the yoke for oxen, the bit, bridle, saddle and stirrup for horses (all making it possible to exploit animal power), windmills, water wheels, cannon and other firearms. The profoundest change in human life, however, came in the late eighteenth century with the introduction of heat engines.

The steam engine transformed the chemical energy of wood and coal into mechanical energy. There were steam engines before Watt, but they did not exert their power to turn a shaft. In so doing Watt's marvelous engine could drive looms and other machines and launch the industrial revolution. Toward the end of the nineteenth century other heat engines emerged: the internal-combustion engine (which first relied on the chemical energy of gas and later on that of petroleum) and the steam turbine. Even the nuclear reactor is a heat engine, in that it transforms nuclear energy into the heat of a turbine-driving fluid such as steam.

Turbines, in which a shaft is rotated by an impeller resembling a windmill, are generally more efficient than reciprocating engines, in which the shaft is rotated by the back-and-forth motion of a piston in a cylinder. In other words, they transform a larger fraction of the chemical energy of the fuel into mechanical energy of the rotating shaft. The reason is that they can operate at a higher average temperature because the hot fluid that drives them is not cooled with each stroke of a piston. A modern steam-turbine electric-generating plant can be 40 percent efficient; a modern automobile engine is about 25 percent efficient. An exception, however, to the efficiency advantage of turbines is large diesel engines, such as those used to propel ships; their efficiency can be well above 40 percent. In all these engines the remainder of the energy goes off as waste heat.

The original advantage of the internal-combustion engine was that it dispensed with the weight of a boiler and water and could therefore transform more energy per pound of engine. Such an engine was much better suited to smaller vehicles such as automobiles and airplanes. Thirty years before the Wright brothers' flight of 1903 practical people could see that the future of human flight lay with a heavier-than-air craft with some kind of stationary wing, but they did not know of an engine that would be capable of generating enough power to get both the airframe and itself into the air. One of the Wrights' great achievements was building a light internal-combustion engine that could do the job. By the same token the jet aircraft engine of today—a gas turbine—is an internal-combustion engine.

An epochal development toward the end of the nineteenth century was the fuller application of another form of energy: electricity. It is a curious fact that even after the development of the electric telegraph, the electric motor, the electric generator and the telephone no one thought of using electricity to transmit power any distance. As late as the 1870s magazines such as *Scientific American* were full of ingenious mechanical schemes for getting power from a distance: water or compressed air pumped through pipes, long chain drives and so on.

The electric generator is based on Michael Faraday's discovery in 1831 of electromagnetic induction: If a magnet is moved at right angles to a wire, it induces in the wire an electric current. Conversely, if a wire is wrapped around a piece of iron and an electric current is passed through the wire, the iron develops a magnetic field and exerts a force. You can see how a wire-wrapped armature rotating inside a wire-wrapped ring can translate the force of rotation into an electric current (a generator) or translate an electric current into a force of rotation (a motor). The story goes that one day Faraday was showing William Ewart Gladstone a primitive generator. Gladstone asked: "What good is it?" Faraday replied: "Soon you will be able to tax it."

Less than four years after Thomas Edison got his first successful incandescent lamp in 1879, he was operating a system in downtown New York for distributing electricity to 10,000 lamps for 400 customers. His generator was driven by a steam engine, and the electricity was distributed over copper bars in the form of direct current: current that flows in only one direction. It quickly became apparent to others that what would be much better for the purpose would be alternating current: current that reverses direction many times a second.

The reason is that direct current cannot actuate an electric transformer and alternating current can. Therefore a low-voltage alternating current can be transformed to a higher-voltage one and vice versa. Since more power can be transmitted over a conductor at a higher voltage than can be transmitted at a lower one, the economics of electric-power distribution was greatly enhanced. The trend to higher voltages has continued up to the present day, when electric power is routinely distributed over long lines at 765,000 volts. At the same time it has been found that very-high-voltage direct current has advantages for long-distance transmission, even though it must be converted from alternating current and back again.

Edison was an obstinate man, which may be one of the reasons for his success as an inventor. He hated alternating current. He argued that an electric shock from alternating current was more dangerous than one from direct current. At one point he, the leading electrical personage of the day, was approached by a New York group who wanted to introduce what they thought would be a humane form of execution: the electric chair. He advised them to use alternating current; since it was more dangerous than direct current, it would be more effective for the purpose. So it was that in 1889 alternating current was applied (with ghastly difficulty) to accomplish the first deliberate electrocution.

Today electrical technology is on the threshold of pervasive change because of a largely empirical discovery. Although metals conduct electricity readily, at normal temperatures a certain amount of the electrical energy is lost (as heat) to electrical resistance. At temperatures close to absolute zero metals become superconducting: they conduct electricity totally without resistance. Although ceramics are normally electrical insulators, certain complex ceramics have been made in the laboratory that are not only conductors but also superconductors.

Moreover, these materials are superconducting at temperatures much higher than those near absolute zero. Before their discovery superconductivity was known only in materials cooled with liquid helium, which liquefies at 4 degrees K. (4 degrees C. above absolute zero). Afterward it was known in materials cooled with liquid nitrogen, which liquefies at 77 degrees K. To put that initial advance in the simplest economic terms, liquid helium costs $11 per gallon and liquid nitrogen costs 22 cents.

Exactly what the advance will bring is still in engineering dreamland, but the dreams have mostly to do with supercomputers, ultrafast transmission of computer data, ultrapowerful electromagnets and power lines that can carry electricity for long distances without loss. Watching the advance of superconducting technology in the twenty-first century is going to be a wonderful spectator sport.

Bits and Pixels

The first practical application of electricity was the electric telegraph. When Thoreau heard that Maine and Texas had been linked by telegraph, he wondered what Maine had to say to Texas. Judging by the instantaneous success of the telegraph, the telephone, radio and television, people have an enormous amount to say to one another. In fact, communication may be the technology that is the purest extension of human behavior.

The telephone is now so embedded in human behavior that it is hard to imagine what life was like without it. At the same time it has shaped human behavior. Many Europeans have observed that Americans seem to have an overpowering urge to answer the telephone, even if they are in the midst of business that may be presumed to be more important. This behavior may have a distinct historical origin.

The cost of a telephone call—not the charge to the customer but the cost to the telephone company—depends partly on the length of the call. In order to handle x calls with an average length of y the company needs z facilities. Therefore if y is longer, the company needs more z, and if y is shorter, the company needs less.

At the time of the First World War thoughtful analysts working for the Bell system realized that if people would answer the telephone just a little faster than they were accustomed to doing, the average length of the calls would be a little shorter and a little less facility would be needed. The small savings, multiplied by the company's vast number of facilities, would add up to a substantial amount of money.

The company launched a vigorous advertising campaign urging people to answer the telephone faster. Since there was a war on, the appeal was put on the basis that tying up telephone communications hindered the war effort. The campaign worked like a charm. It is said that the man in charge of it later remarked: "I can state that I am personally responsible for making the American people the only people in the world who will interrupt sex to answer the telephone."

Engineers are normally regarded as people who apply the findings of science rather than invent scientific theories. There are important exceptions, and one of them is modern information theory. Telephone engineers have always been concerned with noise in the telephone circuit, and early in this century they introduced the concept of the signal-to-noise ratio. The idea is that if the ratio of the signal—dots and dashes, the human voice or what have you—to the noise is low, the noise tends to drown out the signal. The interesting thing about the concept is that it applies to *all* forms of communication. A well-produced book written by a scholar, for example, has a higher signal-to-noise ratio than a tabloid newspaper.

Other general concepts flowed from the experience of communication engineers. One is that in any form of communication there is between the source (the transmitter) and the sink (the receiver) a channel. In human conversation, for example, the channel is the range of sound frequencies generated by the human voice. Such a range of frequencies is called a band, and the greater the range of frequencies, the larger the bandwidth. A wide band of frequencies can transmit more information per second than a narrower band; hence bandwidth is a measure of any channel's capacity to transmit information.

A case in point is the following. When you listen to your favorite anchorman on the evening television news, he cannot talk any faster than about 100 words per minute. When you read a book, if you read at a typical speed, you should be able to do 300 words per minute. Therefore the bandwidth of written communication is three times larger than spoken communication.

Writing is one of the ancient technologies that have become so embedded in human behavior that they are never outmoded. The earliest written texts are credited to the Sumerians of 6,000 years ago. Denise Schmandt-Besserat, a French scholar now working at the University of Texas at Austin, traces their origins back even further. She has demonstrated that the symbols devised by the Sumerians are closely related to small clay tokens that served for the keeping of accounts as much as 11,000 years ago.

Another means of keeping accounts that goes back to antiquity is the abacus. Surely anyone who could manipulate an abacus could imagine a machine that did the same thing with much greater speed and capacity. The realization of the modern computer, however, had to await the evolution of electronics.

Computer engineers made their own contribution to information theory. They applied the concept of the binary digit, or "bit." It is the fundamental particle of information: either a 0 or a 1. Later engineers working on computer graphics introduced the concept of the pixel, the fundamental particle of pictures. The dots that make up a television picture are pixels, and so are the ultimate constituents of a painting, a photograph or any other picture.

Computer engineers also introduced the powerful concept of random access. An old-style phonograph record does not have the feature of random access; in order to gain access to part of the record you have to play it up to that point (unless you want to ruin the record by putting the needle down in the middle of it). The computer diskette on which I am writing this book does have random access; I can find a page or a line or a word, wherever they are on the disk, simply by pecking in a specification. The most awesome of all random-access devices is a newspaper such as *The New York Times*. It would take you weeks to go through every bit of information in it, but by its architecture of sections and headlines you can find what you want in at most a few minutes.

The telephone people also made profound contributions to the computer. The essence of all modern digital computers is a switch: a device that will either pass an electric current or not pass it, equivalent to the digital 0 or 1. One such device is the electromechanical relay, in which a hinged piece of metal closes an electric circuit when it is pulled down by a current flowing through an electromagnet. Until recent years a telephone exchange consisted of rack after rack after rack of relays. During the Second World War large arrays of telephone-company relays were assembled into machines for computing firing tables for artillery.

In the late 1940s I visited such a machine at the Aberdeen Proving Ground in Maryland. The remarkable thing about this early computer is that you could *hear* it working. Over in the corner of a large room filled with racks of relays I would hear the sharp "bip" of one relay closing. Then from other parts of the room there would be a fusillade of answering bips. It was about as close as one can get to having the sensation of being inside a working brain.

Actually I had gone to Aberdeen to visit the famed ENIAC, the first large, general-purpose electronic computer. In ENIAC the switches were not relays but 18,000 glass vacuum tubes. Since the vacuum tubes generated a lot of heat, one heard the hum of large cooling fans. It almost seemed as if ENIAC was some kind of heat engine! To be sure, one should not forget that computers, like all other tools, are energy transformers. The amount of energy they transform is small, but considering the increase in efficiency they bestow on many human activities, the amplification is vast.

It was hard to conceive that vacuum-tube computers could be made much larger than ENIAC, and in fact they weren't. Providentially the telephone connection brought the transistor. As is well known, the transistor was invented by William Shockley, Walter Brattain and John Bardeen at Bell Telephone Laboratories. They were not looking for a switch; they were physicists studying the properties of semiconductors. One of the advantages of having a large, successful organization as a patron is that the patron can take the long view. It is a good lesson in the support of basic research; by any standard the invention of the transistor should repay the operation of even an establishment as large as Bell Laboratories for a long time.

The first transistors were about the size of the eraser at the end of a pencil. Nowadays they are tiny areas on the surface of a microelectronic chip. To me one of the most remarkable things about the chip is that, seen under a low-power microscope, it looks not like an electronic device but like a *diagram* of the device. The diagrams of the electronic circuits of yesteryear were wonderfully neat, but the circuits themselves were a wiry jungle. With chips form follows function so exactly that you can almost read them. For example, a memory chip looks like a regularly patterned textile, whereas a processor chip looks like a complex rectilinear city seen from the air.

Like writing and the telephone, the computer is now so embedded in human behavior that it is hard to imagine what life was like without it. Can you imagine operating a bank without computers? Such functions are well understood and taken for granted by everyone. The frontier that beckons is artificial intelligence. Exactly what is meant by artificial intelligence depends to some extent on what expert you talk to, but I think I have a test for it.

A writer is working at an advanced word processor, one so advanced that it not only corrects his spelling but also repairs his grammar and gives him a running critique of his writing, with tart comments such as "You already said that" or "This really belongs at the beginning of the piece." At the end of the day's work the writer, feeling rather inadequate, is musing at the keyboard. Suddenly it occurs to him to peck into the machine a question: "Do you think this program can be said to have the same kind of intelligence a human being has?" There is a distinct pause as the program processes the question. Then there comes on the screen: "That reminds me of a story." It seems to me a program spontaneously capable of such a response could be said to be intelligent.

But in a technology evolving as rapidly as information technology it is difficult to predict what will happen next. In the late 1940s I was visited by three men from the Haloid Corporation of Rochester, New York. They said they wanted to show me something. They got out an old camera with a plateholder in the back, and into the plateholder they put a piece of ordinary paper. They snapped me with the camera, removed the paper and put it in an aluminum tray holding some kind of powder. They shook the paper around and fished it out of the tray. On it I could see the dim outline of a human head. I was too dumb to realize that what I was really seeing was the beginnings of Xerox.

Götterdämmerung Technology

It is not possible to reflect on technology without thinking of the technology that is capable of ending all technology. I refer, of course, to nuclear-weapon technology. To be sure, not a great deal can be said about the technology itself because much of it is secret, if not to Russian nuclear-weapon designers, then at least to the ordinary citizen. What is public knowledge, however, is the following.

When the nuclei of uranium 235 or plutonium 239 absorb slow neutrons, they fission and release an enormous amount of energy. If a sufficient amount of one or the other of those metals is brought together in a hurry, the fission reaction propagates and there is a colossal explosion. A curious sidelight is that the first nuclear explosion—at Alamogordo on July 16, 1945—was not a test of the bomb that according to the Japanese survey killed 122,000 people in Hiroshima on August 6. That bomb was a uranium 235 bomb, and nobody in the know doubted it would work. What was tested was a plutonium bomb, about which there *were* doubts. A second plutonium bomb killed 73,000 people in Nagasaki on August 9. (I mention the numbers of dead because they are so large that in people who are not Japanese they seem to induce amnesia.)

The nuclei of hydrogen release an enormous amount of energy when they are brought together and fuse. Fusing nuclei of ordinary hydrogen (hydrogen 1) calls for a temperature in the millions of degrees C. Fusing nuclei of hydrogen 2 (deuterium) or hydrogen 3 (tritium) calls for somewhat lower temperatures, but still temperatures that in a fusion bomb could be provided only by the explosion of a fission bomb.

If a high-school physics student undertook to design a fusion bomb, it might have a core of liquid deuterium or tritium surrounded by a fission bomb. Then when the fission bomb was set off, it would presumably generate enough heat to ignite the fusion reaction. That is definitely *not* what is done. There have been a few public intimations over thirty-five years. One is an article in the Encyclopedia Americana by none other than Edward Teller, "the father of the hydrogen bomb," with an illustration that shows the fission part of the bomb separated from the fusion part.

The implication is that it is not the fission bomb's heat that ignites the fusion reaction but its blast of radiation—light, ultraviolet and X rays. The illustration shows another interesting wrinkle. Whereas uranium 235 can be fissioned by slow neutrons and not by fast neutrons, it is the other way around with uranium 238. And when the fusion reaction is ignited, it shoots out a flood of fast neutrons. Therefore if the fusion material is surrounded by uranium 238, the uranium fissions. Such a bomb is properly called not a hydrogen bomb but a fission-fusion-fission bomb. Important details, however, are still secret. Robert Oppenheimer called the mechanism "technically sweet." One of these sweethearts typically has an explosive yield of one megaton—forty times that of the bombs dropped on Hiroshima and Nagasaki.

The Human Species Is Still Creating Itself

Technological evolution is faster than biological evolution, and yet it seems the use of tools shaped the evolution of early hominids into *Homo sapiens*. Is technology still shaping the biological evolution of the human species? Some people, including a few eminent scientists, passionately believe that cultural evolution is going *against* what they think human biological evolution should be. The argument is that, in preserving the lives of the weak and favoring equality of opportunity, culture evades the rough-and-tumble of natural selection and erodes the human genetic heritage.

To me it has never been clear how natural selection could possibly be evaded. Over a period of time individuals in a population that are "weak" in a given environment—less adapted to that environment—are bound to have fewer offspring than those that are "strong." Yes, I know that poorer people tend to have more children than better-off people, but that has remarkably little to do with the case.

Being poor or being better off evens out after very few generations—even one generation. We are talking about evolutionary effects that in human populations take centuries, if not tens of millenniums, to develop. Very few members of the human population can trace their ancestry back even four generations. There is no reason to believe that on the average the weak produce more offspring than the strong.

Do you know anyone who is extremely nearsighted? If you do, it is almost certain they wear glasses. In a hunting, gathering and scavenging society, long before eyeglasses, such people would have been at quite a disadvantage, and presumably they would have produced fewer offspring than people who had better eyesight. Today, with eyeglasses, they are at less of a disadvantage, and since nearsightedness is genetic, the frequency of the gene or genes that are responsible for nearsightedness in the human population is probably increasing.

Does this mean that technology has enabled nearsighted people to escape natural selection? No. They are still being selected for all kinds of other traits. If a nearsighted person has another genetic trait that confers an advantage over non-nearsighted people, say high resistance to infectious disease, the chances are that that person will produce more offspring than non-nearsighted people who lack that trait.

The environment in which human beings are selected is one they have largely created themselves. Therefore the traits that are being selected are those that favor reproduction in that environment, not the environment of hunters, gatherers and scavengers. If such selection places a lower value on traits that were important in the Paleolithic, who cares? For a human being who was subject, for example, to being attacked by another animal the genetic traits that favor a quick surge of fear and anger were highly adaptive. Today they may not be.

In short, the human species does continue to make itself, both by compensating for human deficiencies with technology and by creating an environment in which the human traits that are being selected differ from those that were selected in earlier environments. The trouble is that biological evolution is so much slower than technological evolution, which for the first time has given the human species the ability to destroy itself. One can only hope that the day will be carried by a genetic trait that arose at the beginning of human history: an unusual capacity for learning.

THE DANGEROUS CHARM
OF CRANKS

I do not agree with the Duke of Wellington politically (he was an awful Tory), but otherwise I find him an attractive figure. People regarded him, as they regard all *very* famous men, as an oracle, and when he said something, it was more than likely to be recorded for posterity. Once he was reviewing his ragtag troops during the campaign against Napoleon's army in Spain. He turned to one of his officers and said: "I don't know what effect these men will have upon the enemy, but, by God, they terrify me." A few years later, after he and Marshal Blücher had defeated Napoleon at Waterloo, he remarked with admirable objectivity: "It was the nearest-run thing you ever saw in your life." Best of all is what he said one day after he had become the most famous man in England. As he was walking down the street a man rushed up to him and exclaimed: "Mr. Jones, I believe!" Wellington replied: "If you believe that, you'll believe anything."

The remark has applications far beyond what Wellington meant. If someone believes something that on the face of it is un-believable, he is a crank. In our own way, however, we are all cranks. Among the people I have known well there are none who did not believe something unbelievable, and whereas I believe *I* do not believe anything unbelievable, others have informed me I am quite mistaken. It is like the classic line: "All the world is mad except me and thee, and sometimes I wonder about thee."

If cranks are so common, why not simply accept crankishness as a human foible and let it go at that? In the preceding piece I mentioned one of the concepts of information theory: the signal-to-noise ratio. If it can be said that one of the main requirements of human life is distinguishing the signal of the true from the noise of the false, then noise that interferes with the signal is a serious matter. Moreover, if tolerance of noise becomes a habit, it can become a *very* serious matter.

It is quite remarkable that many—perhaps most—educated people accept the notion of extrasensory perception, or ESP. A conversation between a skeptic and a nonskeptic might go like this:

Skeptic: "Do you believe in ESP?"

Nonskeptic: "Sure. My wife has it."

Skeptic: "How's that?"

Nonskeptic: "Well, my mother-in-law calls us at almost any hour of the day or night, but my wife and I will be sitting there and she'll say, 'My mother will call us in the next five minutes.' And, you know, it happens every time."

Skeptic: "That's interesting, although you might say your wife is even more familiar with her mother's patterns of behavior than she is aware. But do you know of any *scientific* demonstration of ESP?"

Nonskeptic: "Sure. There's that fellow—what's his name?—Rhine. He proved it."

Skeptic: "What would you say if I told you that since J. B. Rhine started doing his card-matching experiments in the 1920s hundreds of people have tried to repeat them under controlled conditions and no one has succeeded."

Nonskeptic: "Is that so? But didn't he prove it anyway?"

Skeptic: "You know, the whole idea of experimental science is that if someone does an experiment, you don't have to take his word for it. You can repeat the experiment yourself and see if you can reproduce it. If you can't, you can be skeptical of it. One of the key words in science is reproducibility."

Nonskeptic: "O.K., if you say so. But I still say my wife has ESP."

ESP has a history going back well beyond J. B. Rhine. In late Victorian England there was wide interest in psychical research and spiritualism, particularly communication with the dead. Among those who thought such things were worth serious investigation were eminent scientists, including the evolutionary biologist Alfred Russel Wallace and the physicists William Crookes, Lord Rayleigh and Oliver Lodge.

Janet Oppenheim argues (in her book *The Other World: Spiritualism and Psychical Research in England, 1850–1914*) that the reason people were so interested in psychical research and spiritualism is that they were trying somehow to reconcile science and religion. To a society that had lived by a theological explanation of the universe the concepts of physical materialism and biological evolution came as a painful shock. Human beings had lost their immortality and their privileged place in the universe. They might regain them if psychical research could show that there is life after death and there are phenomena other than "normal" ones.

Organizations set up to pursue such research have continued down to the present day; indeed, they are going strong. Among them are the American Society for Psychical Research, the Parapsychological Foundation and the Institute of Noetic Sciences (the last founded by the astronaut Edgar Mitchell). These organizations, however, are by no means the only descendants of the original impulse to seek evidence for the "paranormal."

ESP is one of several alleged paranormal phenomena. Another is psychokinesis, or PK: making something happen by willing it. PK would be even harder to demonstrate than ESP, but it attracted a flurry of notice in the mid-1970s. Uri Geller, a performing magician, wowed members of the staff of Stanford Research International (which is not part of Stanford University) by apparently performing from a distance such feats as bending a spoon and stopping a clock.

According to another magician, James Randi, the magazine *Time* was considering doing a cover article on Geller. A senior member of the staff was skeptical, and prevailed on his colleagues to invite Geller to the office and have him repeat his feats for their benefit. At the same time the staff member arranged for Randi and an amateur magician, Charles Reynolds, to be present incognito. After Geller had gone through his paces, he left. Randi and Reynolds had no difficulty showing that what he was doing was conjuring tricks. *Time* still did the story, but Geller did not appear on the cover.

The remarkable thing about the Geller episode is that the people who took him at face value—and there were many, including reputable scientists—seemed to ignore the fact that he was a professional magician. Surely anyone who has seen a magician in action realizes he can do things that seem magical. Perhaps those who took Geller seriously had never seen a magician in action. There is, however, a saying that goes back to the Romans: *Populus vult decipi, ergo decipiatur*—People want to be deceived, therefore let them be deceived.

Geller marches right along. He published a book about his allegedly paranormal feats in 1986. In addition, he now charges vast fees (according to the *Financial Times* up to £1 million) to sense minerals from a distance, even from maps. In 1987 he had a meeting with Senator Claiborne Pell, chairman of the Senate Committee on Foreign Relations, and Representative Dante Fascell, chairman of the House Committee on Foreign Affairs, to acquaint them with his conviction that the Russians are ahead of us in the "psychic arms race."

Research in the paranormal does not lack for apparent respectability. The American Parapsychology Association is a division in good standing of the American Association for the Advancement of Science. Several leading universities, including the University of California at Davis, have professors of parapsychology, and Ph.D.s in the subject are granted. Although such research has yet to produce anything in the way of a repeatable controlled experiment, its practitioners argue that its revolutionary potentialities justify its continuation. My own feeling is that after a century of total failure it has become a bloody bore.

Laughing at Copernicus

It is a curious fact that most people who have a passionate interest in the motions of celestial bodies haven't the slightest interest in astronomy. The astrologers of the world far outnumber the astronomers. It seems unlikely that many astrologers or many of those who hang on their prognostications have ever looked at the constellations that have lent their names to the signs of the zodiac. Shakespeare put it best: "The fault, dear Brutus, is not in our stars, but in ourselves."

The heavens seem to attract people who do not look at them very seriously. In 1950 the Macmillan Company published a book titled *Worlds in Collision*. It was written by Immanuel Velikovsky, a psychoanalyst. In it Velikovsky contended that at the time of the Exodus of the Israelites from Egypt in 1500 B.C. an encounter with a giant comet caused the earth either to slow down suddenly or to stop spinning altogether. Among the consequences were floods, hurricanes, dust storms, fires, boiling seas, rivers the color of blood, rains of petroleum, the collapse and rise of mountains, the parting of the Red Sea and the deposition of the manna that sustained the Israelites for forty years. After fifty-two years the comet returned, causing among other things the fall of the walls of Jericho. In certain respects an immensely learned man, Velikovsky found evidence for these events not only in the Old Testament but also in the literature of other ancient cultures.

An encounter between the earth and another body in 1500 B.C. is not in itself unbelievable, although there is no nonliterary evidence for it. Velikovsky was convinced, however, that the literary evidence testifies quite specifically to what happened. The giant comet sprang out of the planet Jupiter, had its two encounters with the earth, had an encounter with Mars and then went on to become what is now the planet Venus. Such a sequence of events, quite apart from what Velikovsky believed were the consequences, calls for the abandonment of an entire edifice of observation and theory that physicists and astronomers have built since Galileo. One can almost admire Velikovsky's imperturbable disregard of it.

If that was all there was to it, one might leave the Velikovsky episode to the history of cranks and crankishness. Strangely, however, his eccentric ideas have not faded away. When *Worlds in Collision* appeared, a few astronomers took the trouble to say it was not to be taken seriously. One of them, Harlow Shapley, had been published by the Macmillan Company, and in a letter to his editor he remarked that if Macmillan got in the habit of publishing such books, they might have difficulty getting scientists to write for them.

Macmillan interpreted the remark as an effort at censorship, and said as much publicly. The company did not, however, present two sequels to *Worlds in Collision: Ages in Chaos* and *Earth in Upheaval.* That was done by Doubleday & Company,

which does not publish textbooks. Doubleday continued to publish books by Velikovsky until 1978, and William Morrow & Co.
published him in 1983.

Among those who have defended Velikovsky are a few scientists who felt that his right to be heard was being threatened.
Curiously his defenders have seldom mentioned what he is ad-
vocating, only his right to advocate it. In other words, he became
a kind of civil-liberties case. This raises the question of whether
anyone who has an idea in science has a right to be heard, as
any citizen has a right to be heard. The answer cannot be anything
but yes, and yet some people have less of a right to be heard than
others.

Science is a profession, not unlike engineering, law and
medicine. Few seek medical advice from people who do not have
an M.D. degree; whatever its faults, the degree is evidence that
its holder has gone to considerable trouble to learn something
about medicine. It is like that in science; the Ph.D. degree is
evidence that at the very least its holder has spent considerable
time studying the subject. To be sure, a Ph.D. is no guarantee
the holder is not a crank. I remember a well-known psychologist's
asking me how *Scientific American* chose its scientist authors. I
said: "First of all, we make the assumption that someone who is
a professor at a place like Harvard is not a crank." He interjected:
"I find that rather touching."

The fact remains that Velikovsky made a sweeping claim
about astronomical events, and he did not know very much about
astronomy. If he had, he could not have believed what he believed. Comets do not spring out of planets; the planet Venus is
far larger than any comet; the motions of Velikovsky's comet
violate the laws of celestial mechanics. The physicist Wolfgang
Pauli once remarked about a speculative proposal in physics: "It's
not even wrong." That's the way it is with Velikovsky and comets.

For many people this is not enough. Such a person might

well say: "They laughed at Copernicus." As a matter of fact, very few important scientific advances (including Copernicus's) get laughed at. Among scientists a commoner response is: "Why, of course! Why didn't I think of that?" Consider the double helix. If there is such a thing as a scientific establishment, Watson and Crick were hardly full-fledged members of it, and yet their model of DNA was quickly accepted. At first there were a few who doubted its significance, but skepticism was soon washed away by the sheer usefulness of the double helix for further research.

The longevity of the Velikovsky episode testifies to the vitality of the notion that discoveries are usually made by lonely outsiders; at first everyone laughs and then suddenly they are chastened and laugh no more. As a matter of fact, scientific discoverers have to be insiders. Isaac Newton wrote Robert Hooke: "If I have seen further [than you and Descartes] it is by standing on the shoulders of Giants." Robert Merton has written an amusing book titled *On the Shoulders of Giants*, in which he traces Newton's famous remark back to antiquity. The point is that it has been understood for a long time that no one discovers anything without being well informed about what earlier discoverers have done. That is what was lacking in the work of Immanuel Velikovsky. It is also lacking in the understanding of those who felt, and in some instances still feel, that his ideas deserved an attentive hearing.

Higher-Order Cranks

Crank ideas abound, and many of them last even longer than Velikovsky's. The world owes a great debt to Martin Gardner, who has examined many of them in detail. He has written a classic titled *Fads and Fallacies in the Name of Science* (a revision of his earlier book *In the Name of Science*). Among the fads and fallacies are: a flat earth (or a hollow one), flying saucers, gravity screens, dowsing, orgone boxes and dianetics (also known as Scientology).

A particularly persistent fallacy is that one of the great problems of mathematics is how to divide an angle into three equal angles with a ruler and a compass, as in high-school geometry one erects a perpendicular to a line. Angle trisectors are a chosen few who have never bothered to find out that trisecting the angle is *not* one of the great problems of mathematics. Many angles can be trisected easily. For the Greeks the problem was to find a single method of trisecting all conceivable angles. A completely rigorous proof that finding such a method is impossible was discovered in 1837.

Such beliefs are not hard to attribute to cranks, even if many people hold them. There are other questionable beliefs where the decision is harder.

A not inconsiderable number of academic psychologists believe there is a connection between intelligence and race. Since some components of human behavior are genetic, and intelligence is presumably a component of human behavior, it might seem plausible that intelligence is genetic. And since human groups differ from one another genetically, it might seem plausible that the members of some groups are on the average more intelligent than the members of other groups.

It is a curious fact that those who study the connection between intelligence and race never find the intelligence of the population to which *they* belong inferior to the intelligence of members of some other population. Where the fat lands in the fire is when white psychologists find evidence that members of the black population are on the average inferior in intelligence to members of the white population. One such psychologist, Arthur Jensen, even asserted that his findings have implications for educational policy. Exactly what he meant by that is not clear, but it is hard to put a kindly face on it.

The real trouble is with the concepts "intelligence" and "race." What is intelligence? Everyone knows people who are intelligent and other people who are less so, but that doesn't answer the question. Dictionary definitions are vague, and expert definitions are unsatisfactory to other experts.

Whatever intelligence is, measurements of something purporting to be it are widely made for educational purposes. The justification is that decisions must be made on the advancement of students. The best-known of the tests is the Stanford-Binet, a variation on tests introduced early in this century by the French psychologist Alfred Binet; it is one of the tests scored in intelligence quotient, or IQ. The originators of such tests have mostly been modest about what is actually being measured, but others have been less so. Some take it for granted that what is being measured is intelligence pure and simple.

It is hard to see how it could be. Can you imagine giving such a test to a Bushman of the Kalahari Desert? Even if the test were meticulously explained to him, it is unlikely that his score would be high. Would that mean he is unintelligent? If a Bushman were to devise an intelligence test and give it to, say, an Italian, and the Italian had a low score, would that make the Italian unintelligent? In other words, intelligence tests have to be firmly embedded in the culture and environment of those who devise them.

The environment of a child with poor parents is by definition different from the environment of a child with parents who are better off. In fact, the child with poor parents may well be deprived of important early learning experiences that are a natural consequence of the environment of the child with better-off parents. At the same time the child with poor parents may, in order to survive, develop abilities that are not taken into account in the design of intelligence tests. In the circumstances it is hardly surprising that on the average children with extremely poor parents have lower intelligence-test scores than children with better-off parents.

Having a relatively low intelligence-test score can have long-term effects not only on educational opportunities but also on self-esteem. David Ogilvy, the advertising magnate, tells the following story. He is of English origin, and as a child he was never given an intelligence test. Hearing a lot about IQ tests in later life, he wondered how he might do on one of them. In a test scored by IQ the average score is set at 100. Ogilvy took such a test and scored 96. He remarks: "That is about par for ditch-diggers. If I had known earlier that my IQ was 96, I would have sought a career as a ditchdigger."

Intelligence-test scores also have a powerful influence on the expectations of teachers. In a famous experiment conducted at a school in San Francisco, Robert Rosenthal and Lenore Jacobsen had the teachers administer a battery of intelligence tests, including the Stanford-Binet, to their pupils. The experimenters scored the tests and reported to the teachers which pupils were likely to be "spurters" in the next grade. In actuality those pupils were chosen entirely at random. When the same pupils were tested at the end of the year, they showed substantial gains in their IQ scores. For example, the pupils randomly designated spurters in the first grade had gained an average of 27 points. The teachers had obviously given them special attention; it was what is often called self-fulfilling prophecy.

The concept of race is just as troublesome as the concept of intelligence. The human species, now five billion strong, covers the planet. In the tens of millenniums since the emergence of Homo sapiens, the species has separated into many distinct populations. If one such population has been isolated from other human populations over a substantial period of time, variations in the biological characteristics of its members accumulate. The result is the formation of a race.

A human being of any race has between 50,000 and 100,000 pairs of genes, with one gene of each pair coming from each parent. Two genes in a pair may differ somewhat; that is the stuff of the differences between races and of all other human differences: in height, weight, skin color, blood type and so on. When it comes down to it, the differences are not all that great. The interesting thing about the genetic differences between races is that the differences *within* a human population are greater than the average differences *between* populations.

Some human characteristics, for example certain blood-group factors, are associated with a single gene. In a person having that factor a single gene is translated into the factor substance. Such a characteristic is best described as a trait. Many human characteristics, however, consist not of a single trait but of a combination of them. Therefore such characteristics are associated with a combination of genes.

It would seem highly unlikely that a characteristic as subtle as intelligence could be a single trait. It is much more likely to consist of a combination of traits and to be the result of a combination of genes. If that is the case, the mechanisms of genetics will shuffle those genes with their paired genes from one generation to the next. It would seem that the inheritance of intelligence, if there is such a thing, would be quite complex and not subject to the same simple rules as the inheritance of a blood-group factor.

Against this background, what is the likelihood that one race is more or less intelligent than another? Assuming that there is such a characteristic as intelligence, there are variations in it, as there are variations in all other human characteristics. But how could natural selection have favored a lower average intelligence in any human population? Whatever intelligence is, less of it could hardly have been adaptive in any conceivable environment. It is more plausible that variations in such a characteristic would be individual, not racial.

The facts about intelligence testing and human genetics are well known. This particular layman finds it hard to understand how anyone who is aware of them could pursue the idea that some human groups are more or less intelligent than others. Is someone who pursues the idea a crank? It is a question people have to decide for themselves.

Authority Cranks

I live in Greenwich Village, where walls are plastered with posters advertising pop performers. Recently I saw a poster featuring a picture of a cheerful bewhiskered man with a bandanna around his head and a microphone thrust against his teeth. What made me stop and get out my notepaper was the accompanying message: "The World Presents Copernicus, America's Premier Poet/Performer/Philosopher, with His 10-Piece Band." Boy, I thought, if this guy is as good as he thinks he is, we could entrust him with *all* our problems.

Everyone seems to have a certain craving for authority, a need to be told how it is instead of having to figure it out for themselves. The former is certainly easier than the latter, which can call for an effort that generates fear and loathing. To be sure, authority is often benevolent; there are times when one reasonably puts one's trust in officials duly elected or appointed by one's society. Moreover, no one can know everything, and there are times when one reasonably puts one's trust in the accumulated knowledge of professionals such as plumbers, automobile mechanics, physicians and scientists.

Many find comfort in the ultimate authority: the Deity. Among them are those who have a deep need not only to rely on such authority but also to convince others that their particular belief is the only acceptable one. In recent years these efforts have taken an interesting turn.

Christianity, like other religions, has its sacred literature. The Holy Bible is a diverse collection of writings from two great religions: Judaism and Christianity. In the days before the rise of the physical and biological sciences Christians took these writings more or less literally. Faced with conflicts between Scripture and the new knowledge, many devout people maintained their faith by regarding the Bible not as literal truth but as humane allegory.

Other Christians, mostly those of Protestant denominations in the southern United States, persisted in regarding Scripture as literal truth. Darwin had said in his *Descent of Man and Selection in Relation to Sex*, published in 1871: "The main conclusion arrived at in this work, namely that man is descended from some lowly organized form, will, I regret to think, be highly distasteful to many." What was most distasteful to many was the thought that human beings might be descended from monkeys.

In the 1920s fundamentalists in several southern states succeeded in getting the state government to pass a "monkey law" making it illegal to teach evolution in schools and colleges. The best known of these laws was the Rotenberry Act of Tennessee, which led to the Scopes trial of 1925. John Thomas Scopes, a high-school biology teacher, was tried for breaking the law. In the courtroom Clarence Darrow made a monkey out of William Jennings Bryan, but Scopes was convicted. Thereafter there were many challenges to the Rotenberry Act, but it was not until 1968 that the Supreme Court of the United States declared it unconstitutional.

At that time it seemed that the long struggle of fundamentalists to bar the teaching of evolution was over. *Scientific Amer-*

ican even published an article titled "The End of the Monkey War." In fact the war had barely begun.

A new group had come into the picture calling themselves scientific creationists. Instead of arguing on theological grounds they argue on "scientific" ones. They maintain that the theory of evolution is only a theory, so that an alternative theory deserves equal attention. That theory is that the world and all its living inhabitants were created in the six days of Genesis. (On the seventh day He rested.) Exactly when those days were is not explicitly stated, but they may have been as recent as 10,000 years ago.

At first the technically educated members of the scientific-creationist movement were engineers and scientists in disciplines other than biology, geology and paleontology. In recent years, however, many creationists have pursued studies in those subjects, mostly in fundamentalist colleges. Some have received Ph.D.s. To find evidence supporting their position they do research.

For example, the creationist position requires that human beings and dinosaurs lived at the same time. In the scientific-creationist literature it is pointed out that in the bed of the Paluxy River in Texas fossil dinosaur footprints and fossil human footprints are found side by side. The putative human footprints look human because whatever made them landed on its heels when it walked, whereas dinosaurs were believed to have walked only on their toes. Close examination of the footprints has shown that just ahead of the heel impressions are faint traces of dinosaur toe impressions. It seems that the prints were made by a funny kind of dinosaur that walked on its heels.

Scientific creationists have cited much other evidence to discredit the evolutionary picture built up over two centuries by physical and biological scientists: that the earth formed 4.6 billion years ago and that living organisms have evolved over a period of 3.5 billion years. The creationists have made their case, however, not in the scientific community but in public forums such as school-board meetings. It has been a remarkably effective approach, because many citizens who would not accept a purely theological picture of the world are impressed by people who maintain that they are scientists and that there are scientific flaws in the evolutionary picture. Not knowing very much about biology and geology, such citizens think it is only fair to yield to a creationist demand for "equal time."

"Equal time" is interesting in its own right. The concept that every citizen has a right to be heard is an ancient one, but the idea that a group opposing the views of another group has a right to equal time to be heard is fairly recent. In 1927 Congress passed the Radio Act, requiring that radio broadcasters be licensed so that the natural resource represented by the radio spectrum would be used in an orderly manner. It was thus established that the radio spectrum or any part of it, which cannot very well be owned by any one person or company, is owned by the public. Then in 1934 Congress created the Federal Communications Commission. On the grounds that a broadcasting license is a public trust the FCC required that a broadcast presenting a controversial view give more or less equal time to opposing views.

What equal time means for creationists is equal representation with evolutionary concepts in textbooks, or at the least the elimination of evolutionary concepts in textbooks. Going before curriculum commissions, notably in California, they have on numerous occasions succeeded in convincing the commissioners to accede to their wishes. Textbook publishers must then do the same or not sell their books. And if textbooks are modified according to creationist demands in one large state, the same textbooks are the only ones available in other states; it would be costly for the publishers to put out separate editions.

Where decisions have gone against them, creationists have

resorted to the courts. This points to the heart of the matter. *Creationists seek to have their point of view upheld not by scientific institutions but by political and legal ones.* Since political and legal institutions are not equipped to decide such issues, the result is confusion and tumult. The whole point of the scientific enterprise is that what is true is to be decided not by opinion, majority or otherwise, but by the reproducibility of observation and experiment and by the usefulness of theory in pointing the way to new observations and new experiments.

When creationists argue that evolution is "only a theory," they disregard two crucial points. First, there is a distinction between the fact of evolution and the theory of evolution. To repeat, the fact of evolution, for which the evidence is overwhelming, is simply that the earth and its living organisms have evolved. The theory of evolution is an explanation of *how* living organisms evolved through natural selection.

Second, the modern theory of evolution is not simply a single hypothesis. It is a highly integrated body of reasoning, incorporating the facts of evolution (including the facts of paleontology, genetics and population biology). Like all useful theories, it raises questions, which is a way of saying that it does not have all the answers. It is nonetheless one of the great achievements of the human mind, and theological criticisms going back to the time of Darwin are irrelevant to it. Indeed, if one wishes to believe that the universe and everything in it were created by a supreme being, there is nothing in the theory of evolution to contradict it.

Seen in this light the scientific-creationist movement would seem to be a social aberration, one hardly worth discussing. But the damage done by such cranks is not trivial. Textbooks are polluted, and the impression is given that an all-or-nothing choice must be made between acceptance of evolution and belief in God.

Michael Cavanaugh of Temple University, who has probably examined scientific creationists more intensively than anyone else, cites a recent survey of students at Ohio State University. Eighty percent of them favored the teaching of creationism along with biology. In a way this is a tribute to their fair-mindedness. The trouble is that there is nothing to be taught. One either accepts the literal authority of the Bible or one doesn't.

In 1981 the state of Louisiana passed a law requiring that any public school teaching evolution as science had to teach creationism as science too. In 1987 the United States Supreme Court ruled the law unconstitutional. Many people assumed that this marked the end of the creationist attack on evolution. Judging by the long history of fundamentalist efforts to work through political and legal institutions rather than scientific ones, it seems unlikely.

Moral Cranks

I shall never forget the look of horror on the face of my six-year-old daughter when she learned that what she was eating at that moment had been a live chicken. I also have a vivid recollection of my twelve-year-old stepdaughter's bringing me a handbill with a picture of a small dog with its belly rather badly sewn up after an operation. It was alleged that the dog had been used in a scientific experiment, and the child wanted to write a school paper expressing her disapproval.

I sometimes wonder if the animal-welfare movement does not have its origins in such early experiences. It is surely understandable that a young child taught to be nice to animals is shocked to learn that human beings routinely kill them. It is equally understandable that a child with no knowledge of why animal experiments are done is dismayed to learn that the experiments are done with live animals. Perhaps adults with such concerns are motivated by the same moral verities.

Moral verities do not always fit real life. I have a third daughter, actually a daughter-in-law. She has a Ph.D. in human nutrition, and she began her professional career studying the nutritional requirements of infants both after birth and before. It is a subject of some moment. If an infant is inadequately nourished, it may not develop fully, may never be able to achieve its potential and may be a burden on society.

My daughter-in-law has worked on infant nutrition among poor people in Africa, and she has also had a laboratory at the University of Cambridge. There are crucial nutritional experiments that cannot be conducted with human infants, either after birth or before, and so her laboratory work was done with infant rats and baboons and their mothers. One night in 1983 a fire bomb was thrown into the laboratory by people who later announced they were animal liberationists, destroying many of her records and doing $250,000 worth of damage. The fire narrowly missed destroying the animals as well.

The animal-welfare movement has actually consisted of many movements. Its main origins were in the nineteenth century in England, where a Cruelty to Animals Act became law in 1876. That law has now been replaced by the Animals (Scientific Procedures) Act of 1986, which is broader and more stringent. In the words of the Home Office: "If you are not licensed, you may be committing an offense for which there are very substantial penalties."

Once Sir Geoffrey Taylor, a physicist who studied the behavior of fluids, discovered an important phenomenon: If a rapidly rotating fluid is disturbed, as by being touched at the surface, a column of stationary fluid forms below the disturbance. One way Sir Geoffrey demonstrated this "Taylor column" was to put goldfish into a tank of rotating water and touch the surface of the water with the end of a pencil. When he moved the pencil about, the goldfish swam around the moving column as though it were a solid object they were trying to avoid. It would have been nice, if only for teaching purposes, if Sir Geoffrey had mentioned the demonstration in his published accounts of the work. He never did so, he said, because he was sure that in England he would have gotten in trouble with the authorities or with people who objected to experimentation with animals.

Most animals exploited by human beings do not serve for scientific or medical experiments. Many more serve for the testing of substances that may be hazardous to human beings, and far more, of course, serve for food. The brunt of animal-welfare advocacy has nonetheless been borne by scientific and medical experimenters.

The efforts of animal-welfare advocates in the United States culminated with the passage of the Animal Protection Act of 1966, which requires that experimenters working with animals other than rats, mice and birds be licensed by agencies of the federal government. Enforcement has not been nominal. Following an inspection of laboratories at Columbia University in January 1986 the National Institutes of Health suspended all grants to the University for research with vertebrate animals other than rodents. There can be no doubt that the Animal Protection Act has improved the living conditions of laboratory animals. It has also increased the cost of working with animals, which is largely borne by the public.

Some animal-rights advocates have heeded a call to arms. There have been several episodes in addition to the one in my daughter-in-law's laboratory. In May 1984 animal liberationists wrecked an animal-research laboratory at the University of Pennsylvania; in April 1985 members of the Animal Liberation Front removed documents, vandalized facilities and took away 467 animals at the University of California at Riverside; in August 1987 members of a group calling itself the Band of Mercy broke into an animal experimentation facility of the Department of Agriculture at Beltsville, Maryland, and took away twenty-eight cats and three pigs. There have been other episodes as well.

Many years ago, in 1949 to be exact, there was a public hearing in Baltimore on the question of whether or not the public pounds should make animals abandoned by their owners available to the city's research institutions. No fewer than 3,500 people attended the hearing, which was held in the largest auditorium in Baltimore. Among those who testified at the hearing was a mother whose child's life had been saved by the famous "blue baby" operation, which had been developed by experimentation with dogs. She asked whether those present would prefer to save the lives of children or the lives of dogs. According to an eyewitness account, shouts rang out from the audience: "Dogs! Dogs! Save the dogs!"

The more philosophical animal-rights advocates argue that it is wrong for human beings to be more "loyal" to their own species than to other species. It is hard to see how it could be otherwise. Anyone who has been a parent, particularly a female parent, knows that being nice to members of our own species and putting them first is built into our genes. In other words, species loyalty has been tested by natural selection and found adaptive. For human beings, as the Greeks had it, human beings must be the measure of all things.

When Society Is a Crank

The concept of nuclear deterrence is seductive. If Nation A has at its command powerful forces armed with nuclear weapons and

Nation B is contemplating a move that would be gravely inimical to Nation A, Nation B will be deterred from making the move lest it bring on itself nuclear destruction. The logic is impeccable, yet one wonders if it applies in the real world.

It is worth recalling that when the concept of nuclear deterrence was first propounded, the international situation was quite different from what it is today. In 1945 the United States was the only nation that had nuclear weapons. At the same time the U.S.S.R. had the most powerful army the world had ever seen, and it had just defeated the second most powerful army the world had ever seen: the German army. It was feared that if the Russians should decide to invade Western Europe, nothing could stop them. What might deter them, however, was the threat that nuclear bombs would be dropped on Russian cities. Nuclear weapons accordingly became the foundation of American military policy.

In 1949 the Russians tested their first fission bomb. In 1952 the United States tested its first thermonuclear bomb. In 1955 the Russians did the same. In short order each nation had a large arsenal of nuclear weapons far more powerful than those that had destroyed Hiroshima and Nagasaki. Moreover, in 1957 the Russians launched the first artificial satellite, demonstrating that they had developed rockets capable of firing nuclear weapons from one continent to another. The United States, whose intelligence services had not prevented its being given a nasty shock, was not long in following suit.

What happened to nuclear deterrence then? Clearly the concept that nuclear weapons would deter a Russian ground attack no longer covered the total situation. Such weapons could, however, deter a Russian nuclear attack. To be sure, Russian nuclear weapons would also deter an American nuclear attack. Since it was now a standoff, the concept of deterrence was transmogrified by strategists into the concept of mutual assured destruction (MAD). Under the rule of MAD each side maintains nuclear forces that in the event of a nuclear attack are sufficient to destroy the other side.

The curious thing is that to this day one of the main reasons given for our maintaining a nuclear arsenal is that doing so deters the Russians from a major nonnuclear attack on other countries. One does not have to be a professional strategist to doubt that this doctrine is sound.

Let us say the Russians now invade Western Europe. We (the United States) then have the option of launching our nuclear forces against them. But if we do, they will launch their nuclear forces against us. The net result is that in order to punish the Russians for their transgression, we will have committed suicide. There are some who say: "If that's the way it has to be, that's the way it has to be. We have to stop them somewhere." Others might prefer not to join them in pulling the trigger of the pistol pointed at their own head. There would not, however, be much time for debate.

There are two logical escapes from what I shall call suicide deterrence, although both seem chimerical. One is a preemptive attack—a "first strike"—on the other side's nuclear forces that prevents the other side from retaliating. In the three decades since intercontinental ballistic missiles came into existence, they have become increasingly accurate. It is entirely possible to land a direct hit on one of the other side's missile silos at intercontinental distances.

Neither side, however, has all of its nuclear "reentry vehicles" on missiles in silos; many are on submarine missiles and on mobile launchers for ballistic missiles. Moreover, many nuclear weapons are carried by manned aircraft and unmanned cruise missiles. All of these unensiled systems are hard to keep track of. What is more to the point, each side has more than 10,000 strategic reentry vehicles ready to launch, and it would take only a few of them to inflict catastrophic damage on the other side. If only one thermonuclear bomb exploded over each of the ten largest cities in the United States and killed half the population, which is quite within the bounds of official estimates, the number of dead would be more than 20 million.

The other escape from suicide deterrence is a defensive system that would destroy virtually all of the other side's reentry vehicles before they could reach their targets. The modern version of this concept is the system we named the Strategic Defense Initiative (SDI) or "Star Wars." A curious thing about the SDI is that from the beginning its proponents readily conceded that, even if all their technical dreams came true, the system could never provide a fully effective shield against a large-scale missile attack. Others asked: If the shield could never be fully effective and a tiny fraction of the attacking missiles could inflict catastrophic damage, why have a shield?

President Reagan characterized the SDI as "a system that defends human life instead of threatening it." After he first proposed the system the justifications became more complex. The existence of the shield, it was said, would help preserve our deterrent by discouraging the Russians from thinking they could knock out all of our silo-based missiles with a first strike. In other words, the SDI was seen as defending not human life but missiles. Again, some asked: If a large fraction of our missiles are mobile and not in silos, and if an even larger fraction could be made mobile at a cost much lower than that of a missile defense, why have a missile defense?

It is sometimes argued that by developing new military technologies that require the Russians to follow suit, the United States puts an additional strain on the Russian economy and makes it more difficult for the U.S.S.R. to pursue its aims. The question with the SDI is exactly how the Russians follow suit. Since no shield can be fully effective, the cheapest way to counter one would be to make the attacking forces more effective. There are many approaches; for example, developing a means of attacking the shield just before the launching of missiles, shortening the "burn" time of rising missiles so that the shield has less time to attack them, modifying the skin of missiles to make them more resistant to laser or particle-beam attack, and increasing the number of decoy reentry vehicles carried by each missile. One may wonder which economy would be strained the more.

The avant-garde technology proposed for the SDI obscures the fact that efforts to escape the realities of nuclear war are a primordial psychopathology of the nuclear age. In the 1960s there was a big push in the United States for the development of antiballistic-missile (ABM) missiles. There was little reason to believe that such a system would be of much help in the event of an all-out nuclear attack, and much reason to believe that it would provoke offensive countermeasures. The idea was side-tracked (until the SDI) by the ABM Treaty of 1972. Before that there was the strange mania of fallout shelters, which were sup-posed to enable people to survive a nuclear war that had destroyed their society.

Much ingenuity was brought to bear on fallout shelters, the lunacy of which was brought home to me, at least, by a black-humorous suggestion made by the physicist Edward Condon. He proposed a special kind of pill for the fallout shelter that, in the event it became clear that survival was going to be impossible, could be taken by the occupants. The outer layer of the pill was a tranquilizer, so that the prospect of dying would not make the occupant too unhappy. Then there was a second layer; it consisted of morphine, so that the occupant would feel no pain. The core of the pill was a lethal poison. Condon even had a name for the pill: Dismilin.

It is often observed that whatever one may think about the morality and strategic practicality of nuclear weapons, the concept of mutual assured destruction has so far prevented a Third World War. This may even be true. What is also true is that nuclear weapons make possible a Third World War of such devastating consequences that all other wars will have been mere noise in the signal of human history. Even if neither side wants to commit suicide, it is all too easy to imagine technical accidents—or, even more likely, international incidents—that could brush against the hair trigger.

It takes thirty minutes for a ballistic missile to get from the United States to the U.S.S.R. or from the U.S.S.R. to the United States. The flight time for a missile launched by a strategically placed submarine is considerably less. Whichever direction the missiles are headed in, there is not much time for decision. If the side being attacked believes it cannot risk the loss of retaliatory missiles, it is virtually forced to adopt the strategy of "launch under attack," in which it automatically launches its missiles while the other side's missiles are on the way.

The situation can only be described as a highly unstable and irrational one. How did it come about? Some see it as the result of plots and schemes by one side or the other, by the military, by the defense industry and so on. I myself tend toward the view that it is mostly unintentional social pathology. In this instance the crank is society.

For example, it is hardly surprising that generals and admirals on both sides would like to have the forces—including nuclear forces—under their command as strong as possible. That is what they are hired for. But, you say, in the end decisions on the strength of the military forces are made not by generals and admirals but by civilians. There a curious thing happens. If both sides are scared of each other, a kind of Darwinian process acts to select the particular civilians chosen to make the decisions on military matters. Pessimists, who are usually regarded as being more realistic than optimists, tend to rise in the civilian ranks until their views become national policy. Some little foxes can build an entire career on consistently being more pessimistic than anyone else.

In spite of such social pathology the United States and the U.S.S.R. have succeeded in arriving at a few arms-control agreements. As everyone knows, however, these agreements are a long way from guaranteeing that there will not be a catastrophic nuclear shootout. Reducing 10,000 strategic reentry vehicles on each side to 5,000 or even 1,000 still leaves the situation unstable and irrational. Some experts on arms control have calculated that the maximum number of reentry vehicles needed for full deterrence is 400. Even achieving that number would not cure the irrationality of suicide deterrence.

Attitudes toward arms-control agreements have their own pathology. In view of the fact that both sides have so much to gain by avoiding the shootout, why have they been so reluctant to enter into even modest agreements? On the American side two reasons have often been given. Reason 1 is that the Russians are ahead of us in some respect, so that to enter into an agreement now would put us at a disadvantage. Reason 2 is that you can't trust the Russians to honor *any* agreement.

The flaw in Reason 1, sometimes called the fallacy of the last move, is that there is never any end to it. To put it as charitably as possible, if someone in authority on one side is merely playing it safe and wanting to avoid the possibility of being found in error at some later date, he need only assert that the other side is "ahead" and this is not the time to enter into an agreement. Then, when his side has "caught up," someone in authority on the other side can take the same position. This contrapuntal process is understandable, but it is irrational. It calls for a perpetual escalation in nuclear arms and increased peril to both sides.

The flaw in Reason 2 is the assumption that treaties between nations are solely based on trust. If they were, very few treaties would have ever been signed. A treaty is an agreement between nations, usually for their mutual benefit. If one nation violates the treaty, the treaty ceases to exist. It is often said that the U.S.S.R. violates treaties, but if it is in the interest of any nation not to violate a treaty, it will not do so. And it is very much in the interest of both the U.S.S.R. and the United States to drastically reduce nuclear arms.

But what if the U.S.S.R. were to *secretly* violate a treaty reducing nuclear arms? The only answer is that any such treaty must incorporate provisions to verify that the treaty is not being violated, including direct inspection of the relevant sites. It used to be said that the Russians would never accept on-site inspection, but the necessity of such inspection is now accepted by both sides. Moreover, other means of inspection have become increasingly effective. Seismic stations around the U.S.S.R. are able to detect underground tests within the U.S.S.R., and the Russians have agreed to allow the installation of other stations within the country to better verify that illicit tests are not being conducted. Meanwhile spy satellites have become steadily better at covering an entire country with remarkably sharp pictures.

Studs Terkel, the Chicago oral historian, once observed that when it came to thinking about Russians, most Americans lived in a fifty-first state named Catatonia. Whether or not the metaphor is just, there does exist a state of mind that makes it hard for many Americans to accept propositions that can only decrease the possibility of their perishing in a nuclear war. One proposition is that it is not sufficient to dislike the Russians, or even merely to dislike their government; both exist, therefore they must be dealt with.

Back when the Russians and Chinese were friends, a Chinese personage is said to have observed to First Secretary Khrushchev that the United States was a paper tiger. "Yes," responded Khrushchev, "but the paper tiger has nuclear teeth." It is the same the other way around. Nuclear weapons are the great equalizer.

Another proposition that many Americans find hard to accept is that if elected officials suggest we should try to arrive at agreements with the Russians, it does not follow that they are "soft on Communism." This is no trivial matter; anyone running for office in the United States knows that to risk the accusation is political poison. Yet it is a funny thing about the United States and Communism. If Communism is the enemy, how can it be that we have friendly relations with the largest Communist nation in the world? I refer, of course, to China. If we befriend one Communist nation simply because it is unfriendly to a stronger Communist nation, it suggests that our policy is based not on political philosophy but on fear of a rival power.

Everything I have said in this section is well known to many people. What may be less well known is that some familiar— even cherished—policies and attitudes are irrational, inimical to our interest and potentially self-destructive. It is hard to blame these irrationalities on any one group of cranks; we are all cranks for going about our daily business largely as though those irrationalities did not exist. Some try to do something about them, but it is clear that not enough is being done. Unless there is a basic shift in policies and attitudes, self-destruction will ultimately be achieved.

There is a theme running through all of these types of crankishness. It is an underlying mistrust of one's fellow human beings, whether it be a mistrust of what other people have laboriously learned over generations or a mistrust of entire nations. Sometimes trusting other people is risky, but as a matter of fact it is done by practically everyone practically all of the time. After all, if it were not, society could not function at all. If Americans and Russians cannot take a certain amount of risk in dealing with each other for their mutual benefit, a missing adaptation in the human species will be exposed by natural selection, and the human evolutionary experiment may have little chance to continue.

INDEX

abacus, 212
Aberdeen Proving Ground, 213–14
ABM Treaty of 1972, 44
acceleration, free fall, 44–5, 46
accelerators, particle, 16, 37, 57–60,
    97, 106
accretion disk, 88
acetone, 185
acetylsalicylic acid (aspirin), 192
acid rain, 178
acoustical physics, 52
Acrasiales, 158
acrasin, 158
Acrilan, 198
actin, 149
adaptation, 14–15, 173; behavioral,
    163–4; cultural, 174–5; social, 14;
    technological, 173
adenine, 141, 142
adenosine triphosphate (ATP), 134, 146,
    149
adhesives, 189, 198
Africa, 118; Atlantic coastline, 103–4;
    northward drift, 119
Ages in Chaos (Velikovsky), 225
agricultural chemicals, 182, 189
agricultural revolution, 175, 181–2, 192
agriculture, 173, 174, 181–2;
    beginnings of, 21, 175; employment
    in, 23, 182; green revolution, 29, 182
air, 115, 189; *see also* atmosphere
air conditioning, 197

aircraft, 177, 207; engines, 207–8
air pollution, 178, 190
Alamogordo A-bomb test, 216
alcohol, 80–1; industrial, 185
algae, 157
algebra, 19
alkalies, 191
alkaloids, 135
alpha helix, 137, 138
Alpher, Ralph, 96–7
alternating current, 208–9
alternative energy sources, 179–80
alumina, 190
aluminum, 189
American Association for the
    Advancement of Science, 224
American Dental Association, 10
American Diabetes Association, 10
American Heart Association, 10
American Heritage Dictionary, 11
American Parapsychology Association,
    224
American Society for Psychical
    Research, 222
amino acids, 136–8, 141–3, 145, 148,
    154, 185, 198; side groups, 136, 143
ammonia, 81, 191; in solar system, 107
ammonium nitrate, 191
ammonium sulfate, 191
amoebae, 157–8
AMP, cyclic, 158–9
amphibians, 159

118; currents, 126, 127; interaction
with atmosphere, 120, 122–3, 126,
127–8; level, 124, 130; origin of, 109;
waves, 126–7; *see also* mid-ocean
ridges; mid-ocean rifts
ocean floor, 102–4; sediment, 115, 117;
spreading, 104, 112, 117
oceanic crust, 114–15, 117
oceanography, 101, 105
ocean trenches, 117
octane rating, 190
Ogilvy, David, 230
Ohio State University, 237
oil, 128, 130, 175, 177–8; refineries,
190, 205
Olympus Mons, 113
Omni magazine, 11
"one gene—one enzyme" concept, 139
on-site inspection, arms, 247
On the Origin of Species (Darwin), 161
On the Shoulders of Giants (Merton),
227
open-hearth furnace, 195
open universe, 65, 95, 97
Oppenheim, Janet, 222
Oppenheimer, J. Robert, 19, 217
orbits, planetary, 47, 74, 108; earth, 124
organelles, 147, 148, 157
organic chemistry, 191–2
orgone boxes, 228
Orlon, 198
ornithology, 140
*Other World, The: Spiritualism and
Psychical Research in England (1850–
1914)* (Oppenheim), 222
outgassing, 121
overpopulation, 10
oxen, 206
Oxford, University of, 167, 185–6
oxygen, 80–1, 121–2, 128, 135–6, 167,
191, 192–4; atmospheric, 120, 121,
128, 129, 134, 155; on earth, 112,
120, 121–2, 155; need of animal life
for, 133–4; in red-giant stars, 72; in
solar system, 107; as waste product of
photosynthesis, 121, 155
ozone, 129

Pacific coast volcanism, 118
Pacific Ocean, 118, 125; plate, 113
Pagels, Heinz, 47
pain, 152–3
paints, 189, 198
Paleolithic, 219
paleontology, 17, 234, 236
Palomar Observatory, 67, 91, 93
Paluxy River, Texas, 234
paranormal phenomena, 222–4
Parapsychological Foundation, 222
parapsychology, 222, 224
parsec, 66
particle accelerators, 16, 37, 57–60, 97,
106
particle-antiparticle pairs, 32, 58, 60
particles of matter, 47, 89; kinds of,
31–2, 57–8; predicted, 60; string and
superstring, 60; uncertainty principle,
48; unstable, 32; vs. waves, 48–50,
58, 144
Pasteur, Louis, 25
Pastore, John O., 16
Pauli, Wolfgang, 37, 226
Pauling, Linus, 136–7
Payne, Jerry A., 167–8
Pell, Claiborne, 223
penicillin, 186
Penicillium, 185–6; *chrysogenum*, 186
Peru, coast of, 126
pesticides, 182
petroleum, 185, 189, 190, 191, 198,
207
pharmaceuticals, 185, 189
phenylalanine, 142
Philippines, 118
Phobos (moon of Mars), 108
phonograph record, 18–19, 213
phosphate, 141
phosphoric acid, 191
phosporus, 128, 189, 196
photinos, 60
photons, 31, 32, 41, 43–4, 47, 48, 58,
60
photosynthesis, 121, 129, 134, 146,
155–6, 157
physicians, 25–6